C000214468

THE RETURN OF THE STRONG

Also by Robert Harvey

The Undefeated: The Rise, Fall and Rise of Modern Japan
Fire Down Below: A Journey of Exploration from Mexico to Chile
Portugal: Birth of a Democracy

AS EDITOR

Blueprint 2000: Employment and Technology in the Next Century

ROBERT HARVEY

THE RETURN OF THE STRONG

The Drift to Global Disorder

MACMILLAN

First published 1995 by Macmillan London

an imprint of Macmillan General Books
Cavaye Place London SW10 9PG
and Basingstoke

Associated companies throughout the world

ISBN 0 333 61208 6

1 3 5 7 9 8 6 4 2

A CIP catalogue record for this book is available from
the British Library

Typeset by CentraCet Limited, Cambridge
Printed and bound in Great Britain by
Mackays of Chatham PLC, Kent

To Alan and Millicent

CONTENTS

CONTENTS

PART FOUR
RESTORING ORDER

ACKNOWLEDGEMENTS

This book was prompted by the dangers, as I see them, arising from current global developments. It draws on sixteen years' experience as a commentator on politics, economics and foreign affairs for, first, *The Economist* and then the *Daily Telegraph*, as well as four further years in the House of Commons, three of them as a member of the Foreign Affairs Select Committee. An enormous number of people have helped either directly in the preparation of the book over the past two years, or indirectly through interviews and discussions over two decades in helping to shape the views contained in it. Needless to say, responsibility for the opinions and contents of the book is entirely mine.

Among those I am chiefly indebted to for helping to shape my thoughts are, in Britain, the Rt Hon. Kenneth Clarke, the Rt Hon. Michael Heseltine, the Rt Hon. Richard Ryder, the Rt Hon. Lord Howe of Aberavon, the Rt Hon. Lord Prior, the Rt Hon. Chris Patten, Sir Anthony Kershaw, Sir Anthony Meyer, BT, Jim Lester MP, Richard Shepherd MP, Sir Ivan Lawrence QC MP, Bowen Wells MP, Gerry Malone MP, Mark Robinson MP, Keith Raffan, Stephen Milligan, Bill Emmott, Andrew Knight, Brian Beedham, Gordon Lee, Jonathan Fenby, Jim Meacham, Iain Carson, Dr Edwina Moreton, Simon Scott-Plummer, Trevor Grove, Nicholas Comfort, Nigel Wade, Andrew Williams, Peter Lloyd, Patric Dickinson, David Warren, Robert Lyle, Hugh Ehrman, Dr Jonathan Wright, Professor Alan Ryan, Professor Peter Oppenheimer, Peter Pulzer, Oscar Wood, Tim Card (who gave me my first grounding in economics), Peter Lawrence, John Peake and Patrick Croker.

In the United States, General Alexander Haig, Zbigniew Brzinzki, Admiral Stansfield Turner, Barber Conable, Ernest

Stern, Moeen Qureshi, Jacques de Larosiere, Senator Bill Bradley, Congressman Jack Kemp, Senator John Tower, Congressman Charles Schumer. Ambassador Ray Seitz, Ambassador Tom Pickering, Jeffrey Record. In Russia, Mikhail Gorbachev, Leonid Zamyatin, Boris Ponomarev, Lev Parshin, Anatoli Danilitski.

In Europe, President Mario Soares and Prime Minister Cavaco Silva of Portugal, Professor Diogo Freitas do Amaral, Adelino Amaro da Costa, Manuel Frago, Santiago Carrillo, Giulio Andreotti, Amintore Fanfani, Bettino Craxi and Ciriaco de Mita, Bruno Trentin, Luciano Lama, Professor Giovanni Magnifico, Paulo Baffi, Achille Occhetto, Luciano Barca, Giorgio Amendola, Giovanni Russo and Count Paulo Filo de Torre, General Volcker Ruhe, Horst Telschik, General Wolfgang Von Altenberg and Carl Bildt of Sweden.

In South East Asia, Singapore's Lee Kuan Yew, Cambodia's Prince Norodom Ranarridh, Thailand's General Prem. In Japan Toshiki Kaifu and Ambassador Yukio Satch. In Israel Prime Minister Yitzhak Rabin, Yitzhak Shamir, Abba Eban, David Kimche, Ambassador Gideon Rafael. In Iraq deputy prime minister Tariq Aziz. In Saudi Arabia, Sheikh Mohammed Abalkhail, Sheikh Ibrahim al-Sheikh and Sheikh al-Qurraishi. On debt problems, Professor Dragoslav Avramovits of Serbia and Senator Roberto Campos, and Delfim Netto of Brazil. In Latin America generally, General Golbery do Couto e Silva, Alberto Tamer of Brazil, General Omar Graffigna, Admiral Emilio Messera and General Roberto Viola of Argentina, General Augusto Pinochet of Chile and Hernan Cubillos, President Violeta Chamorro of Nicaragua and ex-presidents Luis Echeverria of Mexico and Vinicio Cerezo of Guatemala.

I owe very special thanks to Gillon Aitken, as good a friend as an agent, encouraging, painstaking and constructive editors, Jon Riley and Tanya Stobbs; my tireless assistant, Jenny Wills; my wife, Jane, son Oliver, and my mother for their support and patience; my mother-in-law Millicent; and finally Christine (and Richard and Emma) who kept us supplied during the last winter of writing the book.

The author and publishers would like to express their gratitude to the following who have kindly given their permission for the use of copyright material.

America's Military Revolution by William Odom, American University Press, 1993
The Challenge of Europe by Michael Heseltine, Weidenfeld & Nicolson, 1989
The Culture of Contentment by J. K. Galbraith, Penguin, 1993
A Fate Worse than Debt by Susan George, Penguin, 1988
A History of Political Thought in the English Revolution by Perez Zagorin, Routledge and Kegan Paul, 1954
Max Weber: Essays in Sociology, translated by H. H. Garth and C. W. Mills, Routledge and Kegan Paul, 1948
Max Weber and German Politics by J. P. Meyer, Faber and Faber, 1956
The Mind of the Strategist by Kenichi Ohmae, Penguin, 1983
Modern Organizations by Stewart Clegg, Sage, 1990
Trojan Horse by Barrie James, Weidenfeld & Nicolson, 1990
Where There's a Will by Michael Heseltine, Hutchinson, 1987

Every effort has been made to trace all copyright holders, but if any have inadvertently been overlooked, the author and publishers will be pleased to make the necessary arrangements at the first opportunity.

INTRODUCTION

AT THE CLOSE of the nineteenth century, more self-confidence and exuberance emanated from the capital of the world's largest empire, London, than at any time in history. The industrial world, while far from free of war, appeared more tranquil than it had been for centuries. The global economy was in a state of sustained expansion, with Britain's industrial revolution being imitated in the United States, Germany, France and, to a lesser extent, Russia. Capitalism was at its zenith, bestriding the major economies and their colonies. The volume of international trade had multiplied twenty-five times in a hundred years. It was an era of growth, progress and self-reliance.

The great European wars had washed past earlier in the century; the American Civil War was over. It was possible to believe in a new world order where civilization would gradually clothe the less developed parts of the world in peace and material advance. While Britain began to indulge in social reform to cushion the excesses of capitalism, the United States was experiencing the first huge benefits of railways, mass production and thrusting entrepreneurship. When the twentieth century began, there was little reason to fear the future. As the strait-laced energy of the Victorian age mellowed into the comfortable respectability of the Edwardian, security, prosperity and progress seemed assured.

Within two decades, the whole booming, peaceful, bourgeois façade was shattered as the wave of prosperity was dashed on to the jagged rocks of nationalism and, a little later, communism. The First World War plunged Europe into an almost entirely futile slaughter of nationalist ambition and destroyed the old order.

Meanwhile communism seized control in Russia in 1917,

and threatened to spread across much of the globe. The second great chapter of the twentieth century had begun. The capitalist world went on an economic roller-coaster, from postwar recession through the booming 1920s to protracted recession in the 1930s, dazing millions of people into seeking extremist solutions. As a reaction against the threat of socialism in Europe, but also against the coldly impersonal forces of capitalism plunging the globe into economic tumult, Fascism took power in Italy in 1922, Nazism in Germany in 1933 and Francoism in Spain in 1939. In the Far East, an increasingly militarist Japan embarked on a policy of imperialist expansionism that culminated in war with China and, eventually, America and Britain.

In Europe, German expansionism ignited war with France, Britain and eventually Russia, drawing in the United States. The three decades between 1914 and 1945 were times of trouble, marked by some of the most unstable political and economic conditions the world has ever known. The twin ogres of nationalism and communism bestrode continents, putting millions to the sword and enslaving hundreds of millions. While nationalism was to some extent self-generating, communism arose almost entirely out of extreme economic conditions that had been neither understood nor addressed.

After the defeat of Germany, Italy and Japan, two global superpowers – the United States and the Soviet Union – were left straddling the smoking ruins of postwar Europe. Almost by historical accident, the third chapter of the twentieth century began. The world settled into a gridlock where East and West confronted each other under threat of nuclear annihilation, each with client states over which they exerted some control. For the first time since the early twentieth century a kind of global political and economic order, and an unprecedented surge of prosperity and development, were restored. Over the period the volume of trade increased some twelve times while world output jumped six times.

In place of world war there were occasional confrontations, often by proxy, in the developing world. The first was Korea in the early 1950s, where the superpowers drew back from the brink of world war. Hungary in 1956, the perpetual stand-off over Berlin, the Cuban missile crisis in 1961, Indochina throughout the 1960s and early 1970s, Czechoslovakia in 1968, Angola in the mid-1970s, Afghanistan and Central America in 1979, and successive Middle Eastern crises brought the superpowers to eyeball-rolling confrontation; but the unspoken rules of the game kept them from conflict.

Between 1987 and 1991, the Soviet Empire fractured spectacularly apart, and the triumph of good over evil seemed complete. Poland, Czechoslovakia, Hungary, East Germany, Bulgaria and Romania fell like skittles as it became apparent that the Soviet Union would no longer shore up their unpopular bureau-dictatorships. The Baltic Republics, the Ukraine and the southern republics broke away from the weakening embrace of Russia. The Soviet system was exposed for the bureaucratic, incompetent, authoritarian mastodon that it was. To some, Western liberal democracy and free-market values reigned supreme. The 'end of history' had arrived.

In fact it was the end of the struggle between rival ideologies and the beginning of the fourth and last chapter of twentieth-century history (the first of the twenty-first century). For within months, the hounds of ethnic nationalism were unleashed again, vigorously, destructively and murderously; and global capitalism displayed similar insensitivity towards ordinary people as it had at the beginning of the century, which had led to the decades of turbulence that followed.

As the millennium closes, the same seeds of global disorder, even anarchy, that grew into the years 1914–45 are being sown. Racialism and ethnic nationalism are already on the rampage. Bigger powers show signs of going their own way. America is blindly and dangerously disengaging from Europe, Britain viewing the Continent with scepticism, Germany and Japan becoming more assertive, Italy reinventing itself and China rearming.

Global chaos is entirely avoidable, through the kind of long-sighted security policies that kept the post-1950 era from holocaust, and the economic imagination and vigour that led to a half-century of unprecedented growth. So far, in the post-Cold War era, Western governments show little sign of responding to any but immediate local threats – but the major challenge is an international one, both on the economic and security fronts.

On global strategy, we face a dangerous period of lowered guards and an escalating possibility of conflict. As Eugene Rostow has written, 'In the short term the Soviet collapse, like the fall of any empire in history, has radically destabilized world politics.' Economically, global capitalism may be at a stage not far different from that of national capitalism at the end of the last century: its authoritarian nature, disregard for national and personal sensitivities, enormous power and – as the world debt crisis in the 1980s showed – incompetence, could give rise to a perilous reaction: the birth of a new 'communism'.

The old communism collapsed because it was imbued with the same faults, but on an even bigger scale, as the old capitalism. The modern capitalist corporation more nearly resembles the communist corporation than it would like to think, and is in danger of going the same way. Communism, a truly monstrous system, was created by the inhumanity of early capitalism. An equally deformed global changeling could be born of today's capitalist failings. Global capitalism shows a similar tendency to escape international control as it did in the 1920s and the 1930s.

The major powers at the end of this millennium, as Cold War memories fade, exude the same complacency and self-congratulation as at the end of the last century. Unless action is taken as the warm glow of sunset on the twentieth century is replaced by the pale dawn light of the twenty-first, we will gaze upon the same horizon of global horrors as our great-grandfathers, this time through a nuclear haze. The world is a much more dangerous place than it has been for nearly half a century.

PART ONE

The Other Side of Brandenburg

CHAPTER ONE

THE THAW AND THE FLOOD

On 4 October 1990, I joined the orderly human torrent that poured through the Brandenburg Gate to a Germany no longer split after forty-five years of division. It was one of the biggest street parties the world has ever witnessed. Two million West Berliners flowed through the neoclassical baroque edifice, past the balloon sellers in the city's most celebrated street, the Unter den Linden. Behind, in the shadow of the Reichstag, Russian uniforms and caps were on sale for a pittance, as the departing occupiers tried to earn a few marks to take back with them to their economically devastated homeland. Beyond lay the stately drab edifices of East Germany's showpiece, now thronged with würste and sauerkraut sellers catering to the crowds.

The day was free of clouds, blue-skied above the rejoined throng below; the mood was unecstatic, subdued, friendly, with families taking an afternoon promenade – not a celebration. You could tell the Westerners by the expensive open-necked casualness of their clothes, in contrast to the easterners' shabby suits or jackets and ties. The Westerners were a little edgy, as if they knew that freely crossing the magic threshold, which few had ever expected in their lifetimes, was not the fulfilment of a dream but entry into an uncertain looking-glass world where all was parallel but inverted, and would take decades to reorder. There was guilt at witnessing the conditions of down-and-out, dignified poverty in which their blood relatives had lived for so long, as well as apprehension about the cost of taking them under the West's wing, and contempt for their submissiveness.

I passed Berlin's ornate Comic Opera where a champagne bottle had been inserted into the crook of the arm of a sculpted nymphet on the façade. A little further on, across the road, was the cathedral where an exhibition was being staged – surely not coincidentally? – of photographs of Berlin from the first fierce philistine Nazi frenzy of the 1920s to the cemetery-city of 1945. I skirted looming, dreary bronzes of Marx and Engels in a park, where a silly street-theatre was being staged by Euro-enthusiasts – on second thoughts perhaps it struck exactly the right note of mockery for that life-freezing, apocalyptic pair. The only intrusion of violence or politics was a minor bit of shopfront smashing beyond by extreme left-wingers, which some thirty busloads of jittery German police inched forward to control.

Far from the placid crowd, I took the overground, open for the first time, back across a city which had been divided for two generations. The acned Bronx-like tenements of the East, hunch-shouldered greycoat slabs pockmarked with windows fronting the river, were sliced abruptly short by the Wall, dead-ending purposeless streets. With its raked-sand moats, minefields, spikes, fences and now empty machine-gun turrets, the Wall had been a killing ground seared across the heart of a once-elegant European city. The little railway bore me across to the raucous glitter of a largely American garrison town, where gaudy strip shows vied with supermarkets for hoarding space. I had taken a fifteen-minute, one-mark journey from the 1940s to the 1990s, and it was not entirely clear that the neon glitter of the West was an improvement on the stately shabbiness of the East.

The crowds went on their three-mile pilgrimage because they knew human history was being made across the breeding ground of some of the most terrible events this century. Reunification might be just a matter of Germany regaining its national identity – or was it the joining together of two elements that would ignite a critical mass of explosive proportions? The night before, which I had spent in a provincial town to the sound of firecrackers and carousing, the West German flag had been raised over the Reichstag, to make the point that Germany was not being 'reunified', but that the East was being absorbed into the West.

*

THAT WAS THE end of communism, that was, the 'end of history', in the rather foolhardy phrase of American commentator Francis Fukuyama. German reunification was the climax of a chain reaction across Eastern Europe in which Poland, Czechoslovakia, Hungary, and to a lesser extent Romania and Bulgaria, had found their freedom, while shortly afterwards the Soviet Union began its meltdown towards no one knew quite what. The West had triumphed, the East had lost. The free market was victorious, state socialism lay in self-inflicted ruins. Mrs Thatcher trumpeted the victory, President Reagan celebrated it, President Bush had a splash of coffee.

It had all been so simple. All that was now needed was for the East to adopt free-market economic solutions, the faster the better, to catch up with the West, and become part of a streamlined, competitive world econony. The 'peace dividend' could be carved out of the successful armies of NATO; soldiers could go home; the threat of nuclear holocaust had disappeared. The huge ideological struggle of the second half of the twentieth century was over; communism had been crushed by capitalism; not so much the end of history, but the end of argument.

Rarely can partying have turned so quickly to depression, unease and hangover. The 'new world order' supposedly ushered in after the Cold War soon looked more like global disorder. 'Disorientation was pervasive after the fall of the Berlin Wall,' one of Western Europe's most respected foreign ministers told me. It was as though the thawing of the Cold War had unleashed a thousand torrents of hatred. Where once superpower confrontation acted as a restraint on nationalism and extremism, for fear that any outbreaks could escalate into superpower conflict, now there were the beginnings of a free-for-all.

Of course, the end of the Cold War remained a staggeringly positive achievement, removing as it did the largely hypothetical fear of nuclear war and mass military confrontation in Europe. But it lifted the lid on other potential sources of conflict. If early twentieth-century developments in the Soviet Union will be seen as the maturing of a semi-backward society founded on primitive ideology, force and arms, so in the 1990s there stepped from behind it other similar models.

It was possible, too, to talk of a new age of nationalism. The suffering caused by the ideological challenge of communism was probably second to none in the world's history. Yet as communism began to atrophy and become less murderous, so the East–West confrontation imposed its own strange order on global affairs. Rogue countries and extremist organizations were careful not to offend their superpower masters. Countries usually engaged in furious competition with each other in Europe and Asia co-operated in the face of a common threat.

The end of the Cold War transformed the landscape: self-interest became the guiding principle of nations. Where once men struggled and died for the rights of freedom or equality, now they fought for turf, hatred of other ethnic groups, economic advantage, jealousy. There is nothing new in this: history has frequently alternated between ideological struggle – the wars of religion, the struggles for independence, the revolutionary wars of the nineteenth century – and periods of naked self-interest. Human nature is an incubator of both noble ideals and selfishness; it is hard to decide which has caused the more suffering.

The end of the Cold War did not just release the impoverished people of Eastern Europe and the Soviet Union. The United States, by a hasty, substantial and unnecessary reduction in its commitment to Europe and the world, threw into doubt its very status – unchallenged after the collapse of the Soviet Union – as sole global superpower. Admittedly the trend was already evident. A senior NATO foreign minister dates the 'American disengagement from the European land mass' as having started at the Reykjavik summit of 1987, when America and Russia nearly did a deal over Europe's head. 'Even Shultz supported Reagan . . . all considerations were now being made primarily from a US point of view . . . This is a longstanding shift within America.' Desperately, in an effort to re-engage America, Britain, Germany and France launched their proposal for a balanced military–economic partnership in February 1995.

For those who have long looked for postwar inspiration and leadership from the United States, it would be hard to exaggerate the disappointment felt at the moral turpitude and failure of leadership of foreign policy under the Clinton administration.

Of course, State Department professionals under the Secretary of State, Warren Christopher, have helped to broker much good around the world – from the Middle East to Southern Africa.

But the Democrat Clinton has combined a traditionally Republican preoccupation with America's business interests abroad – most notable in his cynical abandonment of human rights in China in pursuit of what American commerce secretary, Ronald Brown, has labelled with grandiose rhetoric 'commercial diplomacy' – with a policy of steadfast non-intervention in major contemporary security crises. Speak loudly and carry a little stick – a policy calculated to bring respect for America to its lowest ebb since Warren G. Harding. Only when public opinion or electoral interest spurs the Clinton administration to foreign policy action does America react. In an area where leadership is usually required and respected, the cart has been pulling the horse.

The ultimate cynicism of this approach was exposed by American Caribbean policy in the autumn of 1994: in response to the pitiable mass exodus of Cuban refugees, the Clinton administration rescinded America's open-door policy under political pressure from the southern states, and then negotiated a tawdry deal with its perennial foe, dictator Fidel Castro, to keep his people penned in on the island.

Simultaneously, America staged an occupation of Haiti to guarantee the 'right' of its people to democracy, in defence of a dubious democratic leadership; Haiti, whose endemic and repellent tyrannies had been neglected by the United States for decades, differed from Cuba only in that its ramshackle armed forces were an easy prey for American military might. (The 'right' of China's people to democracy did not, of course, even register on the balance sheet against America's commercial interest there.) An easy display of military force against a tinpot dictator might, of course, be a boost for Democratic candidates in crucial mid-term congressional elections; it could hardly restore the drooping prestige of America abroad. Intervention in Haiti was intervention at the wrong time in the wrong place and for the wrong reason.

In the event the occupation had overtones of a tragi-comic

opera. Invited in at the last minute by the very military junta it was designed to overthrow, after an ultimatum from ex-President Carter, American troops were initially instructed not to intervene as government thugs attacked the country's democratic forces. Pentagon spokesmen announced with relief that 'massive bloodshed' had been averted – which hardly seemed likely in any confrontation between overwhelming American military force and Haiti's ramshackle 7,000-strong militia, with only six artillery pieces, one propeller plane, one helicopter, four working armoured personnel carriers and a handful of voodoo spells among them.

President Clinton, who had earlier described the country's dictators as 'thugs' and having created a 'nightmare of bloodshed' and a 'reign of terror' was left averring that it was 'plain wrong' to call the country's military leader a dictator. In the end the junta departed; but democracy's hold on the country depended upon the presence of American troops, which might be withdrawn at any time.

Ordinary Americans reflected their leader's new reluctance to interfere abroad. According to one survey in November 1993, Americans were vastly more concerned with such issues as crime, unemployment and health care than foreign policy. Fewer than one in ten believed America should act as sole global superpower. A major survey across four nations in April 1994 found that while the British and Germans overwhelmingly considered war the world's most serious problem, only 8 per cent of Americans did, compared to 17 per cent listing crime at the top. In America, Britain, Germany and Spain a large majority considered the world more dangerous after the end of the Cold War. More hopefully, only in Japan was there a majority against sending troops on UN missions, and around two-thirds or more of respondents in America, Britain and Germany favoured UN military intervention in trouble spots.

Japan has begun to shake off its postwar inhibitions to become increasingly self-assertive not just in respect of its neighbours, but towards the United States. China has cynically shed its communist shell to emerge as a nakedly authoritarian system, striving for economic and political power, while unashamedly embracing consumerism. This cannot last; any system needs legitimacy, and the Chinese do not have any.

Germany has been unified, and is beginning to behave with the arrogance of the biggest boy in the class, and no longer quite so guiltily remembers the misdeeds of former generations. Italy, a country polarized by the Cold War, has seen its political system virtually disintegrate in a disconcertingly populist, even fascist, direction. Britain exhibits some of the same kind of fussy, freezing disdain for continental entanglement that so disastrously characterized its policy between the wars.

It is certainly a new age of narcissism, of self-absorption, of selfishness. The grim confrontation of forty years has collapsed, all has changed, and instead of grasping new opportunities, nations are withdrawing into their shells, resorting to petty expressions of their ego. Unless they re-emerge, the current confusion will be followed by serious danger.

THE END OF confrontation in Europe was hailed specifically as marking three milestones: first, the establishment of a 'new world order' presided over by a single benevolent superpower, the United States, in place of superpower competition and regional wars; second, the triumph of free-market capitalism; and, third, the triumph of liberal democracy. All three 'victories' dissolved with remarkable speed to reveal much grimmer realities. Euphoria swiftly turned to disillusion; the sweet taste of Western victory to ashes.

With a little poetic licence, let us take one of the cruise missiles that were once stationed in Europe, disarm it, and attach a camera to it. Let us launch it, on a course dictated by a computer-programmed path, and, starting from Germany, let it hug the ground on a zig-zag curve eastward.

This peace missile would film first the city of Solingen on 28 May 1993, where a young Turkish woman and five sisters were burnt to death in an arson attack by neo-Nazis. A thousand such attacks had taken place in just eighteen months, directed both against the Turkish 'guest workers' brought in to help the German economy, and granted virtually no rights and very little possibility of acquiring citizenship, even after two generations, unless they can pass a battery of assimilation tests, and the 250,000 or so refugees from Eastern Europe who may be granted fuller rights. The Solingen attack provoked the first militant reaction among the Turks, 3,000 of whom rampaged across the city centre and were vigorously repulsed by the police, whose own campaign against extreme-right arsonists had been feeble and had produced few results.

While Germany deserved some sympathy for the refugee problem – although not the Turkish one, which is an exploitative one of its own making – the Kohl government's failure to act decisively against the far right seemed to many to represent the moral bankruptcy of post-reunification Germany. In the first nine months of 1992 there were 1,480 attacks on foreigners, compared with about 70 in 1980. Around 67,000 Germans were members of neo-Nazi organizations. The more moderate right is already dictating the German agenda: in November 1993, Edmund Stoiber, the Bavarian prime minister, called for 'a halt in European integration' because Germans had no further need to seek 'an identity' as Europeans. To him, the Second World War 'is past now'.

Domestically, German reunification had been expensively secured by the opportunist handling of the issue by the Kohl government. Taking advantage of the euphoria generated by reunification, the chancellor generously permitted a one-to-one exchange between West German marks and East German ones, worth probably a tenth as much, which generated huge inflationary pressures. While this ensured a massive endorsement of the government by the East Germans in the following election, Kohl flunked the tax increases needed to pay for the package in a non-inflationary manner.

The largely autonomous Bundesbank was instead drafted in to dampen down inflation through its sole available mechanism – high interest rates, which had the effect of stifling growth in the rest of Europe, running down their currencies in favour of the mark and, finally, putting the German economy itself into a tailspin. Meanwhile, friction and disillusion between former East and West Germans grew apace, while the East became a centre of rapidly closing industries and unemployment.

As Soviet troops departed, in closed trains to avoid attacks from the local population, the outlook for former East Germans looked grim, and, if they moved to the West, they seemed condemned to hard work on low pay. A great deal of this was inevitable; and the reconversion of East German industry was a necessity. Even so the German failure to provide a more exalted national lead and their assertion of self-interest at the expense of the rest of Europe was a serious downer after the high of reunification.

IF OUR PEACE missile now veered south-east, it would come across an horrific indictment not so much of man's inhumanity to man – that has been present through the ages – as of decent man's penchant for passing by on the other side. By mid-1993 the siege of Sarajevo had become a cliché, even a bore; yet the continuation of a conflict to the point of tediousness disguised deeper suffering rather than the reverse. By then some 200,000 people, mostly Bosnian Muslims, had been killed, more than one million forcibly removed from their homes, and some 50,000 women systematically raped.

These cold statistics masked stories of individual tragedy, like that of a forty-year-old woman who told of dozens of women and guards being shepherded into the hall of a building where:

> They tore off their clothes, pulled their hair, cut their breasts with their knives. They would cut the belly of the women who wore the traditional Muslim baggy trousers. Those who screamed would be killed on the spot.
>
> In front of a few hundred prisoners they raped and tortured women and girls for days. It was unbearable to watch girls being raped in front of their fathers. In the evening, after heavy drinking, the Chetniks would come into the hall with lamps. Stepping on us, they would look for girls, not older than twelve, thirteen. The girls cried, holding on to their

> mothers. As they were taken, pieces of their mothers' clothes remained in their hands. While doing that, the Chetniks would shoot at us.
>
> Later they would leave the girls' dead bodies in the hall, so we had to see them. We cried until morning. Then they would throw the bodies in the river. Every day the same picture was repeated; they would rape and kill in front of hundreds of us.
>
> Once a young woman with a baby was taken in the middle of the hall. It was in June. They ordered her to take off her clothes. She put the baby on the floor next to her. Four Chetniks raped her; she was silent, looking at her crying child. When she was left alone she asked if she could breast-feed the baby. Then a Chetnik cut the child's head off with a knife. He gave the bloody head to the mother. The poor woman screamed. They took her outside and she never came back.

Horrific as such descriptions are, they are nothing new: man, since the beginning of time, has shown how little encouragement he needs to return to bestiality, particularly in times of war. The aggression of Serbia and the opportunist savagery of Croatia are nothing new either; petty tyrannies and ethnic hatreds are phenomena as old as human history. What is missing, in the last decade of the twentieth century, is the will of outsiders to deter, as though they had learnt nothing from every previous conflict in the century. One by one, the excuses for appeasing evil had been reasserted with the kind of stubborn ingenuity that suggested that international relations had taken a giant leap back into the 1930s.

The conflict within Yugoslavia was initially described by the non-interventionists as a 'civil' war; in fact Yugoslavia had always been an artificial creation and the aggression of its strongest component, Serbia, against first the Croats and then the Bosnians, was plain from the first. Once Tito had died and the Eastern bloc crumbled, there was no possibility of holding Yugoslavia together; the only issue was how much of it would be run by Serbia, which controlled the bulk of the country's armed forces. There could be no excuse for dismissing the war as an 'internal' affair when the international community had already granted recognition to such 'internal states' as the Baltic Republics and even acknowledged an obligation to protect the stateless Kurds.

There was then an attempt to equate the three communities; it was said that this was an ethnic war between three sides equally guilty of atrocities. The fact that some appalling acts were carried out by Bosnia's Muslims could hardly obscure the overwhelming aggression and racial war – 'ethnic cleansing' – carried out against them; even the Croats, helping themselves to a piece of Bosnia, had themselves been victims of major Serbian attack. As early as November 1992, Tadeusz Mazowiecki, the respected former prime minister of Poland, reported to the United Nations Commission on Human Rights that 'the collective evidence leaves no doubt as to who is responsible for the horror (in Bosnia); the Serbian political and military leaders in Bosnia–Herzogovina, supported by the authorities of Serbia'. The West pointed to the undiplomatic manner in which the Croats, and then the Bosnians, had voted to secede from Yugoslavia; thus the overwhelming desire of a people to be free through their own democratic choice was cynically dismissed by the democratic powers (Germany excepted).

The military establishments of the Western nations, in particular the Pentagon, were wheeled in to assert that military intervention in Bosnia was impossible, requiring an overwhelming commitment and small possibility of exit. In fact there was little evidence that the Serbs were particularly effective fighters; they were mainly successful in terrorizing civilians and shelling cities without retaliation. On the few occasions that well-equipped UN troops were allowed to retaliate to Serbian attacks, the effect was devastating. While the nature of Bosnia's terrain would certainly not render the intervention a quick or casualty-free operation, it was no Vietnam either. Intervening forces would have had the vehement support of a clearly defined section of the population which, because of the policy of ethnic cleansing, was geographically concentrated; unlike Vietnam, the enemy would thus be visible and in front, not invisible and behind; the country was rough, but not jungle.

There must be some doubt that UN troops in Bosnia were

really so exposed – heavily armed British tanks, for example, have proved virtually invulnerable to the firepower of irregular Serb forces, as in attacks on convoys near Tuzla. The UN force at Vitez would have been within range of Serbian 155mm guns in the hills, but if they had opened fire, these would have been quickly subject to observation with advanced radar and heat-sensing equipment that could pinpoint them for air strikes. Moreover, artillery could have been provided to shore up UN positions. Initially, playing up the threat of Serbian retaliation against 'vulnerable' UN forces seemed principally an excuse for staying out of the conflict.

The Serbs, effective at murdering unarmed civilians though they were, did not have an impressive record in real fighting. During the battle of Vukovar in 1991, for example, around 1,500 Croats, equipped only with rifles and handguns, held off 25,000 Serbs equipped with tanks, Migs and heavy artillery for three months, until running out of ammunition. Far from being effective hand-to-hand fighters or guerrillas, the Serbs relied heavily on tanks and artillery in old-fashioned Soviet fashion; some nine-tenths of the casualties they inflicted were from artillery and tank guns. Although some of the guns could be hidden, they had to emerge to fire, and the number of available sites – flat areas near roads – were limited in the mountains.

If Serbian firepower was exposed, so were their supply lines, across just half a dozen bridges spanning the Danube and the Drina. It was worth noting that the war between Serbia and Croatia only stopped when it reached a rough military stalemate – 'level killing fields' – tilted ones provide every incentive for the more powerful to continue to take territory. This, of course, is not a new doctrine, but one which dominated all Cold War planning, based on mutual assured destruction or, more simply, 'deterrence'.

Short of major intervention, other options existed, such as air strikes against Serbian artillery and the interception of supplies from Serbia into Bosnia. Neither was ever threatened or tried until too late. Publicly aired doubts about the difficulty of intervening, before Serbian aggression really got under way, sent a repeated message to the beast of Belgrade, President Milosevic, that there would be no retaliation.

George Kenney, acting chief of the Yugoslav desk at the State Department, who resigned in protest at American inaction as far back as August 1992, angrily alleged that it was cold political calculus that explained why the Americans had kept out of Bosnia. 'The administration, I believe, made a basic decision at the highest levels that politically it had more to gain from not getting involved in a very messy foreign conflict where it cannot count on an easy or quick solution but risks getting the blame for failure.' He argued convincingly for limited military intervention:

> Would US military involvement lead to a quagmire? Unless we were extraordinarily inept in our deployment of force, I doubt it. Although I am not a military expert, I believe that the forces in Bosnia are poorly disciplined, loosely organized and to a large extent nothing more than wild young men who have gone on a mass killing spree. These are the disgruntled who have no stake in what was normal society in Bosnia or in Serbia. But they have the guns and, for now, face only weak opposition. I am convinced that they would not stand up to a strong attack.
>
> We do not have to take the ground and hold it. That is the Bosnian government's problem. But we could undertake a number of limited military actions that would greatly support the Bosnian government in its efforts to reclaim its territory.

All these suggestions were in fact considered when it was probably too late to affect the course of the fighting; Kenney's analysis has an uncomfortable ring of truth.

The prime movers behind the policy of non-intervention were the military establishments. In the United States, a post-Vietnam policy of non-intervention, except where American forces can be overwhelmingly deployed at very little risk, was still in force; the Gulf War had been a confirmation, rather than a departure, from this. In Western Europe, military establishments still in rivalry with one another, incapable of co-ordination except against a now-departed Soviet threat, proved unable to rise to any other occasion. America and Europe swapped recriminations about where responsibility for Bosnia lay.

America's Secretary of State, Warren Christopher, in an almost exact echo of Chamberlain's famous comment about Czechoslovakia on the eve of Munich, spoke of 'a humanitarian crisis a long way from home in the middle of another continent'.

The United States is departing from years of precedent in suggesting that it will recognize Bosnia's new, shrunken boundaries. In 1931 the then American Secretary of State elaborated on what became known as the Stimson doctrine: America would not recognize political or territorial changes made by force – in this case China's occupation of Manchuria. This was later applied to Nazi conquests from 1938 on, as well as to the Baltic Republics seized by Russia in 1940.

The Europeans retorted that it was global superpower America that should give a lead; on Bosnia, Britain, America's traditional ally in conflict, insisted that, as long as the United States was unwilling to commit ground forces, the only policy was damage limitation. By the time there was some will to act, particularly on America's part, the presence of UN forces provided another let-out; these would be attacked by the Serbs, it was asserted, if the West intervened.

Certainly the UN forces, in particular the large British and French contingents, behaved with courage and professionalism and saved possibly hundreds of thousands of lives in the winters of 1992–3, 1993–4 and 1994–5; but their capacity to resist attack was never tested, and the right kind of intervention could anyway have protected them. Military intervention would have been difficult, cost lives and perhaps lasted years. But to assert that the West had no business to resist was to rule out intervention in nine-tenths of the globe; to give aggressors everywhere a blank cheque.

It was asserted that the Balkans were of no strategic significance to the West, and that the war was a small, local one which would not spread. Aside from the flagrant immorality of this assertion – the Second World War broke out over Poland, after all, another country of no great strategic interest to the Western powers – it was wholly mistaken. Serbia's war against Croatia had already spread to Bosnia, and Kosovo and Macedonia were tinder dry for conflagration to the south, with the further possibility of drawing in the Greeks and the Turks. The wider implications of permitting potential aggressors around the world to believe they could get away with it, like the Serbs, were never addressed. For any European government to assert that aggression and genocide within Europe was of no strategic importance seemed remarkably short-sighted.

Finally, in as classic an act of appeasement as ever occurred before the last war, an arms embargo was imposed on all sides, which in practice prevented Bosnia's Muslims from resisting the aggressor Serbs, who were fighting with the arsenal of the Yugoslav army behind them. To arm the Bosnians would be to create 'level killing fields' – a tasteless play on an American business cliché. Better to continue to twist the arm of the victim, Bosnia, to accept dismemberment, than to help him fight back. In virtually every postwar conflict from which the West has decided to abstain, it has armed its own side or the perceived victims of aggression; Afghanistan's mujaheddin and Angola's non-communist guerrillas are examples. Later it became impossible to remove the embargo without fuelling the flames. But the initial decision was indefensible.

The West's attitude to Bosnia seemed to suggest that it was preferable that one side, the aggressor, applier of systematic ethnic cleansing and atrocities, be given the freedom to win, so as to get the killing over as quickly as possible. The new doctrine was to apply pressure on the loser to stop fighting. The consequences of such a course being applied in the Second World War, or any other conflict, do not bear thinking about. What if Roosevelt had decided not to level the killing fields between Germany and Britain by denying the latter Lend-Lease in 1941?

Truly, initial Western policy towards Serbia represented the very bottom of the barrel in postwar international relations, a combination of ignorance, selfishness, inertia (foreign ministry spokesmen in Europe and America poured scorn on those who advocated 'doing something' to help; the converse was to do nothing), amorality and tolerance of pure evil that will forever besmirch the nations principally responsible for it.

In July 1993, Eugene Rostow, the Reagan administration's director of the Arms Control and Disarmament Agency, devastatingly attacked American policy over Bosnia in the *International Herald Tribune* (other critics included Reagan himself and George Shultz, his Secretary of State):

> The Gulf War was fought not only to ensure America's access to the oil of the region but to defend a far more fundamental national security interest – that of resisting aggression. Mr Bush has said many times that if aggression is allowed to stand, the practice spreads until it threatens the general peace; and, therefore, that the world community must enforce the rule even against relatively small violations.
>
> This has been the basic theme of American foreign policy since the time of President Harry Truman.
>
> Enforcing the rule of international law against aggression does not require the United States to send in the marines every time a leaf falls . . . But the major powers and the world community should take all substantial acts of aggression seriously, and move decisively against those that threaten regional or world stability.
>
> Serbia's aggression against the former Yugoslav republic more than meets that standard. The most vital goal of US security policy is to help build a system of world public order, managed by the major powers, in accordance with the rules of the United Nations Charter.
>
> In an effort to escape from the challenge of the Yugoslav tragedy, some now contend that the collapse of the Soviet Union makes it less important for the Western allies to enforce the law against aggression than in the days of Soviet Union expansionism. A few even argue that because of the recent changes in Russian policy, the rule against aggression has become 'optional'.
>
> This view is in error. A scrupulous respect for the rule against aggression is more important to the Western allies

> today than it was before the Soviet collapse began in 1989. In the short run, the Soviet collapse, like the fall of every other empire in history, has radically destabilized world politics. It will take an alert, perceptive and flexible Western foreign policy to make sure that the system emerges with a structure favourable to America's abiding national interests.
>
> During this period of transition, hostile or unfriendly combinations of states may come into being, threatening to become hegemonies – combinations between Russia and Germany, for example, between China and Japan, or between Russia and China. This is no time to behave as if the end of the Soviet Union has guaranteed perpetual peace. A reasonably peaceful world order can only be built on the foundation of a favourable balance of power or, even better, a true concert of the major powers.

To repeat, if such policies had prevailed in the late 1930s there would have been no Second World War – just German domination of Europe; Britain would have been vulnerable to invasion and occupation; and the cause of Hitler would have triumphed. Fortunately, there is reason to believe that what happened in Bosnia will not set the pace for international relations; the West was caught on the hop by the end of the Cold War without the necessary deterrent structures for defusing regional conflicts and it misjudged the extent of the problem. All of these things can be solved, as will be suggested later. For if Bosnia is the pointer to the future, global anarchy threatens to become reality indeed.

The whole cruel farce of Western policy towards Bosnia reached its nemesis on 5 February 1994, when a mortar shell was lobbed into Sarajevo market, killing sixty-eight people, from a distance of less than a mile (leading to suggestions that the Muslims had acted to provoke Western retaliation against the Serbs). The television pictures of the carnage were ghastly, shocking even to Western publics that had become blasé about the suffering in Bosnia in the light of their own governments' lumpen inaction. That single massacre – a drop in the ocean of a slaughter that had claimed maybe 200,000 lives – prompted the United States to go into fast reverse on policies of pusillanimity dressed up as sage and statesman-like caution. The West had found a leader at last, not a prime minister, but 'prime time television'.

President Clinton was suddenly persuaded of the need for air strikes – but not of American ground troops – as was the French government. Britain went along reluctantly; we were at least consistent. Miraculously, in a 180-degree change of policy, the market-place massacre had changed Western policy from do-nothing to do-something (the exact policy so long derided). It was decided that the previous objections to allied air strikes on Bosnian Serb artillery outside Sarajevo no longer stood up. The risk to UN forces on the ground was no longer an overriding reason for staying out. Military action was no longer seen as dangerously open-ended. NATO was no longer deemed to lack the authority to act 'out-of-area'. Serbian artillery was no longer seen as untargetable, Serbian fighters as an overwhelming foe, air attacks as risking too many civilian casualties.

No one resigned and no heads rolled as a number of foreign ministers solemnly ate their previous protestations as to the dangers of threatening force. Unlike, say, finance ministers forced to put their policies into reverse by events, their diplomatic counterparts were finely skilled at chocolate-coating the abandonment of a policy as an effortless progression towards an always consistent goal. NATO, with a new British commander on the ground, General Sir Michael Rose, finally summoned the will to issue an ultimatum against Serbia to withdraw its artillery from a twelve-mile exclusion zone around Sarajevo, under threat of air strikes. President Clinton rallied Western resolve after the massacre with the stirring cry: 'Until those folks get tired of killing each other over there, bad things will continue to happen.'

A remarkable thing did happen, as the ragged Chetnik militia of civilian slayers faced the threat of massive attack from the most sophisticated air forces in the world – the Serbs complied. Their crumpled, amiable, double-crossing and mendacious leader, Radovan Karadzic, admitted that they were 'not so stupid' as to take on NATO. Not a single Western serviceman was required to die to achieve what had been declared as unachievable only days earlier; just a show of Western resolve, of the kind that had characterized the postwar decades, which over the past three dog years of Western diplomacy had been entirely lacking. Of course this was but a beginning, and many more trials lay ahead. But it was an enormous step forward for those who had long argued that Western political and military leaders should be less spineless. And it begged the question – how many lives might have been saved if NATO had acted a year or two earlier?

Sarajevo settled into an uneasy semblance of normality; the war wound down slightly elsewhere. The high hopes aroused early in 1994 began to dissipate as it became clear that Western forces would retaliate only if public anger back home was aroused. The Bosnian Serbs taunted the UN by helping themselves to military supplies early in the summer, provoking only a token response. In the summer of 1994 the devious Milosevic abruptly imposed an embargo on Bosnia's Serbs for refusing to agree to the latest Western plan for carving up the country; it seemed that sanctions were at last having an effect on Belgrade.

Congress prodded President Clinton into setting a deadline for lifting the arms embargo on Bosnia's Muslims – which the Europeans argued would set off a new phase in the war. Certainly the timing would be wrong, if it resulted in renewed fighting and a withdrawal of UN forces before the onset of winter; a delay past the winter was essential. Yet, failing Bosnian Serbian acceptance of the plan – itself a nauseating legitimization of many of Serbia's conquests – lifting the embargo in the long term, particularly if UN forces were withdrawn, seemed the only course likely to give the Muslims a fighting chance.

Barring any willingness by the West to station large numbers of troops in Bosnia indefinitely to police an immoral and indefensible border, future fighting seemed inevitable. Even in the improbable event of Serbian agreement, the Muslims seemed unlikely in the long term to abide by the rape of large parts of their land. Peace with dishonour could but be a postponement; and in the next round, the victim should surely be equipped to defend himself against the well-armed aggressor, as he should have been in the first.

In late 1994, under intense Congressional pressure, President Clinton announced that American forces would no longer help enforce the arms embargo on Bosnia. NATO air strikes against Serbian positions were also stepped up. Bosnian forces staged their first major effective offensive on all fronts of the war. This triggered off a savage Serb counter-attack, and fierce fighting at Bihac.

Western policymakers could not argue that their damage limitation exercises had shortened the war. The Bosnian crisis, in truth, served as an awful – if limited – example of the dangers of appeasement and the failure to instal proper post-Cold-War security structures – 'one that got away,' as Jim Lester, senior member of the House of Commons Foreign Affairs Committee, aptly defined it. Would that it were the only one.

BY EARLY 1995, the outlook was bleak indeed. With President Clinton and the new Republican majority in Congress united in continuing to rule out the despatch of large numbers of ground forces, and the Europeans insisting that they would send only peacekeepers in America's absence, the UN force had become the flimsy railing that prevented the whole country hurling itself over a cliff: a decision to withdraw would inevitably lead to all-out conflict.

The policy of sending UN peacekeepers, instead of a Western intervention force with a mandate to act against aggression had been wrong from the beginning. But peacekeepers were better than no force at all; no foreign minister, understandably for once, would wish to be responsible for a decision to withdraw that could spark all-out war. The new Republican majority in Congress pressed for such a withdrawal, then quietened down as it began to realize the consequences. Britain's Defence Secretary, Malcolm Rifkind, let it be known that withdrawal was under active consideration, possibly as a tactic to concentrate the minds of the warring factions.

For the issue was not so much whether the UN should withdraw, but whether the warring factions would allow its forces to stay. The Serbs had always disliked and harried the peacekeepers, but permitted them to remain out of fear of Western military retaliation. By 1995 the prospects of any but limited Western air attacks were fading, which loosened the restraints on Serbian forces to behave themselves. The Croat president, Franjo Tudjman, threatened to force out the 12,000 UN peacekeepers between his forces and the Croat Serbs who had seized the enclave of Krajina in order to absorb it into Greater Serbia; inevitably, Milosevic would come to their defence against the Croats. Only the Bosnian Muslims had an interest in retaining the UN presence; however, their demand for an arms embargo would, if met, probably trigger off an all-out Serbian offensive which would require the withdrawal of UN forces under fire.

Western policymakers were thus boxed into a corner of their own making. It seemed clear that they should take no action – withdrawing UN forces, lifting the arms embargo – which at this stage might precipitate all-out conflict. The only sensible course was to prepare plans for the enforced evacuation of UN troops, itself a tricky and dangerous operation likely to take up to a year and involving the commitment of American ground forces.

Prospects for a settlement looked forlorn, with the Serbs refusing to talk and the Croats threatening to attack the Serbs; in repressed Kosovo, meanwhile, the pot, in early 1995, reached boiling point while the throttling embargo on Macedonia was bringing Greece and Turkey to the edge of conflict. Barring a determined effort by both the Americans and the Russians to force the three sides to a settlement backed up by the threat of military action, all-out war in the Balkans seemed in prospect. If the UN forces were forced out, the West would have no further excuse for denying the Bosnians the arms they sought against aggression.

An all-out war would be a terrible headstone for the failure of leadership that has taken place over the past four years. In the beginning, there were three options: military intervention against the Serb aggressor; peacekeeping; or staying out and permitting a full-scale war. The first was never tried, the second is failing, the third beckons.

OUR DISARMED peace cruise missile, with its camera, might continue on its course north-eastward, over to the Black Sea, where Russia and the Ukraine have been locked in conflict over possession of the Black Sea Fleet and the Ukraine's stockpile of nuclear weapons, then directly northwards to Moscow, where the reform process has been anything but smooth.

The remarkable thing about Russia has been, in truth, not that reform has gone badly, but that it has survived at all. On the night of 18 April 1991, the current chapter in Soviet postwar history began with the coup attempt that sought to depose the architect of Russia's reform programme, Mikhail Gorbachev. Up to that point, it was possible to argue that Soviet reform was proceeding constitutionally, if slowly. In fact, it was blocked and Gorbachev was straitjacketed by the limits of his own beliefs. A courageous leader in Soviet terms, and a great reformer, he still could not envisage a Soviet Union that was not dominated by the Communist Party and traditional institutions, albeit in updated form. In particular, Gorbachev had failed to establish a popular base for his leadership, this being frustrated at every turn by apparatchiks in the State and Party. Essential economic reforms had time and again been stalled. The Gorbachev regime was going nowhere fast.

It was the old guard, overestimating its strength, that broke the log jam. The images of the coup attempt are familiar the world over – the slurred, blurred television images of the bleary hangdog plotters – Gennady Yanayev, Valentin Pavlov and Boris Pugo; Boris Yeltsin's defiant stand aboard a tank, assuming the leadership of the democratic forces in Gorbachev's absence; the tense stand-off outside the White House – the seat of the Russian government; the rescue of a grim-faced Gorbachev from Yalta, the immediate and contemptuous public upstaging of Gorbachev by Yeltsin.

With the Communist Party's dissolution and Yeltsin's seizure of power, a watershed had been crossed: it had been proved that the old guard no longer possessed the force – in particular the unqualified support of the armed forces – to prevail against Russia's new, articulate middle class and more assertive working class. Yet Yeltsin was not trusted by everyone to pursue unashamedly reformist policies and the old guard resorted to every trick in the book by manipulating a Soviet constitution towards which, when they were in power, they had shown scant respect.

By early 1993 the struggle had crystallized into one between Yeltsin and Ruslan Khasbulatov, the ambitious, crude spokesman of the Russian Parliament, supported by others such as the martinet vice-president, Alexander Rutskoi. Yeltsin at first appeared impotent, sacking his first reformist prime minister, Yegor Gaidar; then he seized the initiative by staging a referendum in support of his position. He won by much larger margins than thought likely, even on the economic reform programme.

At first he seemed to bow to enormous political pressures to moderate free-market economic reforms. In September 1993, he moved decisively against his opponents, declaring emergency rule, in effect dissolving Parliament, and scheduling parliamentary elections for December, with a presidential one promised for the spring. Under the old parliamentary rules this was unconstitutional, and Khasbulatov responded by having Rutskoi sworn in as president. Yeltsin, labelling Khasbulatov 'a cockroach', restored Gaidar to manage the economy, ignored the new parliament, cut off its electricity supply, and, with the support of the army, proceeded with business as usual.

Within days, a bloody confrontation ensued which Yeltsin, backed by a newly assertive army, won. However, the December elections, while granting Yeltsin greater powers, resulted in a Parliament only narrowly dominated by reformists, with old-style communists and new-style fascists, headed by the ludicrous and dangerous Vladimir Zhirinovsky, who won an unexpectedly high share of the vote. A month later the brakes were on economic reform, Gaidar was again ousted, and a more assertive Soviet foreign policy was announced.

The new Soviet toughness found its most dramatic expression in the brutal suppression of Chechnya's attempted secession in the winter of 1994–5. Yeltsin sought to impress upon the Chechens his determination to crush any outbreak of Islamic militancy in the former Soviet Union, but in doing so revived the old image of Russia as a savage, clumsy bear. Encouragingly, there was bitter opposition to the Chechnya campaign in Russia itself.

After the Cold War Eastern Europe can be divided between sheep and goats: the ones that are genuinely democratic and have embarked upon real reform and the ones – the 'nadi' – led by old communist apparatchiks pretending to be nationalists. In the former camp is Poland, which although now run by the ex-communists in opposition to the benignly eccentric and increasingly unpopular presidency of Lech Walesa, have permitted half the economy to pass into private hands (probably two-thirds if the black market is taken into account).

In Hungary a rather colourless but popularly elected prime minister, Joszef Antall, ruled until his death in 1993; his lacklustre successor was massively defeated by the reformed Communist Party the following year. The Czech Republic is run by a brilliant economist, Vaclav Klaus. All three have suffered smaller declines in GDP than forecast as a result of the economic reforms – around 10 per cent – and are already recovering. All three are moving close to the economic requirements of European Union membership. Bulgaria and Albania too seem to be performing surprisingly well.

Of the Baltic States, Estonia has the most successful economy under free-market reformists. Lithuania has fallen into the hands of Soviet-style apparatchiks. Latvia is doing reasonably well, but the Russians have 25,000 troops stationed there against 'external threats', and are angry about the refusal of the government to grant citizenship to the large proportion of Estonians of Russian origin. Russia calls these states part of the 'near abroad'.

However, the regimes of the Ukraine, Slovakia, Serbia, Croatia, Romania and Byelorussia leave much to be desired. The Ukrainian leader, Leonid Kravchuk, presided over the nearest there was to a bankrupt command economy in Eastern Europe until his welcome election defeat in 1994. The Slovak president, Vladimir Meciar, has been waging an unsavoury campaign against the Hungarian minority there. Serbia's Little Hitler, Slobodan Milosevic, presides over an economic shambles and a holocaust as a result of his decision to create a greater Serbia. The Croat leader, Franjo Tudjman, is another hardliner, viscerally anti-Semitic. The Romanian president, Ion Iliescu, has employed miners as his storm-troopers against the opposition, and also persecutes his Hungarian minority.

THE PEACE MISSILE, turning south, would cross the former southern states of the Soviet Union, a region of sporadic, almost unceasing turmoil and bloodshed, with some thirty separate conflicts at the last count. There was, of course, the brutal pounding of Chechnya. In Georgia, rebellions in Abkhazia as well as by the followers of former strongman Zviad Gamsakhurdia left the country's President Eduard Shevardnadze on the ropes and provided a pretext for Russia to intervene to prop him up on its terms (almost certainly, the Soviet army helped the rebellions with this end in view).

To the south-east, Armenia lay blockaded by its neighbour Azerbaijan, as punishment for its support for the Armenian enclave inside Azerbaijan, Nagorno-Karabakh. In order to break this President Levon Ter-Petrosian had to beg for Russian help – which the Russians were willing to grant provided a new Transcaucasian federation, consisting of Armenia and Georgia and – although it is resisting – Azerbaijan was set up. With Russian bases and border forces this would amount to little less than a reconstruction of the Soviet Union in this area.

Azerbaijan itself has lost about a fifth of its territory to the Georgians, who, in five years of savage fighting, have opened a salient up to Nagorno-Karabakh; tens of thousands have been killed and up to a million Azerbaijanis displaced by the war; a slaughterhouse nearly on a par with Yugoslavia, although much more remote. The Azerbaijani leader, Geidar Aliev, has sought Russian help and is prepared to join the Confederation of

Independent States – but not to have Soviet occupying forces in his country. The presence of oil complicates the strategic calculation here, with Western companies eager to move in.

Across the Caspian Sea the cruise missile would reach the vast province of Kazakhstan, more than a third of whose people are Russian, with reported large reserves of oil and gold, as well as part of the Soviet nuclear arsenal. So far the Russians have not interfered much in Kazakhstan, which has been flirting with the Americans. Its president, Nursultan Nazarbaev, is closely allied to the fiercely repressive regime of President Islam Karimov in smaller Uzbekistan to the south.

Karimov's main objective has been to stop Islamic fundamentalism, and in this he enjoys warm Russian support. Further south still, in Turkmenistan on the very borders with Iran, another quasi dictator, Sapurmurad Niazov, also relentlessly represses his Islamic movement and all expressions of dissidence. The most front-line state of all against Islam is Tajikistan, to the east, where moderate Islamic forces were driven out of power in December 1992 by a pro-Soviet regime backed by 20,000 Russian troops bent on suppressing Islamic guerrilla incursions across from Afghanistan. As with Turkmenistan and Uzbekistan, the regime is ferociously repressive: glasnost might as well not have occurred. President Yeltsin has stated baldly that 'this border is in effect Russia's, not Tajikistan's'. In Kirgizstan, to the east, along China's border, President Askar Akaev leads a moderately reformist government which, however, may be threatened by pro-Russian communist party bosses.

Before travelling south to the Middle East, the peace missile would have recorded that, a few years after the collapse of the Soviet empire, it has all but reassembled itself in central Asia from the forge of furious ethnic conflict. Russia, still retaining the overwhelming concentration of infrastructure, wealth and industry of the old Soviet Union, now has its buffer republics back as well; the Soviet Union is quietly resurrecting.

*

IF OUR OBSERVER missile then travelled due south, it would encounter the detritus of the first test of the new world order, the greatest show of strength by the West in the post-communist era: the aftermath of the Gulf War. There can be no doubt that a major victory had been won – an act of unprovoked aggression by a major country upon a smaller one had been humiliatingly reversed. The second great achievement was to frustrate, for a few years at least, Iraq's frenzied attempt to gain nuclear weaponry. These two single facts negated all the downsides to the war.

But downsides there were; it was a disastrously missed opportunity. In the early days of the war, Western forces had Iraq's Eighth Army in the bag, with only the Baghdad–Basrah road to close off, to cut its lines of communications and secure its survival. It was instead allowed to escape not because of the feeble excuse proffered, that allied pilots lacked the stomach to indulge in a 'turkey shoot', but because of an arcane geostrategic calculation by President Bush that Iraq must be wounded, but not so seriously as to tempt Iranian attack. In fact, the chances of that were small. Iran had been exhausted by the Iran–Iraq War and, although capable in time of presenting a challenge, was far too weak to intervene again in Iraq.

Subsequent analysis of the crucial Oval Office meeting of 27 February 1991, when the decision was made to stop the war, confirms the magnitude of the error of judgement involved, suspected by many outside observers at the time. The Chairman of the Joint Chiefs of Staff, General Colin Powell, advised President Bush to take the decision without realizing that the bulk of the Iraqi forces was, in fact, escaping encirclement.

The mistake stemmed from the fact that the Iraqi forces, when attacked by a Marine force to the south, put up little resistance and began to retreat before the main American army units – the XVIII Airborne Corps and the VII Corps – were anywhere near cutting off their line of withdrawal with an assault across Western Iraq. Although this main American advance moved swiftly across the desert, the Iraqis were swifter in retreat.

Alarmed by media criticism that several hundred Iraqi soldiers had been killed by air attacks along the 'highway of death' north of Basra, the administration in Washington determined to end the war '100 hours' after the initial offensives. When asked by his deputy, General Cal Waller, why the ceasefire was being declared now, the American Gulf Forces commander, General Norman Schwarzkopf, replied, 'One hundred hours has a nice ring' – an ironic reference to political concerns in Washington. American forces stopped short of closing the trap, and the bulk of Iraqi forces escaped.

This had momentous consequences: Saddam, who quite probably would have fallen had the Iraqi armies been encircled, survived. In an attempt to overthrow him, the Saudis lent their support to a Shia rebellion in southern Iraq that was crushed with the loss of thousands of lives. Pentagon officials blocked attempts to set up a demilitarized zone in southern Iraq – which might have protected the Shias – for fear of further involvement. In 1994 a huge reinforcement of American forces in Kuwait took place after massive Iraqi troop manoeuvres along the Kuwaiti border, prompting the Americans to seek just such a demilitarized zone. All of these consequences can be directly ascribed to the premature ending of the Gulf War.

Perhaps most tragic of all, in place of military defeat there was substituted, as Western policy, a crushing economic war of attrition directed not at a handful of Iraqi soldiers, but at the country's entire civilian population. A dollar today is worth around 15,000 times as much Iraqi currency as before the war – but salaries have not risen. Iraqi rations are around a third of the World Food and Agricultural Organization's estimate of minimum food requirements. The sins of Iraq's leaders are being visited upon its people – through a Western miscalculation.

Saddam was left in power, although almost certainly American forces were capable of seizing Baghdad (British special forces had been right up to the outskirts). The excuse was offered that, once in Baghdad, Western forces would find it difficult to get out, and Saddam would resort to guerrilla war against them. In fact, guerrilla warfare was thoroughly improbable in a flat, largely desert country; only the north offered possibilities for cover, and it would have been hard to dissuade the Kurds from dismembering Saddam if he fled there.

Within Iraq, the hatred of Saddam that manifested itself in frequent coup attempts – in spite of the viciousness of his repression – suggests that the West would have had no difficulty in installing a more representative government in Baghdad, then withdrawing. Once removed, it is hard to believe the hated dictator would have found the support to regroup; Saddam's Iraq was a place of Stalinist oppression and sullenness; he entirely lacked the charisma and popular appeal of a Nasser. But this would have involved the possibility of casualties and a bigger commitment in a virtually casualty-free war. The West's leaders were unwilling to take this risk.

Instead, enticing Kurds to rise up in the north and Shiites to do so in the south, they then stood by and watched them massacred, intervening at length in Kurdistan to provide protection zones when the plight of its people became widely known. Saddam entrenched himself more viciously than ever in charge of a police state where international sanctions did little harm to himself and his cronies, but a great deal to those at the bottom. Other disquieting questions arose from the Gulf intervention: was the scale of the bombing justified by the West's determination to avoid casualties among its own men? Was an opportunity missed to reform the corrupt state of Kuwait? Were the right warning signals sent to Iraq after it hinted it might move into Kuwait? The benefits of victory, in retrospect, far outweighed those drawbacks; but the Gulf War could have been a much firmer foundation for establishing the 'New World Order'.

LET THE PEACE missile now turn a long way due east to cross the barren mountains of Iran and Afghanistan, the mournful plains of Pakistan and reach the border with China, and then film a remarkable phenomenon – the co-existence of capitalism with a communist-style authoritarian regime. By mid-1993, what the *New York Times* journalist Nicholas Kristof dubbed 'Market-Leninism' was comprehensively being applied – a still authoritarian Leninist regime, which had modestly eased its post-Tiananmen-Square repression under intense Western pressure was providing a degree of market freedom unthinkable in the Soviet Union. Hundreds of thousands of small enterprises were booming, the service sector was thriving from a low base and private schools were permitted. Only the major state enterprises remained under public control.

The Chinese leadership was proving that one aspect of free market theory was wrong – that as an economy grew more pluralistic, so political freedom would inevitably follow. An even bigger gamble was the impact on China's troubled economy. Its rates of growth in recent years have been truly astronomic – 13 per cent in 1992 alone, mirroring Japan in the last years of its economic miracle, but also leading to inflation of around 20 per cent and the creation of massive unrest in the countryside, where the great bulk of China's population live. Those living in the countryside were deeply envious of urban prosperity and now faced an increase in the cost of urban goods, a reduction in the value of their products, and rampant urban corruption.

In the long run, the view of the countryside had always prevailed in Chinese politics and the possibility of a backlash, with political bosses and army warlords regaining control of the Chinese communist party, is not to be ruled out – the crushing of the demonstrations in Tiananmen Square almost certainly occurred as a result of pressure from this conservative wing. The question is whether the market or the rural lobby in China will prevail. If China's policies succeed – it is light years ahead of the Soviet Union in economic reform, partly because its communism, after only forty years, is much less entrenched and bureaucratic than that of the Soviet Union after seventy-five years – the iron link, always intellectually dubious, between political and economic pluralism, will have been broken. Indeed, China would stand as an example of authoritarianism and fast economic growth – something already pioneered, in much more subtle form, in Japan and some other Asian countries.

*

THE CAMERA-CARRYING cruise missile might then veer to North Korea where the world's last Stalinist museum-piece (with the exception of Cuba's Fidel Castro), the late Kim Il-sung and, by all accounts, his even more erratic son, Kim Jong-Il, had been probably developing a crude nuclear device at Yongbyon, just north of the capital of Pyongyang, as well as a missile capable of carrying it. The programme was opposed by every one of North Korea's nervous neighbours, including the Russians and the Chinese and, of course, the Japanese and South Korea. The North Koreans have long been viewed as too unreliable to be in possession of such a weapon, and the fear is that, as the regime comes under increasing pressure from its sullen, impoverished, oppressed people, it could lash out wildly and dangerously on a foreign adventure. Intense diplomatic pressure was followed, in the spring of 1993, by an ultimatum that the North Koreans accept proper nuclear inspection, which was rejected; the Koreans threatening to walk out of the Nuclear Non-Proliferation Treaty.

Just short of the deadline in June, they dropped this threat: the question was whether Kim was playing for time or gently submitting. By January 1994, the Americans had acceded to North Korea's refusal to allow none but limited inspections; the cause of nuclear non-proliferation seemed to have been dealt a potentially lethal blow.

Following a mediation attempt by former President Jimmy Carter, the threat of sanctions against North Korea was momentarily lifted. The death of Kim Il-sung and uncertainty as to whether the younger Kim would in fact take power created further unease in the region. However, in October 1994, North Korea abruptly agreed to satisfactory inspection in return for massive financial aid in converting their nuclear reactors to non-plutonium-generating ones.

South Korea is intensely nervous about any strike against the north from its territory or just outside, fearing that the North Koreans will retaliate with a military attack on the South. Yet the Americans cannot afford to take a soft line on this issue, one of the central ones of the post-communist era; nuclear weapons cannot be allowed to fall into the hands of 'rogue' states like North Korea. Unless North Korea is simply playing for time, there is real hope that the crisis may have been defused.

THUS THE PEACE missile might end its outward journey on the edge of the Asian continent. On its return journey, on a southern trajectory, it would set a course over North Africa, to witness the gigantic issue of militant Islam in countries like Algeria and Egypt. In North Africa, the only country where an Islamic fundamentalist regime has actually seized power is Sudan, so poor that no one but the Egyptians have noticed. But it is far from insignificant strategically. It has become the main training and arms supply base for Islamic militants operating in Egypt and Algeria.

Both these countries are now facing full-scale Islamic insurgencies. In Algeria, now in the grip of civil war, the position is critical, after the government's textbook display of how not to handle Islamic militancy. In 1991 Algeria's first free elections were cancelled after it became clear that they would be won by the Islamic Salvation Front, largely because it was identified as the opposition to the corrupt and brutal coalition of socialist bureaucrats, former National Liberation Front guerrilla members and soldiers that have ruled since independence from France.

The Islamic Front went underground, while two militant armed Islamic guerrilla groups have surfaced, the longstanding Armed Islamic Movement, which has declared a fatwa against the regime, and the more extreme Islamic Armed Groups. Their tactics include murdering foreigners – some thirty have been killed, including twelve Croats who had their throats slit in December 1993 – murdering unveiled women, ransacking bars and burning down schools. Up to 20,000 people are believed to have died, mainly in clashes between these groups, the police and the armed forces, as well as terrorist attacks and death-squad reprisals. There are believed to be around 4,000 Islamic guerrillas.

In March 1994 Alain Juppé, the French foreign minister,

underlined that, the situation in Algeria was 'deteriorating sharply' and 'the news is not good'. The French say the fighting is now more severe than during Algeria's war of independence. Unusually, the United States has distanced itself from the regime, urging dialogue with the opposition. President Clinton's national security adviser, Anthony Lake, recently advised against creating 'a fundamental divide pitting Western liberal democratic traditions against Islam and other religious traditions'. The administration emphasized that the Algerian government 'must find a means of bringing the disaffected elements of the populace into a process to chart a new democratic course for Algeria'. Fine sentiments provided they did not entail appeasement of Algeria's murderous Islamic extremists bent on seizing absolute power.

It is conceivable that a more conciliatory stance by the government at the time of the 1991 election would have resulted in the return of a moderate Islamic government. Now there appear to be only two likely outcomes to the war: a military stalemate between the 170,000-strong armed forces and the guerrillas, who enjoy the support of possibly a majority of the population, or outright victory for the militants. Although the president, General Liamine Zeroual, installed in January 1994, favours negotiations, one of his predecessors, President Mohammed Boudiaf, was assassinated by military hardliners for adopting a similar stance, while the chief Islamic moderate, Sheikh Mohammed Bouslemani, suffered the same fate at the hands of his extremists.

For a long time the hardliners, led by the army chief of staff, General Mohammed Lamari, and the interior minister, General Selim Saadi, had the upper hand. It seemed possible that the regime had no alternative but to fight to the end. In September 1994, however, two prominent Islamic Front leaders were released from house arrest, as a possible prelude to negotiations. The moderates seemed to be making a bid for power. This effort now seems to have petered out and the war to have begun to intensify again.

If Algeria falls to extremist Muslim fundamentalists the consequences will be momentous. Algeria is a significant, although not a pivotal, hydrocarbon producer, the world's fifth producer of natural gas, producing nearly two million terajoules a day, and its fifteenth producer of oil, producing some 1.3 million barrels of oil a day. It is the world's tenth largest exporter of energy, at around 110,000 tons of coal equivalent a year. Still, the world could get along without Algerian production fairly comfortably.

But the knock-on effects of an Islamic revolution in Algeria would be enormous. Firstly, there would be a massive migration of Algerians to Europe, particularly to France, where there are already one million Algerians and some three million North Africans. Secondly, Algeria is strategically situated in the southern Mediterranean: the impact of Iranian terrorism in Europe has been considerable, thousands of miles away; the consequences of a base for terrorism and military threats just 300 miles south of France would be serious.

Third and more dangerous still, Algeria would be a huge base for Islamic militants eager to destabilize neighbouring countries. In particular, Morocco, with a population roughly equivalent to Algeria but an economy about half its size, and tiny Tunisia, with an economy a quarter that of Algeria, would be highly vulnerable.

Libya, with half the wealth of Algeria and a population little more than a tenth as big, under the idiosyncratic, ruthless, and unpopular one-man regime of Colonel Qaddafi, might also be ripe for replacement by a more orthodox Islamic regime. At the very least, Qaddafi might dance to a more fundamentalist tune on such issues as oil production policy. Algeria and Libya together account for some 2.8 million barrels a day of oil production, and some 200,000 tons of oil equivalent in energy exports, making them jointly the world's third largest energy exporters, after Saudi Arabia and the former Soviet Union. Again, this is not pivotal, but it is certainly significant.

The spectre of an Islamic Algeria threatening to export its revolution to Morocco and Tunisia, and acting in tandem with Libya and Sudan, would isolate Egypt along the North African coast. Egypt is under intense pressure from Islamic militants, although the struggle there is still in its infancy.

Islamic fundamentalists in Egypt are supported with Iranian money and have been trained and supported from bases in Sudan. Nevertheless, the movement is largely home-grown. There have been a small rash of attacks against foreigners, which has caused tourist income of some $2 billion to dry up. As well as the attempted assassination of the prime minister, there have been a series of bomb attacks and a number of killings and attacks concentrated around the upper Nile city of Assiut. As in Algeria, many wealthy families have virtually emigrated to Europe. Their reaction seems disproportionate: daily life in Cairo is very little affected and the security forces show no signs of being overwhelmed.

At least three groups are operating in Egypt: Gama'at Islamiya; the Egyptian Islamic Jihad; and the Islamic Brigades to avenge Palestinian Martyrs. Their most extremist leader is the blind Sheikh Omar Abdel-Rahman, placed on trial in America on charges of inciting the bombing of the World Trade Center in New York. Sheikh Mohammed al-Ghazzali is associated with the more moderate civilian Moslem Brotherhood, which is tolerated but not permitted to operate politically. This group is pressing for democratic elections which the fundamentalists would stand a good chance of winning.

The mainstream of the Islamic movement does not support the armed struggle: Egypt is a country which has a much larger middle class than Algeria, a much more impressive private sector, and a more politically sensitive ruling elite, although it also suffers from corruption, bureaucracy and repression of the opposition. Egypt has a long-standing secular tradition, and although Islam has a major appeal for the urban poor, there would be bitter resistance to any attempt to impose the veil in cosmopolitan Cairo.

A more likely outcome for Egypt is that the growing Islamic movement will push the government away from pro-Western modernisers like President Mubarak towards more non-aligned leaders with better Islamic credentials. This may be a better outcome for the West than a polarization between the regime and an increasingly extreme Islamic movement: Egypt has a good chance of avoiding Algeria's fate, caused as much as anything by the mistakes of the corrupt and exclusive ruling elite there.

The West, which has invested a huge amount in Egypt's stability (Egypt receives more American aid than any other country in the world), should be ready to support a government that seeks reconciliation with the mainstream Islamic movement – although not with the extremists. For the consequences of an outright extremist Islamic take-over of Egypt would be catastrophic indeed; with a population of 55 million (more than that of all the countries of the Arab Middle East put together), and a GDP of $44 billion, it is the manpower reserve of the Arab world.

LESS IMPORTANT strategically, but a holocaust of near-Cambodian proportions, has been Rwanda's civil war. Following the death of Rwanda's president in a suspicious air crash in April 1994, its Hutu majority turned on the smaller, but dominant until 1962, Tutsi minority and slaughtered up to half a million people. By July, however, the Ugandan-supported Rwanda Patriotic Front, dominated by Tutsis, had seized control of the capital, Kigali, precipitating a massive exodus by Hutus fearing revenge. Altogether, some four million of Rwanda's 7.7 million population fled their homes, into Zaïre, subsisting in horrific refugee camps, where some 40,000 quickly died of cholera. The new regime installed Hutus as president and prime minister and gave assurances that the refugees would be allowed to return peacefully; as Hutus make up 85 per cent of the population, reconciliation is in the Tutsis' interests – although few of the refugees trust their promises.

The West stood inertly by as the blood bath got under way, its belated intervention restricted to an inadequate, although welcome, refugee aid present of some $250 million primarily co-ordinated by the United States, and a well-intentioned French attempt to protect one section of the refugees. Many local observers believe that limited outside military intervention, before the rebels reached Kigali, might have provided the Hutu regime there with the security not to embark on the massacres and would have led to a negotiated settlement. When the massacres began, there were 2,500 UN observers present. Instead of being reinforced, most were withdrawn. In May President Clinton refused a UN request to send troops after nearly 500,000 people had been massacred.

What cannot be disputed is that, in the absence of any outside interest whatever, the most horrific sequence of events possible followed, leading to vastly more expenditure and a more enduring refugee problem than a 'stitch in time' intervention would have entailed in the first place. President Clinton's reluctance to re-engage in another Somali quagmire and America's wish not to lose a single casualty, even when the lives of hundreds of thousands of non-Americans are at stake, must be judged in the harshest possible light.

Rwanda, of course, was precisely the kind of Third World killing ground that the post-Cold War West has been least equipped and least concerned to prevent. Only the existence of a volunteer, rapidly deployable UN intervention force, or of regional powers like France acting under UN auspices, as suggested later in this book, might have prevented the massacre. Following the UN's experience in Somalia (which, however, was a notable humanitarian success – the mistake was to be drawn into the country's internal politics) neither was on the cards. Another yawning gap in the post-Cold War security structure was exposed by Rwanda; Kigali and Goma were added to the 1990s' hall of shame and horror alongside Sarajevo and Gorazde.

OTHER POTENTIAL global flashpoints abound. The crisis over North Korea has highlighted the issue of nuclear proliferation on a world basis: at least half a dozen other countries are close to accepting the bomb. There is the continuing problem of international terrorism; there is the massive global narcotics trade and its related problem of international crime.

But this missile's-eye view should be enough to convince anyone that the concept of a new world order, an era of peace to follow the end of the Cold War, was illusory. Indeed, one can tentatively conclude that the end of the Cold War has ushered in a new age of disturbances which will be much more difficult to contain. Unrestrained by the fear that one or other of the superpowers will step in to police the globe, militant nationalist regimes could emerge in a host of newly rich Asian states currently engaged in an increasingly vigorous arms race – such as China and Japan and to a lesser extent India and Korea.

Even in Europe nationalist jealousies have erupted as the need to form a common front against the Soviet Union has vanished; the dialogues between Germany, France, and Brit[illegible] have adopted an increasingly acerbic tone which only the fra[illegible] fabric of the European Union holds together.

The picture is by no means entirely bad – the surviv[illegible] democracy among the Soviet Union's former depende[illegible] remains remarkable. The end of the Cold War may have ma[illegible] ally contributed towards the precarious Israel–Palest[illegible] accord in 1993 – although not to that other piece of global news, the democratic elections in South Africa.

But the threat of conflagration remains much more prob[illegible] than during the Cold War era because the rules of the game are so undefined. Saddam Hussein did not get away with it, but Slobodan Milosevic did. There are no deterrent structures, no threats of massive retaliation, no prior warnings issued of the consequences of aggression for the newly unleashed dogs of war. With the globalization of international affairs, regional wars can spill into nuclear threats, terrorism, danger to commodity supplies, mass migration, environmental problems (although these have been overblown) applying to the whole world. Unless acted upon, these threats pose a major danger in international relations and security, from which the developed world would be far from immune.

CHAPTER TWO

THE STRONG, THE WEAK AND THE STATE

THE SECOND GREAT achievement trumpeted alongside the collapse of communism was the triumph of capitalism and of free-market economics. The Soviet Union was seen to have collapsed under the weight of a lumbering system of bureaucratic central planning, unresponsive to the needs of the market and repressive of the spirit of free enterprise that is so central to human nature.

In many respects this was true. But its converse, that Western capitalism had forged a super-efficient free market system, was not. Within months of the fall of the Berlin Wall, the global champion of free-market economics, Mrs Thatcher, had been driven out of office. George Bush, a more lukewarm exponent of the doctrines of his predecessor, Ronald Reagan, was to be ejected from office within two years by a Democrat with much more interventionist ideas.

Under President Clinton, America is going down the Japanese *keiretsu* (cartel) route. In October 1993, the White House announced 'a historic new partnership aimed at strengthening US competitiveness for developing technologies for a new generation of vehicles'. The research and development divisions of General Motors, Ford and Chrysler are now effectively under the supervision of Mary Good, under-secretary of commerce for technology. In addition, President Clinton has bailed out the shipbuilding industry to the tune of some $6 billion in loan guarantees. Shipbuilding is to enjoy a substantial export subsidy – another leaf out of Japan's book.

In France, free-market economics had never operated under the Mitterrand presidency; even with the victory of the right in the 1993 election, these were modified by the country's tradition of central planning and opposition to free trade. Even in Germany, a degree of planning remained a key to economic success, which, by 1993, was faltering under the monetarist restraints of the Bundesbank. In Italy and Spain, state intervention continued to remain the norm. The first flush of free-market experimentation in Poland and one or two other Eastern European countries was quickly reined in by political realities – notably the impact upon ordinary people; the same happened in the Soviet Union in 1994.

In China, Japan and the Asian economies, competition was accompanied by continued massive state direction and a consciousness of the need to disarm discontent through: lifetime employment; safety nets; protected agricultural prices; hidden unemployment and other artefacts. While the extreme form of bureaucratic centralization represented by the Soviet Union had certainly collapsed, it seemed that free markets and free enterprise had anything but triumphed.

WHAT HAD HAPPENED, then, in Eastern Europe? What revolution had occurred if not an assertion of democratic free-market values? George Kennan, architect of the policy of post-war Soviet containment, argued vigorously in March 1993 against the idea that communism had been 'defeated' by capitalism. In fact, what had happened was more fundamental – a triumph of the self, of the human yearning for self-expression – from within those countries. It had been an assertion of independence by a rising middle class, and a crushed working class, against the suffocating weight and conformity of communism, a situation that occurs rarely in history when a system becomes too heavy, unresponsive and blatantly corrupt. The direction of popular feeling was neither necessarily free market, nor democratic, although initially it flowed in those directions. It was nationalistic, ethnic, sectarian, individualist, anti-big.

Soviet communism had long derived its sole legitimacy as an expression of nationalism. Thus, the Eastern European upheaval was directed by suppressed nations against the colonialism of the Soviet Union; within Russia, instead, the pressure for change, while strong, was less than that among its subject peoples. The wave of revolt in Eastern Europe was not so much pro-capitalist as anti-authoritarian, the authority of the remote, absolute state represented by Soviet communism, the kind of elemental force that has spawned furious change throughout history – from the English Civil War, to the French, American and Iranian revolutions.

It can be argued that the collapse of Soviet communism was achieved as a result of a decision imposed from above by President Gorbachev. It does not detract from his historical achievement to assert that he was brought in to defuse what the Soviet leadership already saw were irresistible pressures building up within the system. The eruption of popular anti-communist sentiment in Eastern Europe and the Soviet Union, once the iron hand of repression was relaxed, showed how close both were to a revolutionary condition. Exactly the same assertion of the self would explode against any system that had become too remote and authoritarian for its own good – including other types of political regime, and even the institution of capitalism itself.

The root tension within any social structure is that between self-expression and authority. Contrary to some philosophies, it bears asserting at the outset that both are necessary and, provided they do not get out of hand, beneficial. To go back to the very roots of political theory, there are three elemental bases of any political system: individuals; strong individuals; and the state (society, government).

A few political philosophers have held that in a perfect society, all individuals can be entirely self-regulating, acting with full responsibility, in particular, so as not to impinge upon the freedom of others to do the same. To most political philosophers, and just about anyone with any experience of life, this may be an ideal to be worked towards, but it can often be no more than that. In Hobbes's pessimistic 'state of nature', life was nasty, brutish and could be a short one for ordinary people, who were preyed upon by the strong (Hobbes, like other conservative political philosophers, believed that human nature could not be improved, and did not accept the notion of progress). Whether because, as in some countries, the state became dominant in each society, or whether because, as in others, the weak looked to a benevolent leader to control the excesses of the strong, the central authority came into being.

This was looked upon as the defender of the weak against the predations of the strong – a role it did not always fulfil, often becoming chief predator itself. The triangle is true, of course, of much lesser social organisms than the nation state – anything from a school to a village to a military unit. The ordinary pupils, villagers and soldiers look to the teacher, village headmen and officers to protect them from the biggest and strongest among them. Similarly, in any modern society, people count on the police to protect them from criminals.

All this seems blindingly obvious. Yet it has to be stated to advance beyond the model of free-market libertarianism which has recently become fashionable in America and in Britain. For them the model contains only two elements: the individual and the state. In this scheme of things, the state is a tyrant and usurper of the freedom of the individual. Any society in which state power is minimal is a better society. This neglects the point that in the state of nature – where there is no state – the strong tyrannize the weak. There is no freedom for the majority where there is no central authority governing in the name of society as a whole. Indeed, the state derives its traditional legitimacy, in Anglo-Saxon political theory at least, as guarantor of the rights and freedoms of the individual.

Of course, in an enormous number of cases around the world, this has not worked out in practice. In the real world, the state has shown an all-too-frequent propensity to accumulate power and sometimes work in alliance with the powerful interests it is supposed to be protecting the people from. Over time constitutional safeguards evolved in the best political systems to prevent this happening, hedging about the power of the state and guaranteeing personal freedoms. Over time, too, legitimacy based upon force has not been enough – although even in a democratic state this is an important component. In countries where the power of the middle class or even of the working class is such as to threaten the state, the latter has had to secure their consent to government – usually through elections.

But none of this alters the fact that the state, the central authority, came into being, and derives its legitimacy, from the notion that it exists to protect the rights of the individual from his stronger peers. The state is different from other powerful individuals to the extent that it does enjoy the contractual legitimacy and consent of the people. There is no freedom in the state of nature, the society without the state, because the strong – the warlords, the barons, the big industrialists, the monopoly unions – predominate. In some cases people live in fear of a state which has encroached on individual freedom; but removal of the state as a political entity would result in much less freedom for the individual as the strong bully the weak again.

All parts of the trinity – the individual, the strong individual or interest and the state – are necessary and inevitable. In the ideal society a balance is achieved: the individual is protected, but does not inhibit the strong from acting as the driving force of society; the strong are not permitted by the state to push others about, but their energies are channelled on behalf of society as a whole; and the state is permitted to regulate the strong for the good of society, but not to dominate either them or the weak. There is an equilateral triangle. Conversely, if the equation gets out of balance, instability results. If the state becomes too powerful, an explosion of the self may follow. If the strong overpower the weak, the latter may call for a stronger state. If ordinary people become too self-assertive, there may be a demand for tougher rule from the centre or the strong.

A BRIEF EXCURSION into the basis of political theory is necessary in order to understand the crucial notion of consent. Thomas Hobbes was in every sense the father of modern political philosophy. Before him, the main philosophical and theoretical justification for exercising authority and the power of the state had been religious, best exemplified by the doctrine of the divine right of kings, that God had empowered some to have authority over the rest. This legitimized the exercise of power through family dynasty and brute force. Hobbes, between 1640 and 1651, pioneered three immense leaps in political thinking.

He argued that the source of the state's authority was man, or more specifically his nature, not God (this had the welcome effect of divorcing the Church from responsibility for political affairs, a development which many enlightened clerics welcomed). The reason why state authority was necessary was because in the state of nature the selfishness of men would compete so fiercely that it was in the self-interest of all that order be imposed.

From this he then deduced, most controversially, that the state must have quasi-omnipotent powers; he was widely denounced as the prophet of absolutism for this observation. But, in fact, by rooting the source of the state's authority as deriving from the needs of ordinary people for order and security, he was the forerunner of those who argued that the state only existed to serve the people. For if it failed in its task of keeping order and protecting their interests and, above all, their lives, it forfeited its right to exist.

This presaged the idea of many subsequent political philosophers that there is a social contract between rulers and ruled; the former ruled on the understanding that they delivered good government to the people and if they failed to do so, they forfeited the right to rule. This was a revolutionary idea at a time when the right to rule had been considered God-given, and the ruled had an obligation to obey. The new idea of contract became the foundation of liberal democracy: for it was father to the view that government required legitimacy through the consent of the governed.

Although Hobbes could never have imagined it, he was the father of the Western democratic tradition. For Hobbes, the need for state authority arises from the horrors of the state of nature, where man's passions govern everything in competition with other men (he did not condemn passion – rather, he argued, as future economists were later to argue, that self-interest creates wealth, that the passions are the origin of just action).

As Perez Zagorin writes:

> The state of nature is the hypothetical alternative to the commonwealth and sovereignty. It is a condition, therefore, in which human beings in pursuit of their ends are subject to no power or authority beside what they can casually impose upon one another . . .
>
> A situation is displayed to us of unending and oppressive fear. There is no property, for nothing is anyone's with certainty, nor any arts, letters, sciences, or the comforts of life. An unremitting war of all against all takes place, and every man goes in terror of his life. In such circumstances, the notions of justice and injustice have no place, every man having a right to everything, because everything is, in a literal sense, as much his as it is anyone else's.
>
> The first foundation of natural right is this, that every man, 'as much as in him lies, endeavours to protect his life and members'. Because man's absolute priority is self-preservation, which is not guaranteed in the state of nature, he is prepared to hand over authority to the state, which can guarantee him his life through enforcing the law on those who might threaten it.

Zagorin conclusively exposes the contradiction in Hobbes's theory, and how in fact his theory of absolutism limits the ruler contractually and through natural law:

> However it may have originated, government rests on contract – this is all Hobbes is concerned to argue. Contract, therefore, is a postulate of reason, and need never have occurred as a distinct event. The emphasis here upon the contractual foundation of government is not inconsistent with Hobbes's general position, as has sometimes been erroneously contended. It is, on the contrary, a strict deduction from his previous assertions. His theme has been that men make and maintain

> government as the rational expression of their right to preserve themselves. Government, in consequence, must always presuppose consent; and the hypothesis which corresponds to consent is that of a covenant. For this reason, Hobbes insists upon the covenant in despotic and institutive government alike; it is the correlate to his belief that the political order is unthinkable except as something in which men voluntarily acquiesce to secure life and contentment . . .
>
> But the power of the sovereign is, in practice, limited: no man, says Hobbes, 'is bound to obey a command which frustrates the end for which . . . sovereignty was ordained.' The sovereign, he argues, 'has . . . no other bounds, but such as are set out by the . . . Law of Nature . . . All punishments of innocent subjects are against the law of nature . . . to equity as being a precept of the law of nature, a sovereign is as much subject as any of the meanest of his people'; sovereigns 'may in diverse ways transgress against the . . . laws of nature, as by cruelty, iniquity, contumely and other like vices.'

Zagorin concludes that there was a deep cleavage running through Hobbes's thought:

> This cleavage is nothing trivial. It lies, rather, at the very heart of his political philosophy, and arises from the conflict between two fundamentally opposed tendencies: the stress on natural right, and the desire to validate any government as such. The former is liberalism, the latter absolutism. Between the two, it is the stress on natural right which is unquestionably stronger, for it is that concept on which his theory rests. Even against his will, therefore, Hobbes has forged a revolutionary weapon. If he defended absolutism, it was only on the grounds that absolutism is in the general interest; and should this be denied, as his own thought gives us a basis for doing, absolutism disappears, and in its place is substituted the liberal system for which the philosopher's nineteenth-century utilitarian disciples contended.
>
> It is, then, quite accurate to call Hobbes 'a radical in the service of reaction', and to hold that his ideas contain 'the

> germs of the constitutionalism he combated'; indeed, I should say they contain more than the germs. He has affirmed that men, in virtue of their humanity and apart from every social circumstance, possess a natural right which it is the commonwealth's duty to fulfill. This right involves more than a claim to bare preservation; it is a right also, as we have seen, to 'contentment', to 'commodious living', even to 'happiness', for government is instituted so that men may, as far as their human condition permits, 'live delightfully'. This being the case, we are irresistibly brought to conclude that men will be rationally and morally justified when they reject a commonwealth in which the fulfillment of their right has become an impossibility.

Thomas Locke later built this up by arguing that government had an obligation above that of preserving the lives of its subjects to protect and respect individual rights, in particular that of private property. George Sabine pointed out that Locke interpreted natural law 'as a claim to innate, indefeasible rights inherent in each individual. Of such rights that of private property is the typical case. Consequently his theory was by implication as agnostic as that of Hobbes. Both government and society exist to preserve the individual's rights, and the indefeasibility of such rights is a limitation upon the authority of both.'

Other English political thinkers were to elaborate these beginnings into a full theory of personal rights and liberties. John Stuart Mill was to argue that all individuals possessed absolute rights which they partially submitted to the community in which they lived, and the object of the community was the pursuit of the greatest happiness for the greatest number. The American constitution went one further and enshrined 'life, liberty and the pursuit of happiness' as self-evident rights which the state was bound to respect. The key points about the Anglo-American tradition of political philosophy were, first, its emphasis on individual rights independent of any bestowed by the state, from which the latter derived its authority, and which it could not violate, and its absolute acceptance of the need for a state to guarantee those rights. The two are completely interdependent – without the state there can be no respect for rights in the state of nature; without respect for those rights, the state has no purpose, no legitimacy, and deserves to be overthrown.

IT CAN BE SEEN that, over several hundred years, the principal bone of contention for political philosophers in Britain was not whether the state had a right to exist – that was taken for granted, in fact during hundreds of years of monarchy could not even be questioned – but the balance between the state and individual rights. In some continental countries, notably Germany, political theorists held that all rights derived from the state, a view that was to be terribly warped by the doctrines of communism and national socialism this century. The argument about the balance between the state and individual rights was then quite naturally to evolve into the wider subject of how the state should observe those rights and represent the individuals it had to protect, which then led on to the question of extending the franchise and establishing modern democratic institutions.

However, towards the end of the eighteenth century, parallel to this steady development, there came into being a different line of thought which, while responding to the economic advances of the time, represented a throwback to the political thought of the Dark Ages in its advocacy of the interests of the new 'strong' – confident capitalists. This was the new economic thinking, which was to exercise an enormous and disproportionate importance in the twentieth century, dazzling in its mathematics, but short on insight as to how human beings actually work. The prime purpose of the new economics were twofold: to justify and legitimize the new inequalities of wealth and domination by owner and manager over worker under private enterprise; and rigorously to resist 'wasteful' regulation and intervention by the state.

The first of these two objectives of the new economics was not too difficult to achieve: inequality had been a part of the human condition for recorded time, and the capitalist could argue that he was at least contributing to the common wealth by his enterprise. The second involved much more specious arguments, as a large part of early state interference took place to regulate the appalling exploitation and conditions of the industrial revolution, and another large part existed to prevent small businesses being trampled underfoot by larger monopolistic competitors.

When Marxism emerged as a monstrous child of capitalism, using the pseudo-scientific, anti-individualistic theories of Kant and Hegel to justify its doctrines of state absolutism, the economists that were the intellectual handmaidens of capitalism were quick to elaborate their own equally repellent mirror image. This view proclaimed that the state had no place in economics, that absolute freedom for the market was as perfect a mechanism for creating a prosperous and well-ordered society as Marxists argued that absolute state control of the market was.

For Marx, there was 'dialectical materialism', historical inevitability, a completely 'scientific' view of history, which obeyed laws just as physics or chemistry did. For the free marketeers there was the mathematical precision of the market mechanism, working smoothly, ingeniously and perfectly to ensure that the equation balanced perfectly in the end, whatever appearances and the consequences in the real world outside might suggest. Both theories had in common that they were formulated in academic, intellectual hothouses, far from the coalface of politics and business – although elements of both were to make ample use of such theories.

Marxism was a crude child of the new scientific age, whose philosophical insights were a throwback to sixteenth-century political absolutism. The new advocates of *laisser-faire* went back still further in political insight, to the Dark Ages, the barons and the Wars of the Roses. Both ran counter to the evolution of all political thinking since the time of St Thomas Aquinas (and, arguably, Aristotle).

The new doctrines wrought havoc with the cosy British political system of the time – broadly divided between a party representing town (the Whigs) and country (the Tories). The latter clung to the more structured and paternalist order of the countryside, and enjoyed a deferential vote among the new industrial working classes. The Whigs instead attempted to do all things for all men: to straddle both the new tough-minded capitalist anti-state interests and the cause of social reform and workers' rights. It was notable that while many of the great reformers of the nineteenth century were Whigs (later Liberals), those who put most of the reforms into practice were Tories (later Conservatives).

The Liberals broke spectacularly apart in the early twentieth century, as a result of Lloyd George's unequivocal espousal of the workers: the capitalist component migrated to the Conservatives, its social reformist and worker components to the Labour Party, leaving the Liberals a sorry rump. In the past decade, the Conservative Party has shown signs of being taken over by its ex-Whig, stridently capitalist component with its passionately anti-interventionist message, which threatens to be divisive and to endanger the party's unique cross-class appeal.

The thrust of the argument of the major new economists, in particular Hayek and Friedman, partially elaborated in antipathy to the absolutist state theories of the communist world was, in essence, that the state which governs least is best. Virtually any interference with the marketplace creates inefficiencies and distorts it. The government's job is simply to remove any distortions in the way of the free functioning of the market. Governments have no obligation to alleviate the effects of recession, to stimulate economies out of slowdowns, to impose curbs on wages, to regulate or subsidize business.

In practice this ideological stance was far too severe: governments remained necessary to protect society from the worst effects of the market, which was as much a 'state of nature' as anything envisaged by Hobbes in the political sphere. Certainly this ideological assault had a major effect in cutting back on the fat of bloated government bureaucracies; but in its crudeness, it lost sight of the need to make government more accountable.

Indeed in some respects it developed a momentum as authoritarian as that of the communist systems it so disliked. The new orthodox economists frequently suggested that the market needed no regulation from the state. Instead economics should be left as an autonomous, independent 'state of nature' of its own – as if economic priorities are not invariably determined by political choices. Many new economists argued that the democratic state itself, with its politicians currying public favour in elections, was an interference in the marketplace and was best set aside by benevolent military regimes, independent central banks, and 'technocratic' economic managers. Thus was 1,000 years of political evolution from feudal warlordism to liberal democracy to be swept away by the new 'expert' economists.

The contradiction was that many of those same economists were the most ardent advocates of political freedom in the communist bloc: indeed, political freedom was often identified with economic freedom as being indivisible. This was to boomerang when political freedom began to clash with the tenets of the absolutist free market. In the end, its advocates were grudgingly forced to accept that, in a democratic society, politics represent the preferences and aspirations of society, are dominant and are here to stay. The free market, far from being a new ideal of society, has to accept subordinate status to politics, and is in no sense autonomous and independent. Society cannot, and must not, return to the state of nature in the huge sphere of economic activity, as that represents the model of society in which there is least freedom of all, the tyranny of the strong over the weak; so political philosophers over the centuries have long concluded.

THIS EXCURSION into basic political theory is necessary to emphasize the point that central authority is not in itself bad. Indeed, it is essential, except in a society of perfect human beings. Many wielders of central power are corrupt or despotic, as Lord Acton believed; many are conscientious people grappling with enormous responsibilities. For any country or institution to work, you cannot do without it. Excess freedom from it may be freedom only for the gunmen, the robber barons, the big industrialists, or the monopolistic unions to tyrannize and trample upon the freedoms of the rest of us.

While authority is thus a necessity, self-expression is also an absolutely fundamental human force – arguably the most fundamental. From a very young age the smallest child seeks to express himself, to do what he wants to do without help – even if it is not right. It is not normal for the human animal to do what he is told, even if this is in his own interests and he is unable to see them. It may be necessary for him to be forced to do certain things when he cannot be convinced by reason – hence the existence of a legal system at all.

But the reverse side of the coin to the assertion that authority is necessary – to run a country, company, military unit, village, school, family – is that those in authority who ignore this hankering after individualism, even lust for self-expression and personal freedom, do so at their peril. It can topple authority in an explosion of popular feeling – with, as in most revolutions, usually unsatisfactory results for all concerned, governors and governed. Such an upheaval was the recent one in Eastern Europe, although, unusually, it has generated more freedom than repression, more order than chaos (with some exceptions, perhaps where authority had become so fundamentally corrupt (Romania) or ethnic tensions had been suppressed for too long (Yugoslavia)).

The key point about communism was not that it was based on a specific economic-political credo which another – capitalism – triumphed over. It is that pure authoritarianism had gained control of the credo, utterly detaching itself from ordinary people's yearning for self-expression. Exactly the same could happen to any political or economic system, socialist, capitalist or otherwise, that neglects the need for self-expression. In fact, any glance at the political systems that have grown up around the world shows that all other forms – dictatorships, military regimes, even sometimes excessively bureaucratic democracies – have sometimes lost the consent of the governed. Capitalism as an economic system could similarly fail.

The striking thing about the development of contemporary capitalism is the extent to which its organization, particularly in very large companies, increasingly resembles that of the communist regimes it so detested: the systems have shown marked signs of converging, even if there are important differences. This is not so surprising. Capitalism, like any other structure of authority, works through hierarchy, just as communism and feudalism did. Methods of control are usually much the same: the hierarchical-bureaucratic structure of communism (which itself was rooted in traditional ruling structures rather than Marxism) was its governing force – along with Russian nationalism, which at least gave the system some legitimacy in the eyes of the people. The increasingly hierarchical-bureaucratic structure of capitalism could just as easily prise it away from its roots – the need to sell competitive products in the market.

CHAPTER THREE

FATHER AND SON

But in an even more important way, capitalism itself does not represent the pluralist opposition to communism that it thought it did. The key to understanding the rise and fall of world communism is to realize that it was essentially a child of capitalism: a deformed and parricidal one, to be sure. But communism sprang from capitalism in three key ways: it was, most obviously, a reaction against the working conditions imposed by capitalism; its stormtroopers were – or were supposed to be – the sullen proletariat of the capitalist system, the urban workforce; and its system of organization, while radically different in its nominal responsibility (to the workforce, not the owners) and centralization (to the state, not individual companies) was based in most other ways on the capitalist organizational structure which, in turn, probably had military origins.

In this, as in so much else, Marx got it wrong. He believed that the key to a worker state was ownership of the means of production; in fact ownership, even by his time, was becoming increasingly irrelevant to the control of industry. It was the powerful managers, with a new structure of hierarchy beneath them, who really began to run the businesses; this soon was to be true of enterprises in communist states. Worker control was never a serious Marxist option, except in some sections of the extreme left, and is probably unachievable. But the structure of communist enterprises, although generally much larger and differing from capitalism in some key respects, as we shall see, was modelled on that of capitalist enterprises. Hierarchical management delegating key responsibilities to lower levels of specialized officials ultimately supervising the workforce – bureaucracy, to put it baldly – was an invention of capitalism, not communism.

Max Weber, the father of the study of modern organizations,

normally a subject of extreme aridity, expressed this precisely, and also despaired about it, as he wrote in 1948:

> Today it is primarily the capitalist market economy which demands the official business of the administration be discharged precisely, unambiguously, continuously and with as much speed as possible. Normally the very large modern capitalist enterprises are themselves unequalled modes of strict bureaucratic organization. Business management throughout rests on increasing precision, steadiness and, above all, the speed of operations . . . Bureaucratization offers above all the optimum possibility for carrying through the principle of specializing administrative functions according to purely objective considerations. Individual performances are allocated to functionaries who have specialized training and who by practice learn more and more. The 'objective' discharge of business primarily means a discharge of business according to calculable rules and without regard for persons.

Although capitalism has evolved somewhat more flexibly than he outlines, many capitalist enterprises still recognizably answer to his description. In 1956, he lamented:

> Already now, rational calculation is manifested at every stage. By it the performance of each individual worker is mathematically measured, each man becomes a little cog in the machine and, aware of this, his one preoccupation is whether he can become a bigger cog . . . it is horrible to think that the world could one day be filled with these little cogs, little men clinging to little jobs, and striving towards bigger ones . . . this passion for bureaucracy is enough to drive one to despair.

ANY BRIEF HISTORICAL study of the rise and fall of communism must begin with a look at the system that gave birth to the changeling. Capitalism first evolved with the provision of capital to set up industry. This might be called the age of the owner-entrepreneur in late eighteenth-century Britain. It took place during the mid- to late nineteenth century everywhere else in the developed world (and the process is still under way in developing countries).

As firms expanded, contractual relationships became the norm: workers performed specific tasks for a specific rate, according to contract, and were not employees of the firm. Worker specialization followed, through the introduction of new industrial processes and production lines, as well as an expansion in the size of firms, which required supervisors. Thus the professional manager came into being, at around the same time as the growth of capital markets, in which ownership became divorced from day-to-day management. Middle management – men with the job of telling others what to do, instead of actually producing something themselves – flourished.

Today there is the 'post-Fordist' – that is 'post-assembly-line' – revolution, which is only just beginning and promises to transform the traditional methods, in which the huge vertical structures of capitalism, its bureaucracy and segregated workforces become increasingly unnecessary while information technology and automation make them obsolescent, paradoxically concentrating control in fewer and fewer hands. Of these, the first four preceded or accompanied the spread of Marxism, and directly influenced it.

A glance at Britain's Industrial Revolution starts with capitalism in its first two 'pure' phases, those understood by Adam Smith. The tough, risk-taking owner-entrepreneur, is there with his workers. In this early stage the problem was to find capital: in Britain the Agrarian Revolution both displaced workers from their traditional lands by creating cultivation on a much larger scale, and yielded the kind of profits that could be invested in the new industries. (Other countries like France, Germany and Japan, arriving at industrialization later, used the state to channel capital to industrial enterprise.)

The industrial historian R. Edwards describes the first British phase:

> A single entrepreneur, usually flanked by a small coterie of foremen and managers, ruled the firm. These bosses exercised

power personally, intervening in the labour process often to exhort workers, bully and threaten them, reward good performance, hire and fire on the spot, favour loyal workers and generally act as despots, benevolent or otherwise. They had a direct stake in translating labour power into labour, and they combined both incentives and sanctions in an idiosyncratic and unsystematic mix. There was little structure to the way power was exercised, and workers were often treated arbitrarily. Since workforces were small and the boss was both close and powerful, workers had limited success when they tried to oppose his rule.

Josiah Wedgwood was justly hailed as the epitome of the entrepreneurial class, catering for a new mass market. The historian G. M. Trevelyan wrote:

> Wedgwood, in his Staffordshire works, catered for all classes with his pottery and jasper ware, creating a big market both at home and abroad . . . He experimented ceaselessly with new scientific methods, new moulds and new designs. He was indefatigable in promoting canals and turnpikes to reduce his costs of transport and percentage of breakages, and connect his remote Staffordshire potteries, built far inland, with his raw material of China clay in Cornwall and with the overseas markets he hoped to exploit.
>
> Between 1760 and 1790 he succeeded in filling not only England but Europe and America with his goods. During this period, pewter went out of general use and was succeeded by earthenware plates and vessels, so that eating and drinking became more hygienic and more delicate. In the next generation, men no longer spoke of 'common pewter' but of 'common Wedgwood'. Thus a radical paper writes satirically of 'lords and ladies' as the 'china trinkets of the nation, very superior to the common Wedgwood pottery of the mass of the people'.

In the United States and in Japan, the same phases occurred later. But in Britain in the middle of the nineteenth century, there occurred the third great phase, the specialization of labour. This replaced the subcontracting system which was a feature of early capitalism where enterprises paid people at home to produce goods which a relatively small entrepreneur sold to a bigger one, for a specified contract price. 'Internal contracting' began to decline towards the end of the nineteenth century, being replaced by the more formal system of large companies directly employing large numbers of workers in specialized, usually dreary, tasks made possible by the new technology.

This did three things to capitalist organization: It resulted in the creation of middle management; people whose job was to tell others what to do. Then there evolved the modern bureaucratic structure of the large enterprise based, probably, on that other large organization of the time, the army. People had to do as they were told, middle management had to defer to senior management. A hierarchy evolved.

And it soon became clear that management was much more powerful than the owners of the enterprise who, when they were interested at all, were at one remove from its actual running. The bigger a firm became, the less likely it was to be owned by a single man or family; as it expanded it would require more capital, raised from others alongside the original shareholding. The original owners would be less likely to exert real control over the tentacles of the business. The age of the professional manager had arrived.

Thus, almost simultaneously in the large firm, a large industrial workforce was created, doing largely repetitive work, in accordance with the primitive machinery of the time, and a bureaucracy of only indirectly responsible management with power hierarchies all of their own. As stock markets expanded, the relationship between ownership of an enterprise and its control grew more remote still. Meanwhile, the ethos of capitalism, as preached by men like Ricardo and Malthus, was that the workers were responsible for their own poverty, and should be paid the minimum for the maximum work. The conditions of Britain's Industrial Revolution, which were later to be repeated during the industrialization of virtually every other major nation, were created.

However, in the Britain of Robert Owen and others, an awareness developed of the terrifying conditions which resulted – particularly when it was observed that the fall in the death rate between 1780 and 1810, which was considerable thanks to medical advances, suddenly stopped still over the next forty years because of the unspeakable conditions in the slums.

G. M. Trevelyan sums up the conditions of the time:

> Throughout the 'forties nothing was done to control the slum landlords and jerry-builders, who, according to the prevalent *laissez-faire* philosophy, were engaged from motives of self-interest in forwarding the general happiness. These pioneers of 'progress' saved space by crowding families into single rooms or thrusting them underground into cellars, and saved money by the use of cheap and insufficient building materials, and by providing no drains – or, worse still, by providing drains that oozed into the water supply. In London, Lord Shaftesbury discovered a room with a family in each of its four corners, and a room with a cesspool immediately below its boarded floor. We may even regard it as fortunate that cholera ensued, first in the year of the Reform Bill and then in 1848, because the sensational character of this novel visitation scared society into the tardy beginnings of sanitary self-defence.

Edwin Chadwick, Secretary to the Poor Law Commissioners, argued that:

> The prisons were formerly distinguished for their filth and bad ventilation; but the descriptions given by Howard of the worst prisons he visited in England (which he states were among the worst he had seen in Europe) were exceeded in every wynd in Edinburgh and Glasgow inspected by Dr Arnott and myself. More filth, worse physical suffering and moral disorder than Howard describes are to be found

> amongst the cellar populations of the working people of Liverpool, Manchester and Leeds and in large portions of the metropolis.

As a result of his report, the Public Health Bill of 1848 was passed, a first step towards the social legislation in Britain towards the end of the nineteenth century. These scenes of squalor are today repeated across the world, from São Paulo to Shanghai. The combination of intense misery, which some suggested was less bad than poverty in the countryside (which at least had the virtue of being less unsanitary and often subject to some kind of paternalism), the inhumanity of the new employers and the creation of a large urban population was to provide the fodder for the left – the trade union movement, communist egalitarian revolutions, and the socialist creed of state intervention.

In the circumstances of contemporary capitalism, this was highly understandable; only in Britain, with its tradition of social reform, and the United States, with its pioneering frontier spirit – if you didn't like your lot, you moved elsewhere – was serious unrest avoided. In America revolution reared its head with the Depression, and the 'bonus march' on Washington – only through Roosevelt's skill in defusing social unrest through Keynesian economics was capitalism saved. Elsewhere in Europe and Russia, in the throes of early industrialization, strikes, demonstrations, left-wing attempts to seize power and fascist reactions became common.

Communism, that most appalling authoritarian blight on humanity, was thus a direct descendant of capitalism. Communism, a reaction against the excesses of capitalism, was used by a series of intellectuals and power-seekers taking advantage of the blind rage of the working class to seize power. Communism became an authoritarian system modelled on bureaucratic capitalism but with none of the latter's accountability and efficiency.

The next major development in capitalism – which towards the end of this century has become all the more management-led – is computerization, which threatens the whole tottering system of hierarchy, control and empires of subordinates. 'Post-Fordism', as this is called in the jargon, will do away with thousands of jobs and will concentrate power ever more into the hands of a small management clique. This is being bitterly resisted by many power wielders, whose domination of their own workers gives them prestige; but it is inevitable.

This subject will not be addressed in this book, because it is a challenge beyond, and less immediate than, the danger of global economic and political anarchy in the post-Cold War period. But it is of immense long-term importance, because it will divorce wealth and employment in a socially dangerous way, and because it will lead to further concentrations in the balance of wealth and power which could create a backlash.

Meanwhile, the advent of communism in the early twentieth century can only be understood in terms of the conditions created by capitalism, just as potential social and political disaster in the twenty-first century will have to be explained in terms of the globalization of modern capitalism and its failures. Communism inflicted untold misery on the world, but arose directly from the failings of the crude capitalist system that preceded it.

Capitalism was and is the most productive system the world has ever known – harnessing human energy and self-interest to create wealth. But it is up to public policymakers to channel its crude and vibrant energy in a direction that benefits the whole of society, or at least does not create a revolutionary backlash. Currently global capitalism is reaching a critical mass of irresponsibility and remoteness that could incubate another horrific anti-capitalist changeling early in the millennium. It is in this way that communism, a crude, sub-intellectual theory of no great worth or scholarship, had a huge and fertile breeding ground of discontent to exploit that ignited revolutions, plunged whole regions into war, killed millions and put into place the most tyrannical and repressive regimes the world has ever known.

PART TWO

The New State

CHAPTER ONE

THE SIX STRUCTURES

THE COLLAPSE OF communism in the Soviet Union and Eastern Europe lifted the hand of authoritarian conformity from a large swathe of mankind and, with some justification, led to exultant claims that the world was entering a new era of liberal democracy. Freedom, it seemed, was infectious, breaking out all over: in Latin America during the preceding decade, a gaggle of military governments had given way to elected civilian ones; in the Philippines, the dictator Ferdinand Marcos was toppled while traditionally military-run countries like Thailand and South Korea made tentative steps towards democracy. Even in Africa, a traditional one-party system – that of Zambia – held an election that resulted in the peaceful ejection from office of one of the continent's senior statesmen, Kenneth Kaunda (much to his credit). In South Africa, the remarkable political maturity of two leaders, Nelson Mandela and F. W. de Klerk, permitted the holding of a relatively violence-free election in 1994, and an astonishingly smooth transfer of power to the black majority – so far – over a potential racial powder keg.

Democracy had become fashionable; but huge parts of the world remained under authoritarian rule, and the triumph of the ballot box could hardly be taken for granted. What had gone, with the collapse of communism, was the specious claim that an unelected, authoritarian system of government can impose itself on the people because it represents their – or more specifically the workers' – best interests, and that a government which claims to rule in the name of equality has no need for popular consent expressed through elections, as it can be taken for granted that it represents the will of the people. This was the monstrous lie, the self-deception that was cruelly exposed by the popular revolts in Eastern Europe.

To many free-market ideologues, the collapse of the Soviet

Union and of its empire in Eastern Europe represented the triumph of freedom in its purest sense. People had refused to endure the weight of totalitarianism any longer; and, individually, they broke away to express themselves through an unfettered free market. The power of the central state was everywhere on the run. In fact, this was far too simple a view.

The collapse of the Soviet Union represented the destruction of the absolutist anti-democratic totalitarian model of state control. It did not mark the defeat of the state as such. The role of the state around the world continued to be immense, both in democratic and authoritarian societies. No purely 'free' country exists anywhere – that is, without a powerful central government. Even in international relations, over the past forty years, the rule of law has made a major entrance, governing international agreements and treaties, regulating the extensive contracts between nations, and even the ways in which wars are fought, and seeking to order the relations between states. Only in one field, that of global economics, was any attempt made to assert that this was outside the realm of international regulation and supervision.

Given the power of the state in virtually every country around the world, a power that needs constant checking to ensure that individual rights are not violated, but which nevertheless is here to stay, the issue becomes not one of rolling the state back – except from some economic activities which it should never have strayed into – but one of authority: from what does its legitimacy derive?

This section will look at the six modern sources of state authority: dynasty; imperialism; force; rule by elite or the establishment (aristocracy or oligarchy in the past); confucianist authoritarianism; and liberal democracy. It will conclude that only the last, because it is founded on the consent of the governed, an unwritten contract between ruler and ruled, and a system of rights and the rule of law, has true legitimacy and will prevail in the long run.

As the world slowly adjusts itself to that fact, political explosions and dangerous security crises are likely to occur, contributing mightily to the instability of the post-colonial world. Alongside emergent nationalism, the efforts of doomed authoritarian systems to stay atop the bubbling magma of the demand for popular rights is likely to produce ever more violent upheavals. If liberal democracy seems likely to triumph in the end, appalling security crises, as despotisms struggle to retain their hold, are likely along the way. This part also seeks to identify some of the potential flashpoints and fault lines. Again, the probability here is that unresponsive systems are probably doomed, not that state authority as such is. As long as the state remains powerful – and it will for the foreseeable future – the important thing is for it to become representative, responsive, accountable and respectful of personal rights, not to seek to roll back its authority in favour of forces which are none of these things.

AUTHORITARIAN CREEDS persisted around the world after the fall of communism. A glance at the principal ones seems to bear out the thesis that democracy is the system with the greatest long-term chances of survival, indeed of converting the others to its cause, because it best represents that equilateral triangle spoken of in the last chapter – the balance between the state, the strong and the mass of ordinary individuals. A brief review of political systems around the world suggests that it is indeed possible to be optimistic about the eventual triumph of liberal democracy and happily pessimistic about the perpetuation of authoritarianism.

Apart from communism, there now exist six major models that legitimize the power of the modern state. In spite of the collapse of communism, the modern state continues to exercise unprecedented authority, even in countries like Britain which have recently had governments committed to reducing its role. In fact, the power of the state, and more specifically the socially reformist state, had long preceded communism, and the attack of pure free enterprise theorists upon state intervention as such as being 'socialist', simply displayed ignorance or dishonesty.

The six are: the not quite extinct legitimization of family dynasty, which still applies in many Arab states, a handful of

Pacific islands and some African states. There is the legitimacy – if you can call it that – endowed by force, as practised by one of the most widely diffused, least understood forms of government, military regimes, in some parts of Asia and Africa and, in the past, in Latin America. There is the force still practised in a few areas under colonial jurisdiction, for example, Tibet. There is the system of rule by elites in places like Egypt and Mexico. There is the Confucianist authoritarianism of Japan and much of Asia. And there is liberal Western democracy, which in practice usually consists of rule by the educated middle class with the consent, through the ballot box, of the lower income groups (on some occasions their representatives actually come to power, although this is generally short-lived). This part of the book will look at each in turn and ask whether they are threatened by an assertion of the self, leading to potential security crises.

CHAPTER TWO

THE KINGS MUST DIE

THE LEGITIMACY endowed by family rule lingers on in only a few backwaters. With the exception of a handful of small, tightly knit communities, such as Tonga, and the constitutional monarchies of Western Europe, where kings and queens represent continuity and tradition without power, only in the Middle East are there monarchs that rule as well as reign. To understand why, and to judge their prospects of survival, one must look briefly at the peculiar history of the region.

But first a glance at why the legitimization of family dynasty has failed elsewhere. It is, probably, the world's oldest form of government, and certainly the one that has survived the longest. Without offering too many hostages to social history, in the most primitive societies, the notions of family, paternal authority, and a hierarchical ordering of class seem to have been one of the earliest forms of human organization. While other forms certainly existed in ancient times – Greek 'democracy', Roman rule by consuls, then emperors – hereditary monarchy seems to have retained enormous appeal across the centuries, sustained by not quite believable theories about the 'divine right of kings', yet sometimes in vigorous opposition to the Church.

How was this achieved? Regal behaviour, fine clothes and dazzling displays of pomp were only part of the explanation, because they do not sustain monarchy today. In largely rural societies, the three most important sources of power were ownership of the land; the ability to raise armies – which was partly related to ownership of the land, through enlistment of those who worked upon it; and the dispensation of patronage and favours, including landed estates.

In early societies, the most important landowner of all – although rarely achieving a monopoly – was the king. Where land ownership and wealth were the most important factors in royal power, it was natural that the traditional means of passing them on, inheritance, should apply too to royal power. Hereditary rule was a natural extension of the hereditary right to property.

Yet when one of the three sources of royal power came under challenge, the Crown's authority was diminished, as it was if there was any challenge to the monarch on grounds of heredity, by, say, another claimant, or because of the Crown's failure to produce an heir. Thus if coalitions of large landowners could be assembled against a king or queen, along with the men they could raise in arms, the monarch's powers of patronage would count for little (although a victorious king could create a new class of supporters by stripping his opponents of their lands and distributing them to his supporters).

With the evolution of a middle class, in the shape of yeomen (independent) farmers and merchants, for example in England in the sixteenth century, the king, from being *primus inter pares* among the landowning class, based his claim to rule on his desire to represent the wider interests of his countrymen, both in regard to overseas threats and to the selfish interests of his fellow landowners. This worked for a while; indeed it represented the final brilliant fling of royal power, the absolutist dazzle of the renaissance prince.

With the seventeenth century in England, and a little later elsewhere, came the realization by the new middle class that they were the backbone of the nation, the new source of power, and when vain and inept rulers like James I, Charles I and James II tried to rule without consent, the gentry rose in opposition. By the end of the seventeenth century in England – again a little later in most countries – real royal power was a thing of the past (as was rule by the big landowners), although the façade was preserved. The middle classes ruled – because they were more numerous, independent and wealthy as a class. As their size grew, so the political system became more complex, reasserting itself through the limited vote, the extended vote and, eventually, as the pressures from women and the working classes made themselves felt, universal suffrage.

Royalty by now was a mere spectator, enjoying its privileges only on sufferance from the middle classes. The monarchs that clung to absolute power in the face of this inevitable social change tended to get overthrown – with greater violence the longer they clung – as in France or Russia. Huge though royal landholdings might still be, the middle class as a whole now controlled infinitely more wealth, the previously loyal royal army increasingly owed its allegiance to the nation rather than a particular king, and patronage was now largely exercised by the government in office, not the king.

So why has absolute monarchy defied the laws of political gravity in the Middle East? The answer is twofold: the sheer poverty and primitivism of the region, until this century; and oil, an enormous and peculiar form of extreme wealth. It is hard to underestimate that poverty in the past. More arid than any region except Saharan Africa, the bulk of the Middle East afforded a living only to hardy nomads moving from oasis to oasis. Permanent settlement was possible only in three principal areas: the fertile Palestinian coastland; the Yemeni upland; and relatively fertile and irrigated Northern Iraq and some parts of Syria and Lebanon.

Unsurprisingly, these were the most developed and populous regions, rich in architecture and civilization. Perhaps because of the relentless pressures of their existence, the Arabs and the Jews, both an extremely talented people, had created great civilizations in Jerusalem, Sanaa, Babylon, Damascus – and the fount of three of the world's greatest religions: Judaism, the oldest; Christianity, with the widest following; and Islam, with perhaps the greatest appeal for the world's poorest people; (unsurprisingly, as it was born in the sparsest and most impoverished land of all, the Arabian peninsula).

The power of the Middle East's religions, alongside the vastly sophisticated civilizations they spawned in ancient times, has to be set against the desperate struggle for existence in pitiless terrain of most of the region's inhabitants. Between the overcrowded cities with their tilted tower blocks with several storeys in the feudal uplands of Yemen and the placid greenery of Northern Iraq overlooked by Alpine-style mountains lies a vast sea of sand where small, hardy groups of Bedouin swirled about, romantic in appearance but to the few settled peoples of the Middle East, the lowest of the low, without property or land and condemned to wander, as nomads. While undoubtedly attractive in the mould of other wanderers – gypsies, cowboys, the tribes of central Asia – Bedouin social organization was as primitive as could be imagined: familial, clannish, the organization of primitive man throughout the ages – only the sophistication of Islam as a religion leavened it.

By the beginning of this century there was little to suggest that this forsaken, inhospitable corner of the world was ever going to escape hardship or ignorance. Most of it was under the control of the vastly corrupt and centralized Ottoman Empire. While a world war was being fought in Europe, the Turkish grip was relaxed as Britain gave its support to the Arab revolt and installed the most prestigious Arab family, the Hashemites, direct descendants of the Prophet, to rule Iraq, Syria and Jordan. The Arabs' natural leaders were installed in place of the Turkish imperialists; they were, above all, a family dynasty, representing the prime source of social allegiance of the region. In Saudi Arabia, a new and powerful tribe, the al-Saud, installed itself in control of that peninsula, ousting the Hashemites. The primitiveness of the region was underlined by the way the British carved up the new countries with lines on a map.

WITHIN YEARS, a revolution had occurred: oil, the fuel of modern industry, had been discovered in large and unbelievably readily exploitable amounts under the poorest parts of Arabia: Saudi Arabia, the Gulf states, Southern Iraq and, on the Mediterranean, Libya. The derided nomadic peasant warriors of Saudi Arabia, capable only of living in tents, were suddenly, vastly, the richest people in the Middle East. They were cultivated by the Americans, who were relentlessly determined to chase the British out of Arabia. Within a few decades, with the quadrupling of oil prices in the early 1970s, followed by their doubling at the end of the decade, the Arabs' wealth was, quite literally, mind-boggling.

Meanwhile, the traditionally rich, civilized, developed parts of Arabia – Egypt, Palestine, Yemen and Northern Iraq – were reduced to the status of poor relations. Populated, sophisticated and hard-working, they were blocked from sharing in the wealth of the desert by the frozen colonial boundaries, and were reduced to the status of supplicants. Perhaps no greater irony has ever existed in modern history: Egypt, cradle of modern civilization; Yemen, certainly home to the loveliest Arab architecture; Syria, cradling one of the most beautiful cities in the Middle East, Damascus; Palestine – shorn by the creation of Israel of its richest lands, but actually containing the most developed of the Arab peoples – was reduced to begging for alms from the nomads it had despised for millennia.

For their part, the nomads and the scruffy trading statelets of the Gulf responded to the oil bonanza in the time-honoured way of any humble man winning the pools. They went wild. Gin palaces were erected by a people that lacked any architectural tradition of their own around the shores of the Gulf, creations not of ancient Arab but of the flashiest British interior designers.

The Saudis, busy demolishing what was left of the old city of Riyadh and erecting dreary, Dallas-like skyscrapers in its place, built one of the world's largest airport terminals at Jeddah shimmeringly, and not entirely ineffectually, based on the design of the sole architectural inspiration the Bedouin could call their own, the tent. Kuwait, built upon perhaps the most torrid and bleakly sunbaked part of the Gulf, a combination of mudflats and scrub desert with a climate dominated by overheated sandstorms, founded a large, featureless skyscraper city, with a network of motorway rings, as extensive as those around a large Western capital, that dwarfed the few cars that used them.

Unsurprisingly, given their wealth, the inhabitants fled their overheated, bogus cities for older, more attractive ones – London, Paris or Rome – for months at a time. In the Arab societies that had contact with the real world, uninsulated by the oil wealth, tumultuous change resulted. The French mandate in

Syria and Lebanon was finally forced out in 1946. Iraq's monarchy was toppled in 1958. Egypt's bloated and corrupt King Farouk had already gone. Libya's elderly and unworldly King Idris followed in 1969.

Appalling as most of the successor regimes were, they followed the general rule that absolute monarchy in a modern, complex, pluralist world is a thing of the past. Monarchy lingered only in the Gulf and in two largely desert kingdoms: Morocco and Jordan. Kings Hassan and Hussein owe their survival to skilful diplomacy and political shrewdness, the support of a feudal and loyal praetorian guard, and the essentially desert and underdeveloped nature of their countries.

Gulf royalty owes its survival largely to money. Unlike the ownership of land – the traditional fount of royal power in Europe, later overtaken by merchant and industrial wealth, thus undermining the monarchies – the oil is entirely owned by the state, which meant the royal families concerned: any benefit from it is enjoyed by those families, and by no one else. Any who seek wealth or patronage have to go to those families.

The populations of the oil-rich states are necessarily tiny: the nomads had been few, the territory vast. Citizenship of states no one could ever wish to migrate to but for their wealth has been hard to come by: as the Gulf states grew oil-rich, the destitute from places like Pakistan and Bangladesh were conscripted by their own misery to do the menial work. The lowest Kuwaitis employ such servants, and expect to retire at forty on generous welfare payments. There are huge amounts of money to be dispensed to very few people. Revolutions are usually made by the economically desperate. There are none of the latter in the oil states; provided they conform, they are treated very well. But after the initial euphoria and shock of wealth wears of, there are signs that the ambitious are beginning to assemble.

The keys to the survival of the Gulf monarchies are also their probable long-term undoing: the control of oil revenues and the wielding of huge powers of patronage and a degree of ownership that no medieval monarch could aspire to: no British king, for example, ever controlled three-fifths of his country's income, as Saudi Arabia's King Fahd does. The small populations involved represent another means of control: even a people of fourteen million scattered across Saudi Arabia cannot be bought; but it is easier to try to do so than with a population of fifty million. In fact, of course, total control is impossible even over a few hundred thousand; in the desert societies of the Gulf, there is little evidence that the rulers enjoy popular esteem.

The current generation may be rendered docile by their rags-to-riches rise to wealth. But now a new generation has grown up which sees little reason to accept archaic systems of government and the near-monopolist control of the main source of wealth. Unless the oil states adapt, the danger is that change will be violent, extremist and sudden. Oil, previous poverty and small populations have pickled the monarchy in aspic in the Gulf, in a way which has not occurred elsewhere; but this will not necessarily last.

A glance around the Gulf confirms this: every Arab country on its fringes that lacks oil possesses the rudiments of a modern economy and has lost its monarchy, usually violently; only the desert kingdom of Jordan, with its scant economy, survives by the skin of its teeth. Instead the Gulf is dominated by one large monarchy, Saudi Arabia, and a host of lesser princedoms. The region provides the potential for the globe's biggest security crisis early in the next century.

Of these, the kingdom of Saudi Arabia bears the nearest resemblance to a modern society, possessing two major cities – Riyadh and Jeddah – and substantial industry and infrastructure made possible by the oil price rises of the 1970s. Saudi Arabia is ruled through a complex system of control based upon patronage, repression, Islam and tribal links. The patronage is lavishly distributed by the state, which is wholly identified with the al-Saud ruling dynasty (the name of the country enshrines this). It is immense, in the form of a generous welfare state, lavish state support for private industry, a large bureaucracy and special assistance for such groups as the Bedouin.

Repression is of a fairly standard kind: there is no free press, broadcasting or political activity, ostensibly in the name of religion; independent political movements or meetings are suppressed, while Islamic police are used for surveillance, to enforce personal morality, and to administer punishments. The strict enforcement of Islamic law gives the authorities *carte blanche* to police every aspect of Saudi life: the dual police forces are further buttressed by the existence of two armies, the regular army and the National Guard. The point of having two is to prevent one seizing power, as happened in Iraq in 1958.

THE DESOLATION shrieks in the wind at the traveller as his car follows the tarmac strip across miles of dull red rock, through miles of travelling sand, loosely rippled across the rock and then into the monotonous dunescape of the deep sand. The emptiness stretches, beyond his sight, for hundreds of miles in every direction. The desert is empty by day beneath a dusty yellow horizon fading into merciless bluish glare, and by night beneath a star-studded, crystal-clear blackness. The Saudis tell you that when it clouds over and rains, it pours. You have only their word for it.

It is one of the world's greatest wildernesses, a sand continent the size of India, the pasture around the occasional oasis too sparse to persuade the Bedouin trekking interminably from the overpopulated Yemeni mountains of the south-west towards Northern Arabia, to settle. In the desert, humanity was stripped to the essentials. Arabia's heartland was the preserve of a hardy few, driving flocks of sheep and goats from one patch of grass to another, eating camel's flesh and lamb's butter. Scarcity dictated ferocity: they had to be tough fighters, able to hold their own against other tribes. Religion dictated cleanliness: when they came to water, they had to wash before they drank.

The strict rules of Islam grappled with the anarchic sides of their nature. Islam alone united a people bereft of a written culture. Then, early this century, the al-Saud, a tough clan from the village of Riyadh in the centre of the country, successfully bribed, browbeat and battled the other tribes into submission. The head of the clan, Ibn Saud, little knew that his wasteland contained the world's largest reserve of black gold. When his successors learnt that, life did not change much at first for the Bedouin.

It has now. Today, emerging out of the emptiness at night to reach the ancient capital of the al-Saud, the Arabian traveller suddenly comes upon a sea of light, an urban sprawl some forty kilometres across, a grid of giant three-lane highways and flyovers down which Park Avenue Buicks coast line abreast. The city boasts two enormous airports, its skyline bristles with slim, austere minarets, plump watertowers and busy yellow cranes.

Creating a city of two million people at the heart of a desert seems mad. Its location is purely symbolic, as the capital of the al-Saud tribe and the geographical heart of a country which has been unified for little more than half a century. No matter that crops must be fertilized and irrigated at enormous cost to grow at all around Riyadh, no matter that most of the city's needs must be brought 900 kilometres from Jeddah (the Saudi development plan even provides for the 'air transport of cows'). Never mind the cost of digging for water for the city. With the rest of the world picking up the bill, the Saudis could afford their Xanadu.

Is the capital of oil, lacking all life support but money, doomed one day to be reclaimed by the desert, as Brazil's rubber capital, Manaus, was reclaimed by the jungle in the last century? Will puzzled archaeologists of the future pore over the ruins of the Marriott and the Intercontinental Hotel as they do the sand-immured cities of South Afghanistan and Iran?

It depends. It depends on whether the Saudis destroy the market for the oil they possess in such abundance; on whether intelligent men in the governing class realize in time that an anachronistic system of government, even a cleverly run one, cannot survive for ever; and on whether the standards of international self-restraint that have allowed a very few people to squeeze the rich and poor world will long endure when the people doing the squeezing show such lack of self-restraint.

*

'THE VERY RICH', Scott Fitzgerald once observed, 'are different from you and me.' 'Yes', replied Ernest Hemingway, 'they have more money.' The Saudis have been very rich. In 1992, Saudi Arabia's GDP was around $10 billion – about one-ninth as much as Britain, a country which has been developed for a long time with four times as many people, or about three-and-a-half times as much as Egypt, an Arab country with four times as many people. The Saudi government admits to having some $110 billion in holdings abroad and may have $20 billion more than that. Private Saudi investors are reckoned to have some $50 billion abroad.

The Saudis are different. The fact that they have been very rich for so short a time makes them more so (in 1970 they had only $600 million in the bank). They have passed from rags to riches without having to strive and lack the rough edges of men who have to work for their fortunes. They have tried to carry the simplicity of their former pastoral poverty over to their new lifestyle. The plain white ankle-length Arab tunic is as egalitarian a dress as Mao uniforms were once in China. Seniority in Saudi Arabia is denoted only by the silver and gold borders of their black shoulder capes.

The two-storey royal palaces are curiously low-key. I once visited a successful Saudi multi-millionaire's home which was striking for the simplicity of its stark Moorish style. There is a sense of *noblesse oblige* in the way Saudi offices are open to all comers, whether they have appointments or not – with the result that those that do have them can be kept waiting for hours.

The Saudis are soft-spoken, shy almost, utterly different from their excitable Northern Arab brothers. As Bedouins, they used not to push themselves very hard; as millionaires they do not need to. No demand on their hospitality (once it has been extended) is too outrageous, a legacy of the days when you shared or somebody went without.

Yet their unhurried approach to life can also be maddening. The defensive distance they affect comes dangerously close to arrogance and their offices, manned by male secretaries, work with awesome incompetence. They are as sensitive as lilies about what is said about them, but compel observers to speculate by keeping the facts from them, and can be secretive and ambiguous in their pronouncements.

The secretiveness, the ambiguity, the commitment to a way of life no longer relevant to their material circumstances are defence mechanisms. Because the old way of life was so stark and empty, the void is being filled by Dullsville, USA. Underneath, in private, Saudis talk, live and behave like the American oilmen they have come to know so well. As video sets, peanut butter and Pepsi-Cola threaten to become the Saudi way of life, so they cling all the more desperately to the two closely interwoven roots they have always possessed: the family and Islam.

The family was the social unit of the desert: and now that money has come tumbling down from above, dispensed as patronage by heads of family, its authority has, if anything, been strengthened. The family abides by the strict rules of Islam: the mother has no life outside it, apart from her women friends. In the most liberal Saudi household, she may receive male guests, but will then withdraw. But she gets money – and so independence and power – as of right. And she gets her own back on this sexual apartheid by wielding absolute power over her children until their late teens, by which time she has probably wrested control of her husband from his mother as well. Then the father rules his sons through the purse strings of a family business partnership.

Islam is both a way of life and the chosen instrument of the government's political control. Ever since the Iranian revolution of 1978–9, the Saudi government has been congratulating itself on the foresight it showed in never relaxing its hand-in-glove alliance with the country's puritan Wahhabi clerics. The alliance was founded in 1744, with the marriage of an early al-Saud to a daughter of Islam's Savonarola, Abdul Wahhab. His strict interpretation of the Prophet's teachings has put Saudi Arabia in a straitjacket since the al-Saud united the kingdom.

After the austere King Faisal was assassinated in 1975 by a disaffected minor member of his clan, the ruling clique, led by the shrewd but self-indulgent Crown Prince Fahd, marginally eased the iron rules of Islam. But Shia disturbances in the country's oil-producing eastern region and the seizure by Muslim fanatics of the Grand Mosque at Mecca in 1979 showed that there was no room for further relaxation. The disturbances have not recurred, largely thanks to a discreet infusion of money into the affected areas; and the Grand Mosque incident has passed into history as a 'Saudi Jonestown' – a group of suicidal zealots drawn largely from a disgruntled western tribe following a self-appointed imam. Their profaning of the holy places outraged most Saudis.

The Koran provides handy weapons of political control. The censor, it is explained, is a guardian of Islam, not of the nation's rulers. Yet his pen strikes as vigorously at political grumbles as exposed calves. Stick-wielding religious policemen patrolling the streets are a constant reminder of the presence of authority. Publicly administered floggings and executions are as effective in deterring political as well as ordinary crime.

Cinemas are banned as potentially corrupting, but in reality it is because the Saudis do not like crowds to gather. Potentially more corrupting private video sets are allowed. Strict Islam, with its catalogue of 'thou-shalt-nots', is a big brother forever tapping on the shoulders of ordinary Saudis. As the then minister of justice, Sheikh Ibrahim al-Sheikh (a descendant of Abdul Wahhab), once remarked to me: 'Public security dominates the whole place.'

Saudi law is at least punctiliously observed in the traditional way. There is an absence of the extra-legal brutality – the midnight disappearances, the summary trials, the torture – that are common to most countries which have undergone revolutions in the region. The minister of justice, a grave, reflective man, insists that even the king is subject to the law. The forms of punishment, while horrifying to Western eyes, are at least publicly admitted (and administered). They can be defended on the grounds that they belong to Saudi Arabia's feudal age, which abruptly ended only two decades ago.

The principle behind the law is simple: Saudi Arabia used to be a country of tribal blood feuds. The house of Saud took the enforcement of the law out of the hands of individuals and placed it into the hands of the state. The state must be seen to administer retribution to keep its citizens from taking the law back into their own hands. Now, said Sheikh al-Sheikh, 'there is less crime here than in any other nation'. This is almost certainly true.

Chopping off heads and hands concentrates the minds. In an age when officially sanctioned non-legal killings in many Third World countries can be counted in their hundreds, Western indignation about punishments in Saudi Arabia is overdone. About a dozen people are executed a year. The method is usually beheading, though the execution is sometimes carried out by a firing squad, or by the method the murderer used against his victims or, in certain cases of adultery, by stoning.

Due process is closely observed: capital punishment is administered only when a killing has been premeditated and the killer has confessed. He has a right of appeal: the supreme council of the judiciary, a body of between ten and fifteen Islamic scholars, must give their approval. The king must give his. Even then the sentence can be commuted in cases of mental disorder or if the family of the victim exercises its prerogative to waive punishment.

As for wayward princesses, only one person has been stoned for adultery during the past twenty years. And no wonder: the Saudi delegation at a human rights dialogue with European jurists some years ago defined the Koranic circumstances in which stoning applies as being:

> Only when the culprit, prior to his delict, had contracted a legal marriage and if four witnesses known for their righteousness and their integrity were present at the complishment of the sexual act in a manner which would exclude the possibility of doubt: it would not have been sufficient, namely, that they had seen the accused completely naked and stuck together.

After all, the Saudi jurists pointed out:

> If the act was accomplished in the presence of four witnesses, the judgment is that public order has been seriously

> offended . . . It is always improper for the sexual act to take place in public . . . We suppose that if such a thing had happened in the street of a capital of a civilized country, passers-by would have taken it upon themselves to lynch the perpetrators.

Whereat Mr Sean MacBride, heading the European delegation, was moved to reply: 'It is here, in this Muslim country, that human rights should be proclaimed, nowhere else.'

Just as the king is subject to the law, so is he subject to his people. This delightful fiction is based on the hallowed institution of the *majlis*, when any subject, high or low, can present his (but not her) request in written form to the king, shake hands, and maybe have a word or two. The petition may range from a grievance to a personal request for money from the king to finance, for instance, a prostate operation abroad – because no government subsidy exists for the purpose. Something will usually be done. The *majlis* is brandished by Saudis as evidence of democracy. The fact that there are more than 5,000 princes is flourished as evidence that the government is in contact with the people.

Both claims are nonsense. But it is true that power in Saudi Arabia is oligarchical, and does not hang on one man, as it did in Iran. The power structure is hard to get to grips with because, like so much about the country, it is unfinished. Even sections of the frontier remain to be inked in. The country's provinces were formalized only during the past twenty-five years. In 1924 Ibn Saud promised the country a constitution and a middle-class consultative council, a *majlis al-shura*, as an 'intermediary between the people and me'. No constitution has emerged, and the council has only just been set up.

The governance of Saudi Arabia remains improvised, and those seeking to understand it could do worse than read Mario Puzo's *The Godfather*, for an idea of how a large clan with money and force at its disposal operates in the modern world. Ibn Saud had forty-five sons by twenty-two different women. The clan has a dramatic advantage over the Shah's one-man rule: it provides a pool of potential rulers, as well as a means for replacing them. The disadvantage is that power struggles take place within the clan. But these have not been murderous because the house of Saud knows that divided it falls.

In 1967, for example, the fun-loving and decadent King Saud, who had duly succeeded Ibn Saud in 1953, was shoved aside by his brothers in favour of his austere younger brother, Faisal. When the latter was assassinated in 1975, the next brother, Prince Mohammed, who had no wish to be king, stood aside. The most obvious contenders for the succession were Prince Fahd, a pro-American moderate, and Prince Abdullah, a defender of the old ways. The family compromised and chose their elder brother, King Khaled, a gentle man of unimpeachable reputation but without intellectual force.

Tall, imposing and with the quickest intelligence among the sons of Ibn Saud, the then-Prince Fahd's defects were sudden bouts of indolence, a playboy reputation, and a liking for the resort of Marbella in Spain. As King Khaled's health deteriorated, he withdrew into a largely ceremonial role. And as Prince Fahd increasingly concerned himself with affairs of state, so Prince Abdullah's power steadily declined even before Khaled's death.

Prince Abdullah controlled a formidable force – the 40,000-strong National Guard, consisting largely of Bedouins. But Prince Fahd's main ally was the defence minister, Prince Sultan, who headed the 35,000-strong army. Prince Sultan expected to slide easily into the job of crown prince when, on Khaled's death in 1982, Fahd became king. But Prince Sultan lacked the tact and grasp of his elder brother, and the other princes tried to block him.

Nominally, Saudi Arabia is ruled by its council of ministers. In fact, the council of senior princes has to endorse any decision before it reaches the council of ministers. Before that, most important decisions have to get past the ruling tripod of King Fahd, Prince Sultan and the minister of finance, Sheikh Mohammed Aba al-Khail. A senior Saudi who wants a major development project approved will go to one of these three. Within every ministry, there are men loyal to the senior princes.

Lesser ministers will seek the approval of King Fahd's man or Prince Sultan's man before making a decision.

POWER IS MONEY and money is power in Saudi Arabia: nearly two-fifths of the national income comes from oil revenue, which goes directly to the government, providing around 90 per cent of its income. The oil money that is not saved in foreign banks is filtered through the budget to ordinary Saudis. About 12 per cent of this goes in social expenditure, the bulk on development. Tenders are the government's to give to its friends.

'Corruption', say critics in the West at once about this sort of thing. What would be called corruption in the West is not so much an unattractive feature of the Saudi economy as the way it works. Government by family sees nothing wrong in business by connection. Patronage is the way the princes get rich; it is also, much more than coercion, the main source of the government's authority.

Money is fast centralizing a country which a couple of decades ago consisted of pretty well independent tribes, studded far apart, bargaining with the al-Saud for favours and freedoms. Regional tribal disaffection is a more pressing concern for the al-Saud than Western notions of democracy. The al-Saud are enormously skilful in keeping the tribes happy while pulling the country together. Air services and roads linking population centres are snaking across the desert. An industrial port has been built at Yanbu on the Red Sea coast, linked by cross-country pipeline to the eastern province in order to dilute the concentration of industry there.

The princes have been trying to improve local government. Tribal disaffection played a major part in the seizure of the Grand Mosque at Mecca in 1979. Early the following year, the government took the rare step of replacing four emirs, or provincial governors, including the governor of Mecca. The emirs of the fourteen provinces are the central government's proconsuls, responsible for keeping the tribes happy. Seven of the fourteen are brothers of the king; five are members of the aristocratic Sudairi tribe, to which the al-Saud are related by marriage; and two belong to the Ilawi tribes of the northern provinces. The emirs are trying to patch up relations with the tribes, which have been unsettled by the way unregulated local branch offices of the ministries have galloped over local sensibilities.

Sensitivity to tribal feeling was, until recently, about as far as the al-Saud family seemed ready to go in sharing power. Under pressure from the United States, in 1980 Prince Fahd dug up the old idea of a *majlis al-shura* – a body of representatives drawn from the rising middle class to advise the king. The proposal was shunted off to a committee headed by the minister of the interior, Prince Naif, who passed it to a subcommittee to draft a formal proposal. Nothing more was heard until 1993, when the idea came under consideration again.

The government's Islamic veil is slipping. In practice, many middle-class, middle-aged Saudis drink – although in private, usually with non-Saudis, and never in front of elderly Saudis. Saudi children devour Western films in high-technology 'family rooms' while the torrent of religion on local television stays firmly switched off. The sight of Saudis taking to their prayer mats five times a day is impressive; but the great majority do not pray regularly. Teenage girls have been caught dressed as boys at the driving wheel (women are not allowed to drive at all).

Cars of the religious police prowl around girls' schools to discourage leering males. The authorities decreed that any youth caught molesting a schoolgirl would be publicly flogged on the spot. When supermarkets close for twenty minutes' prayer women are turned out on to the streets, and offer irresistible targets for frustrated youths in their cars. The police now compel women to go home and return if they want to resume shopping. The Saudi attempt to shut out the moral lassitude, that usually goes with freedom endowed by wealth and technology, is being slowly battered down. Draconian rules are easier to observe when life is spartan.

The erosion of pure Islamic values does not directly threaten the government: those who want to indulge themselves tend to be apolitical and go abroad. But it is eroding the system's moral authority. And moral authority – the Saudis are the guardians of Islam's holy places – is the underpinning this archaic monarchy requires in a world where, as young Saudis must have noticed abroad, emperors have no clothes.

Many Saudis believe that the royal family is breaking the rules it asks them to live by. As the rules are increasingly flouted by those with money, the rules will grow less respected by their subjects. When an eighteenth-century ruling class wrapped in a cloak of moral righteousness loses respect, it becomes vulnerable.

In Saudi Arabia, the forces which could exploit that vulnerability are, in ascending order of probability:

THE 'STREET'. The uprising in Iran was staged by an alliance of anti-Shah mobs which dared his soldiers to fire; they wouldn't. Saudi Arabia lacks such a street, not just because its laws of assembly are harsh. There are too few Saudis too widely dispersed to stage a credible uprising. An uprising in Jeddah would not necessarily provoke one in Riyadh, much less in Dhahran, near the oil.

FOREIGN WORKERS (of which there are up to three million) are expelled at the first sign of trouble. But a flotsam of Yemenis and largely African ex-pilgrims who live in the western provinces, many without a job or the hope of one, might one day make up a street mob, particularly in the port of Jeddah.

THE MIDDLE CLASS. In money terms, most Saudis can probably now call themselves middle class. But few are educated. Their children are being educated, and it is a moot point whether they will in turn be corrupted or end up denouncing the pervasive corruption and the power structure. Both, probably.

ISLAMIC FUNDAMENTALISTS – the most visibly troublesome opponents of the regime today.

Only a handful of men from the non-royal classes – Sheikh Hisham Nazer, the oil minister, Sheikh Yamani, the former oil minister, Sheikh Aba al-Khail, the finance minister – have penetrated the exclusive circle at the top. For them, the rewards of loyalty to the system are stupendous. But there was room for these men. Yamani, who resigned in 1986, has distanced himself from the regime and may become a focus for moderate opposition. How is a whole generation of educated, ambitious young Saudis going to feel about a system where hosts of idle young princes get preferential treatment? Early in the next century there may be 20,000 princes – a huge parasitic class.

The princes suspect everyone. Yet one of their critics within the system has assured me: 'There is no organized movement.' The regime's technocrats are trying to create a middle class based on the private sector, to act as a buttress against revolution, and perhaps one day to take over from the princes. Yamani would make a plausible moderate national leader.

If the princes could see a little way ahead, they might see the advantage of permitting some embryonic political institutions to emerge. Change might otherwise come in the form of a coup. Acutely aware of the danger, the Saudis pay their soldiers directors' salaries and lavish money on military equipment that can hardly be absorbed. In addition, the country's armed forces are split into two – the army and the National Guard – to keep each other in check.

Senior commanders, some of them princes, are none the less gaining in independent influence. A cause that could lead to mutterings among the ranks would be Saudi acquiescence in a Middle East peace that looked like a sell-out to Israel. The princes have thus been careful to move no faster than the Palestine Liberation Organization itself, although they have taken a risk in acquiescing in the 1993 PLO–Israeli agreement.

Nationalism is strong in the armed forces. Saudi Arabia is largely managed by foreigners and relies on American protection. There are grumbles about the depletion of oil reserves. Junior officers may embrace some form of Islamic socialism, like Colonel Qaddafi's in Libya.

With their moral authority waning, the princes are increasingly dependent on the army. In the end, one clever military man – even a prince – could overthrow the system on an ideological pretext. A conspiracy uncovered in 1969 resulted in the execution of a number of officers in thoroughly un-Islamic secrecy. The main deterrent to a would-be Qaddafi is not, however, the executioner's axe, but the fact that America would not allow the wrong sort of coup to happen. Saudi Arabia has become a kind of American protectorate.

THE EYES OF Saudi Arabia's foreign minister, Prince Saud al-Faisal, flicker nervously this way and that; he moistens his lips frequently. His face has the arch look of his father, King Faisal, but is more conventionally handsome. He is less self-assured. He is the only prince with a senior political post to represent the fifty-year-olds beneath the older, reigning sons of Ibn Saud. He is as likely as any to be king one day. Highly American-educated though he is, he says 'Saudi Arabia is non-aligned'.

This statement belongs to the category of other Saudi official pronouncements. In fact, America's relationship to Saudi Arabia is that of father to a growing and increasingly rebellious son. The Saudis can get away with a lot, but the Americans ultimately provide the protection. America took in Saudi Arabia when it was a ragged desert waif from declining imperial Britain. The American success in obtaining the kingdom's first oil concession against British competition in 1933 marked the passing of the torch. America, which offered Saudi Arabia lend-lease aid in the 1940s, became the kingdom's main trading partner and provider of its slight military might.

Today, the bonds are still close. American companies, the Ralph Parsons Company and Bechtel, are building Saudi Arabia's new industries. There are around 400 American companies and 45,000 American citizens in Saudi Arabia. Some 16,000 Saudis are studying in America. The United States geological survey charts the country's mineral resources, its Military Training Mission trains the army, air force and navy. The Americans are modernizing the Saudi National Guard and their corps of engineers manages contracts worth billions for the ministry of defence and the National Guard. Even before the

Gulf War there were around 4,000 Americans engaged on military programmes there.

The Gulf War, and the huge American presence in Saudi Arabia, although kept at a distance from most of the population, has brought Islamic feeling against the monarchy to boiling point. In May 1993 six prominent Islamic clerics from Nejd, in the centre of the country, who set up an embryonic political party, were formally summoned and attacked by Prince Salman, governor of Riyadh. He said formation of the group was unlawful and un-Islamic, and threatened to issue an edict to declare this formally. The committee had reported that: 'The present Saudi model of Islam is not a good model. It is like the last days of the Ottoman empire, a degenerative state. The government should rule accordingly to the Sunnah, by consultation, with elections, and ensuring that everyone's rights are protected.'

The previous December, King Fahd had claimed that 'foreign currents' were behind a campaign to destabilize Saudi Arabia – a barely concealed reference to Islamic fundamentalists in Iran and Sudan. The King lambasted subversive tapes containing outspoken attacks on Saudi policies, including the regime's alleged corruption, nepotism, business practices and its co-operation with the United States during the Gulf War.

Earlier, seven of the seventeen clerics on the Supreme Authority of Senior Scholars, Saudi Arabia's highest religious body, were dismissed for failing to sign a denunciation of a memorandum drawn up by 107 Islamic fundamentalist clerics calling for a much tighter approach to religion in the Kingdom. Fahd's increasingly tough response to the fundamentalists indicates the danger the regime feels it is under. In the summer of 1994, 110 Islamic fundamentalists were arrested for 'spreading sedition'. The government threatened to 'hit strongly anyone who seeks to disrupt security'. Simultaneously, by setting up a long-promised *majlis al-shura* of sixty members, Fahd has sought at last to co-opt the more enlightened Saudi middle class in the struggle against the fundamentalists. This body has no power to criticize the higher policies of government – but petitions it with local grievances. 'We are trying not to rock the boat,' said one member. 'We don't want the council dissolved.' There is an enormous tension in the Saudis' attempt to improve the living standards of the population by adopting Western technology and its efforts to resist the Westernizing influences that could spark a militant Islamic uprising.

So far, in spite of the inherently unstable nature of Saudi rule, the royal family has quite subtly maintained the precarious balance. There may be sense, too, in their refusal to consider even a small measure of popular representation: once the principle is conceded, the absurdity of rule by hereditary princes would be exposed. However, the land cannot be kept in the past for ever. Sooner or later pressure for change in a society divided between Islamic traditionalists and younger modernizers will surface: the al-Saud dynasty seems likely to become the target for popular discontent.

The ultimate prop of Saudi rule is, rather surprisingly, the West. The United States has shown little historical fondness for hereditary monarchs: but its fear of the country falling into the hands of militant Islam or Arab radicals is so great that it passionately supports the al-Saud – although the Americans sensibly have contacts with the moderate middle class groups they ought to be supporting. The stakes in Saudi Arabia are immense: the Gulf War took place primarily to protect Saudi Arabia, which President Bush feared would be the target for invasion in the first few hours of the Iraqi occupation of Kuwait.

Saudi Arabia is not just the Gulf's 'swing' oil producer, capable of providing as much as all of the rest put together and thus – as has frequently happened – moderating oil price swings throughout the market. It also sits astride overwhelmingly the largest potential oil reserves in the world. As only a handful of oil-bearing areas around the peninsula have been properly explored, its proclaimed oil reserves are probably only a fraction of the real total. Aramco's estimate in 1980 was that Saudi Arabia had proven reserves of 114 billion barrels and probable reserves of 178 billion barrels. Sheikh Yamani, the former oil minister, has calculated that proven reserves are more likely to be 180 billion barrels, and as for probable reserves: 'Fasten your seat belts; you would be amazed.' In 1981, he claimed that

Saudi Arabia had at least twice as much oil as generally thought.

Aramco itself has developed only two of its six concession areas. Saudi Arabia has forty-seven oilfields, but only fifteen are in production. Rock dome formations suggest that oil is present in many unexplored parts of Saudi Arabia. The country's probable reserves would not be exhausted until the end of the first quarter of next century even if Saudi Arabia produced at maximum capacity.

If Saudi Arabia has as much oil as Sheikh Yamani thinks – 350 billion barrels? – reserves will last until around 2070. It costs Saudi Arabia about $1 a barrel to tap the oil, but it is sold at around $15 a barrel, a mark-up of more than 1,500 per cent. Saudi Arabia used to justify this by pointing out that it was running out of oil. And now? The prize is immense; the prospect of Saudi Arabia falling into extremist hands is, in the opinion of the Americans, unacceptable.

This provides for a very major potential crisis early in the next century, where the Americans might have to avail themselves of air bases expressly designed to take their aircraft to step in on the side of an anachronistic feudal monarchy to suppress an uprising. It is a huge irony that the most republican of nations should be prepared to prop up the al-Saud, but it is nevertheless true. The danger is that the ruling family, with its narrow base of support, might be unsustainable in the face of an uprising, and the Americans would get sucked into the kind of fighting they have sought to avoid since Vietnam. A civic insurrection against an unpopular government would result, with all the commitment of ground troops and casualties this would entail. All the same, in view of the stakes, it is hard to see what choice they have.

The only – slender – way out of this dilemma would be for America to encourage the moderate modernizers in the country, prompting them to forge a viable alternative should Saudi rule finally collapse under the weight of its own bloated corruption – and there are signs that the house of Saud enjoys as little popular support as the Shah of Iran did. Certainly the cultivation of a moderate alternative to the al-Saud seems advisable, or the United States risks being tainted with the Saudi hatred for their own ruling dynasty, and going down with the sinking ship. The Saudi conundrum has the makings of a major international crisis and military conflict drawing in the West – one second to none over the next two or three decades.

THE OTHER sheikhdoms around the Gulf are much smaller in size, wealth and oil reserves, and vary in the good sense of their rulers. Oman's Sultan Qaboos, with the smallest oil reserves in the Gulf, is commensurately more moderate and sensible in his rule. He presides over a sparsely populated country of some 500,000 people, mostly concentrated in smallish oasis settlements not too seriously disrupted by accelerated oil-fuelled development. Unlike the Saudis, who won most of their territory by comparatively recent conquest, his ruling family are of long-standing in the territory and enjoy genuine support among the largely homogeneous tribesmen in its rural settlements.

Qaboos used British support between 1965 and 1975 to stave off radical Yemeni attacks in the west of his country, and this proved sufficient. It is hard to detect any substantial opposition to his rule, which co-opts the small middle class of Oman. The combination of a tribal base, a small country, a traditional society, plus a commonsense approach to government realistic development goals and a fairly light repressive hand, is healthy. Islam is less strict than elsewhere in the Gulf, partly because of Oman's racial connections with India. The country is more outward-looking towards the nations of the Indian Ocean than the inward-looking countries inside the foetid Gulf waterway.

The discreet British connection will help to ensure that the Omani dynasty will be one of the longest surviving in the region, as long as agreement can be reached about a suitable heir – as Qaboos has no children. If the Omanis prove flexible in modernizing their government, the dynasty could re-emerge one day as a constitutional government. The only visible threat today is the old Iranian attempt to destabilize the government, born of Oman's strategic position in the approaches to the Gulf.

Iranian subversion is much more evident in Dubai, and to a lesser extent in Abu Dhabi and the other United Arab Emirates: the presence of a considerable minority of Shias, coupled with a transient trading population of Iranians, has led the rotating emirs of this oil-rich corner to be carefully Islamic, as well as their being the most pro-Iranian of the Arab Gulf States. Oil prosperity has disrupted the traditional life of the emirates much more visibly than in, say, Oman. In addition there are tensions between the rival emirs of the UAE and their tribesmen, as well as with Saudi Arabia, such as the traditional dispute for possession of the Buraimi Oasis. The small population (300,000) and the comparatively great shower of oil wealth has permitted the rulers to buy off their populations – for the moment; but it would be naïve to believe that these dynasties will last long into the twenty-first century.

Moving further up the Gulf is probably the politically frailest of the Gulf States, Bahrain, run by the al-Khalifa dynasty. Bahrain contains a large Shia population which is well-organized and unafraid of making itself felt and many observers there believe the regime would fall if given a serious push by the Iranians; it also has its share of Arab socialists. Relatively rich, highly urbanized, the al-Khalifas for the moment survive off the tolerance of their peoples, rather than through repression; their island status has reinforced their hold.

This has been compromised recently with the construction of a causeway to Saudi Arabia, which makes Bahrain the foremost destination for Saudis, as well as people as far away as Kuwait, a popular destination for a weekend of excessive behaviour. The spectacle of young male Saudis in long white robes wildly drunk, as only those unused to alcohol can be, in the bars of Bahrain, is not for those with weak stomachs. Bahrain is one of the most cosmopolitan, even diverting places in the Gulf; it is also one of its weak links.

The last of the feudal princedoms is Kuwait, recently the subject of invasion by Iraq. The Kuwaitis are perhaps the region's most arrogant and inhospitable people – which is saying something, if Saudi Arabia is included in the comparison. With its searing sands bleached by pitiless sunshine in off-white skies, the city of Kuwait is as characterless a collection of modern skyscrapers surrounded by underused beltways as can be seen anywhere in the world; the romance of Arabia is entirely absent from this Detroit-on-sand.

Kuwait, a major trading port for the northern Gulf powers, Iraq and Iran, was historically the first to shower its small population with oil revenues. The vast majority of Kuwaitis live a *rentier* existence off the interest from their wealth (the Koran's ban on interest has long since been circumvented). Men retire at forty with lavish welfare provisions, and live off the work of stateless foreigners – who comprised a majority of the population before the Iraqi invasion. As much as half the population spends several months abroad each year.

Faced with a comparatively well-off and educated people, the ruling al-Sabah dynasty was the first Gulf princedom to concede a kind of consultative assembly elected by male Kuwaitis, which was quickly rescinded when it took too independent a view. After fierce criticism of the al-Sabahs' behaviour during the Gulf War – first out when the Iraqis invaded, last back in after the Iraqi defeat would be a not unfair description – and under American pressure, the ruling dynesty has conceded another assembly, one in which the opposition secured overwhelming victory despite the rules being stacked against them.

It remains to be seen how far this gesture of the al-Sabahs will extend – or whether they have the power again to close it down. If they try, the al-Sabahs might find themselves the first Gulf dynasty to have to back down in the face of democratic pressure. Although there were elements of militant Islam and radicalism in the new assembly, the majority elected were the well-heeled bourgeoisie of Kuwait, somewhat contradicting the oft-stated contention that Arabs are unfit for democracy, too backward, ill-educated and immature for such Western nostrums, inevitably a prey to extremism.

The emir is elderly, vacillating and has a short attention span for work, which hardly commends him to his people.

Paradoxically, Kuwait may be the state best fitted for an experiment in constitutional government. A constitutional success in Kuwait could quickly prove an example for the other city states of the Gulf and lead to pressure for an opening in Saudi Arabia – which is one reason why King Fahd would be the first to back the despised al-Sabahs in any confrontation with their parliament.

Thus the picturesque medieval emirs of the Gulf linger on, with their camel races and falconry and tents within palaces, exuding nostalgia for a nomadic Bedouin past of poverty that does not quite ring true beside their obvious enjoyment of the best things money can buy, an anachronism in the twentieth century, preserved for now, but not forever, by oil wealth. It is impossible to predict when the deluge will come, but come it will; and when it does, it seems likely to be violent and fast, blowing the whole collection away almost simultaneously, not so much like dominoes as like the elegant pieces on the chessboard in Alice in Wonderland, this time toppling the whole white-skirted collection of emirs, beglerbegs, sultans and kings.

It is just possible that the Gulf states will reform themselves sagely and in time; but it may be too late – an opening could self-fulfillingly release pent-up hatreds that are the fuel of extremism – and anyway the monarchs show no signs of sagacity. The Gulf's rulers are the exception that proves that the end of dynastic rule has arrived.

DYNASTY HAS attempted a comeback this century. Some modern rulers have tried to found new dynasties imitating the systems they have often usurped themselves. Almost invariably, these attempts have failed. In Iran, Reza Pahlavi, a sergeant who took over the country in 1921, handed the 'peacock throne', ludicrously revived from Iran's imperial past, on to his son, the Shah, who with the *nouveau rich naïveté* of the second-generation enthroned himself in astonishing ostentation while modernizing his country in an accelerated manner with a fine disdain for all its traditional power centres and constituencies.

He succeeded in uniting Islamic fundamentalists, the middle

classes, radicals, the bazaar merchant class and large sections of the urban population against him. Even the army would not rally to his banner at the end. He was toppled in 1979, in a revolution that began bloodlessly and soon developed its own gruesome momentum.

In China, Deng Xiaoping long harboured ambitions for his son to succeed him; but the latter, a victim of repression during Deng's political eclipse, was patently not up to the job. In Singapore Lee Kuan Yew carefully paved the way for his son to succeed, but internal resistance among Lee's own lieutenants may yet block him. In North Korea, Kim Il-sung's son, Kim Jong-Il, precariously succeeded his father in 1994.

In India, Nehru's daughter, Indira Gandhi, created a second generation of rule through her iron will which also, after her assassination, carried her son Rajiv to the top, until his own murder. Sympathy and support for the Gandhi dynasty is still so considerable that if a suitable candidate could be found – Rajiv's widow, for the moment, demurring – it could yet rule again. In Pakistan, Benazir Bhutto's first spell in office proved a disappointment in the wake of her damagingly populist father, the executed Zulfikar Ali Bhutto; but she has acquired the toughness (excessively so, her mother would say) and staying power, to make what looks like a more mature comeback.

Even in republican America, there was a brief flirtation with dynasty – not that of the Roosevelt cousins, both equally talented in different ways, but the Kennedys, who boasted one supremely talented politician, Jack, one tough-minded but skilful political fixer, Robert, and a rather weaker third brother, Ted. Yet the failure of the latter to stage a serious presidential bid underlined the fact that the two elder brothers were, unusually, both hard enough to make it to the top.

The failure of modern dynastic rule – except in the Indian subcontinent – stems only in part from the fact that this no longer commands the popular legitimacy that it did in the past: it also arises from the propensity of modern societies to permit only those strong and able enough to get to the top. Dynasty does not guarantee that one strong leader will be succeeded by another; the Achilles heel of the hereditary system is that it does not necessarily yield an heir who is up to the job, or even necessarily wants it; and if he has not had to fight for it, he is not usually tough enough.

In spite of its glamour and glitter, dynastic rule seems likely to linger on in only a few of the world's backwaters. Sadly, because of their lack of receptiveness to popular pressure, their myopia and their repression, it seems likely that Arabia's monarchies will one day be replaced not by constitutional democratic rule, but in bloody revolutions by radicals and fundamentalists.

CHAPTER THREE

EMPIRES OF SAND

IT IS PERHAPS the world's most beautiful place, a remote upland plateau the size of a small continent, fringed by the highest mountains on earth, peopled by six million belonging to an ancient race and culture inspired by a gentle Buddhism that, for hundreds of years, was its very government. It has one of the most spectacular capitals in the world, Lhasa, with the cascading multi-tiered Potala Palace as its centrepiece, and some magnificent monasteries as its adornments.

Yet it is a place of sorrow, oppression and fear, ravaged by one of the most vicious colonialist regimes the world has ever known, for more than forty years a massive concentration camp and charnel house. It is Tibet, occupied by China in 1951. Unlike other colonial occupations or acts of international aggression, it is hard to see this one being reversed: the Chinese have brought in eight million of their own people, and now outnumber the Tibetans.

The purpose of the Chinese colonization has been simple in the extreme: to seize a huge swathe of territory extending to India. The conduct of the occupation has been as ruthless as any in history. It began gently, with Tibet's spiritual leader, the Dalai Lama, being received by Mao in Peking. The picture changed when the eastern part of the country rose up against the Chinese in the late 1950s and was ruthlessly put down. In March 1959 the Dalai Lama fled, fearing arrest. The Chinese reacted by killing thousands of his loyal monks and supporters, and arresting thousands more.

A social revolution began: landowners were arrested, expropriated or executed and the survivors turned into 'blackhats', a kind of underclass deprived of all rights. The Tibetan provinces of Amdo and Kham were absorbed into China. The province of U-Tsang, the size of France and Germany combined, was renamed the Tibetan Autonomous Region, but was similarly controlled by the Chinese, who used the schools to indoctrinate their language and propaganda into the people. The Chinese also seized Tibetan harvests in the early 1960s, causing mass starvation.

This terrifying regime could hardly get worse: but it did with the Cultural Revolution in 1966: a frenzy of slaughter and pillage ensued. Perhaps a million people died, some 300,000 in fighting, some 400,000 dying of starvation and some 300,000 being executed or dying in captivity; relative to the population, this was the most savage horror the world had seen before the killing fields of Cambodia in the late 1970s – but it attracted much less attention. The 3,000 monasteries and nunneries strung across this ancient and spectacular land, which had housed some 100,000 clergy, were destroyed, leaving just eight, and a clerical population of some 1,000. This was an act of cultural genocide without precedent.

Only with Mao's death in 1978 did the terror abate. Hu Yaobang, his reformist successor, came to Lhasa and admitted that 'mistakes' had been made: some of the monasteries were restored and some 10,000 monks and nuns returned. The collective farms were broken up and political repression slightly eased. In 1987, after the Dalai Lama, gathering international support, presented a 'peace plan' to the American congress, demonstrations broke out in Lhasa. They were suppressed, with at least 200 Tibetan deaths and thousands of arrests, and were instrumental in Hu's downfall in China. Many protesters were sentenced to long periods in prison and many were tortured with electric shocks.

In 1992 the Chinese made plain their utterly ruthless approach: 'The central government will not make the slightest concession on the fundamental issue of maintaining the motherland's unification. Any activist sabotaging stability and unity in Tibet will be cracked down on relentlessly.' It is an irony of history that the world's last major surviving example of colonialism is one of the most horrific ever experienced.

*

THE SECOND GREAT source of modern state authority has been colonialism, the imposition of rule by one state over another based on military superiority. Today, with the collapse of the Soviet Empire, this is nearly extinct. There are a number of small enclaves under 'colonial' rule, where the inhabitants themselves are reluctant to lose the protection of their foreign masters. For Britain, these are Hong Kong (soon to be relinquished), Montserrat, Anguilla, Bermuda, the British Antarctic Territory, the British Indian Ocean Territory, the British Virgin Islands, the Caymans; the Falklands, Gibraltar, the Pitcairn Group, the St Helena Group, the Turks and Caicos, South Georgia and the South Sandwich Islands. For France, these are French Antarctica, French Polynesia, Guadaloupe, Guiana, Martinique, Mayott, New Caledonia, Réunion, St Pierre and Miquelon, Wallis and Fortune. For Holland, these are the Antilles and Aruba; for Spain, these are Ceuta and Melilla; for Portugal, Macau; and for Denmark, Greenland. All of these might be described as 'voluntary colonies'. The French dependencies have some two million people, the British, excluding Hong Kong, just 150,000.

Russia stands accused of colonialism in the enclaves in which it has lingered – particularly Chechnya – sometimes on the pretext of preventing civil war; in others its re-engagement is actively sought by one side or another – for example in Georgia and Nagorno-Karabakh. It is possible to argue that Kurdistan is an enclave occupied by several colonial powers, although the Kurds have never had a state. Some African tribal minorities argue that they are colonial pockets of the majority. Yet so far Eritrea's justified dash for independence has not multiplied across the continent. Indonesia has certainly made a colony of East Timor. By far the biggest and most obscene is the continuing Chinese domination of Tibet.

BUT THE CONTRAST between the world now and that at the beginning of the century is truly awesome. Then, the British empire dominated one-quarter of the world's population, occupying a quarter of its territory, including much of

Africa, a large swathe of the Middle East, the Indian subcontinent, relatively large parts of Asia through trading proxies, and it had major commercial interests in Mexico and Argentina. France dominated a large swathe of North Africa and the Middle East. Germany had its African possessions. Italy had minor colonies, while Belgium had the Congo. The Portuguese empire in Africa and its enclaves in Asia were considerable. The United States had a number of proxy colonies in Latin America. The Austro-Hungarian empire extended into the Balkans, the Russian empire into Asia.

Imperialism was the norm at the beginning of the century; today it is treated as a joke, an utterly repudiated notion, almost vanished for good. This is not the place for a major survey of traditional imperialism, as opposed to economic imperialism (which continues and will be discussed later) because it is so rare a source of contemporary state authority and will almost certainly be a spent force for the future. But it is worth glancing at some of the trends that caused such a complete transformation of the map of the globe.

The key point about colonialism is that it was a more complex phenomenon than appears from the virtuous stereotype at the beginning of this century and the hostile one at the end. There were at least four strands to classic colonialism. First, chronologically, there was economic colonialism: the expansion of trade between more and less developed societies leading to the use of force by the former to secure their interests, particularly when the 'natives' were viewed as little more than savages and pagans.

Second, there was the religious motive, which was equally important in the Europe of the sixteenth and seventeenth centuries, viewed as a mission to proselytize Christianity around the world. While the first kind had been motivated exclusively by commercial greed and self-interest, the latter, although often even crueller in its consequences, was partly idealistic and led to the kind of missionary idealism that characterized the last stages of colonialism and was in many ways its best feature.

Third, there was – as with Clive's conquest of India in the eighteenth century – the belated imposition of rule by the colonial state to protect its interests and to regulate the countries involved, and even to protect the inhabitants from predatory commercialism.

Finally, there was competitive, and often defensive empire-building pure and simple, as the industrial nations rushed to seize areas of the world, to pre-empt their trading rivals and secure their commercial interests there.

Colonialism was made possible by one simple fact: the superiority of European arms over those of the peoples they subdued. It was reversed largely for one reason: as those colonized acquired arms, in particular small arms that could be diffused among whole populations, it became impossibly expensive for the occupying powers, both financially and in terms of lives, to maintain adequate protection for their enclaves there.

As one colonial war after another erupted into bloodshed, the major imperial powers understood they had no alternative but to leave, covering their tracks in clouds of idealistic and hypocritical rhetoric. Another major factor in the collapse of the European empires was the opposition to them of both the United States (with huge global interests of its own) and the Soviet Union (itself an empire), the one providing fierce criticism, the other offering arms and assistance to anti-colonial movements.

Was there ever any legitimacy other than force to be attached to the imposition of rule by one people upon another? There was certainly a legacy of modernization, infrastructure and education that colonial society indelibly left upon the more backward colonized societies. There were certainly a great many involved in the colonial administrations, as well as their political masters back home, that saw their mission as a civilizing one and harboured high ideals of protecting the inhabitants from naked commercial interests.

Yet the assertion of political independence by the subject peoples, even while often directly contrary to their own economic interests, was an entirely elemental expression of the self. Without a monopoly of military force, minority colonial administrations could not survive. The empires that lasted longest were those most ruthless in flexing military might and prepared to suffer the highest casualties – Portugal, the Soviet Union and China. With modern weaponry now diffuse and guerrilla techniques well understood, no colonial regime could survive today without virtually genocidal ruthlessness.

Traditional colonialism, while virtually extinct, was replaced by two more subtle forms: economic domination by external business interests which frequently benefited from the absence of skilled colonial administrators to check them, as well as from the distance of concerned opinion in the home country; and, latterly, a growing realization on the part of the governments of developed countries that their political expulsion from the colonies did not enable them to abdicate responsibility for the less developed countries, and that they had a role in volunteering assistance to their former subjects.

The exceptions to the end of formal colonialism are East Timor and Tibet. East Timor has its own special corner in the graveyard of recent colonial atrocities. On 7 December 1975, after Portugal had abruptly departed from its former colony, Indonesian troops entered the capital, Dili. The single faint radio report received in Darwin, 300 miles away, was Nanking-like in its horror: 'The soldiers are killing indiscriminately. Women and children are being shot in the streets. We are all going to be killed. I repeat we are all going to be killed . . . This is an appeal for international help. This is an SOS. We appeal to the Australian people. Please help us.' Later the Bishop of Dili, Costa Lopez, reported that: 'The soldiers who landed started killing everyone they could find. There were many dead bodies in the street – all we could see were the soldiers killing, killing, killing.'

Some 200,000 people, approximately a third of the population, were slaughtered in the next few years, in a wholesale colonial annexation based on terrorizing the population. By 1994 a tiny, 400-strong guerrilla movement, with widespread popular sympathy, formed the only challenge to the Indonesian yoke. The peace of the graveyard, and of the concentration camp, reigns there now.

As for Tibet, why does this huge area and population of six million people continue to endure a colonial yoke shrugged off throughout the rest of the world? The major factor, undoubtedly, is China's determination: for strategic reasons, China regards Tibet as critical to projecting its power into central Asia and as a buffer state against any threat from India. Thus the Chinese have been prepared to devote a huge commitment to the region, in terms of oppressive military force and millions of settlers.

Human rights and casualties are of no great concern to the Chinese; nor have the traditionally pacific Tibetan people managed to halt the systematic destruction of Tibet's national identity. There is no sign of any lessening in China's determination to hang on to Tibet. Given Tibetan traditional non-violence (although an increasing number of the Dalai Lama's followers are advocating armed action), and the size and ruthlessness of the Chinese force in Tibet, it may be the one major colonial enclave that, tragically, endures. But this exception stands out from the collapse of virtually every other major colonial experience. Classic colonialism, if it ever enjoyed legitimacy other than through force, does not now and is consigned to the past. The diffusion of arms to less developed countries makes it highly unlikely that it will ever be revived.

CHAPTER FOUR

RULE BY THE JACKBOOT

MILITARY RULE is a truly grim, depressing experience. Take Argentina's ordeal. In September 1973, Argentines of all classes flooded the Plaza de Mayo, in front of the presidential Pink House, parading uproariously down the avenue, which is overlooked by the parliament house. They were celebrating the return to power of Juan Domingo Perón, eighteen years to the month after they had poured into the streets to celebrate the tyrant's overthrow. At the age of seventy-seven, after nearly two decades of comfortable exile in Madrid, Argentina's former dictator had won a staggering sixty-two per cent of the popular vote.

The middle classes voted for him because they thought he was a bulwark against revolution. The working classes, whose view of Perón had grown rosier through glasses clouded by years of army rule, remembered him as the man who gave them some sense of dignity. The far right supported him as the world's last authentic fascist, apprenticed in the 1930s on a military mission to Mussolini's Rome. The Marxists thought of him as a gaga old man of whom they could take advantage.

Because the army had barred Perón from taking part in the elections the previous March, a left-wing stand-in, Héctor Campora, was elected president. Campora promptly freed every Argentine jailbird, political or otherwise, and invited Perón back. El Lider, as Perón was called, insisted that new elections be held and picked as his vice-presidential running mate his wife, Isabelita, a dancer with some of the looks and none of the political savvy of his second wife, the legendary Evita.

In March 1976, laconically and with a week's advance notice, Argentina's army reluctantly took power over a Hogarthian bedlam of a country. Annual inflation was 600 per cent. Isabelita Perón, who had succeeded her husband to the presidency on his death in 1974, was on the verge of a nervous breakdown, being attended by Svengali-like courtiers including José Lopez Rega, an astrologer. Politicians and union leaders had left by plane, their suitcases stuffed with looted cash. Once-tranquil Buenos Aires suburbs were reverberating to the sound of explosions and gunfire as extremist groups battled it out. The day after the army took over, many absentee civil servants reported for the first time in months to their ministries for fear of losing their jobs. Fistfights broke out between those claiming the same desks.

In September 1979, General Luciano Menendez, the commander of the Third Army stationed in Córdoba, called a press conference to demand the resignation of the army commander, General Roberto Viola. General Menendez was angry about the government's decision to release from house arrest Jacobo Timerman, the former editor of the newspaper *La Opinion*. Although allegedly linked with far-left terrorists, Timerman was never formally charged with any crime after his 1977 arrest. He was tortured and, after an international outcry, placed under house arrest. In September 1978, he was put on an airplane to Israel after receiving members of the Inter-American Commission on Human Rights, who were appalled by his story. His book, *Prisoner Without a Name, Cell Without a Number*, was to bring the horror of Argentina to world notice. General Menendez was outraged by the government's 'weakness in releasing Timerman'.

Menendez was immediately relieved of his command – but not before he had set out for Jesus María, a small town in the hills, to rally his forces for a march on Córdoba. Asked by General Viola over the telephone what he was up to, General Menendez replied, 'routine manoeuvres'. These manoeuvres included assembling a force of 750 military engineers and anti-aircraft gunners, who marched, Quixote-style, on the 15,000-strong Viola garrison in Córdoba. When his contingent was surrounded, General Menendez was persuaded to come to his senses and surrender.

He was then forced to fly to Buenos Aires and apologize in person to General Viola in order to restore the respect due to that officer. For openly attempting to overthrow the government by force, General Menendez was sentenced (in a country where editors under suspicion were tortured) to sixty days of dignified confinement. This bizarre story of an armed rebellion, of the military feathers it ruffled, and of the magnanimity extended to the barons but not the serfs, was straight out of the Middle Ages – or perhaps Bolivia.

But Argentina is neither Bolivia nor the Middle Ages. Argentina is modern and wealthy. It is the world's eighth largest country with only 33 million people to share its riches. It has a mild climate and its humid pampas are considered one of the world's five richest agricultural areas. In addition, the Patagonian plateau is ideal for sheep grazing and Argentina is the world's second-largest beef exporter. The nation could be one of its largest grain producers if it cultivated its pampas, and it is its fourth-largest wine producer. Its gross domestic product per head, some $2,800, is perhaps the highest in Latin America. Four-fifths of Argentinians live in cities, and nine-tenths of them can read. Argentina is self-sufficient in its production of oil and has huge natural gas deposits, boundless hydroelectric potential and enormous coal reserves that it does not exploit. Its hills are rich in copper, molybdenum, gold, silver, lead, zinc, barium and uranium, with very little of it mined.

The popular gibe (among Brazilians) is that God lavished natural wealth on Argentina, but other countries complained. So God gave it Argentinians, to redress the balance. This is unfair. But they have made a mess of their politics, and that, more than anything else, stopped Argentina from becoming a paradise on earth.

The juntas that ran Argentina between 1976 and 1982 were unfairly criticized as the source of Argentina's ills. In fact, Perón's uniquely unpleasant legacy of nationalism, populism and military might, have been the source. The subsequent juntas were certainly responsible for acting with the utmost brutality, waging a savage war against the opposition that revolted the conscience of the civilized world. The report on the fate of the disappeared, *Never Again*, compiled by the democratic government of President Raul Alfonsin, makes appalling reading. There is a nauseating voyeurism about books on torture; yet the issue cannot be avoided. This excerpt from *Never Again* will suffice:

> M de M was abducted in Buenos Aires. She was taken for a long distance in a pick-up truck. Judging by the sound of crickets and other details, they took her somewhere in the country. It was like a camp, a provisional set-up, with canvas sheeting and tents everywhere. They left her in a sort of room where she felt terrified and started to scream. Thus alerted, her captors put her into a tank full of water. Her breasts were hurting a lot, as she was breast-feeding at the time . . .
>
> Then they bound her hands and feet with wires and passed electric current through them. She began to have convulsions. They said that was the breaking in she needed in order to confess. Then they stripped her and raped her.
>
> She asked to go to the toilet. They took her naked along an open gallery full of soldiers. She remembers that they all laughed. She also recalls them taking a group of people and putting them into a helicopter; they were thrown out at the end of a rope, and each time they were raised again they were questioned . . .
>
> Teresa Cecilia Meschiati was abducted in the town of Cordoba: 'Immediately after my arrival at La Perla, I was taken to the torture room or intensive therapy room. They stripped me and tied my feet and hands with ropes to the bars of a bed, so that I was hanging from them. They attached a wire to one of the toes of my right foot. Torture was applied gradually by means of electric prods of two different intensities: one of 125 volts which caused involuntary muscle movements all over my body. They applied this to my face, eyes, mouth, arms, vagina and anus; and another of 220 volts called *la margarita* (the daisy) which left deep ulcerations which I still have and which caused a violent contraction, as if all my limbs were being torn off at once, especially in the kidneys, legs, groin and sides of the body. They also put a wet rag on my chest to increase the intensity of the shock.

'I tried to kill myself by drinking the foul water in the tub which was meant for another kind of torture called *submarino*, but I did not succeed.'

YET MILITARY RULE is the third major source of legitimacy for the modern state. Given the large number of countries that have recently undergone the experience of military rule – an area of the map also almost as large as that once covered by colonialism, also founded on the rule of force – this is a much neglected phenomenon.

A decade ago, the overwhelming majority of countries in Latin America were ruled by soldiers; a large number of African countries still suffer a similar experience. It is arguable that some Middle Eastern countries are basically military regimes – Egypt, Iraq, Syria. Military rule has even made its appearance in the Eastern bloc – in Poland. The role of the armed forces in China has been considerable, and in some countries like South Korea, Thailand and Taiwan, dominant. Some of this marching-boot empire has since crumbled, particularly in Latin America.

But military rule remains a real possibility in all of these countries and many others, even including Russia, and begs a large number of questions. Is military rule ever justified or legitimized other than through force? What ideas do military rulers subscribe to, if any, other than repression of the opposition? Why, given the armed forces' monopoly of coercion, are they so often pushed out of office? And is the case of some extreme free-marketeers, that authoritarian rule is actually beneficial when a country is undergoing accelerated economic development, ever justified?

IT IS WORTH briefly examining four controversial examples, although there are many others. In Chile in 1973 a Marxist president elected on a minority three-way vote attempted to push through radical social reform. Social disorder and inflation had occurred as a result, and the country seemed on the brink of chaos. When the army moved in, it had the support not just of the right but of Chile's traditional centrist political party, the Christian Democrats and, almost certainly, the majority of the population. What then happened was that the army stayed in power for a decade and a half, under a tough-minded general, Augusto Pinochet. But this does not invalidate the army's original decision to seize power in conditions of near-chaos in 1973.

Similarly, in Argentina soldiers staged a coup against the blatantly corrupt government of Isabelita Perón, which had presided over economic collapse, hyper-inflation and terrorism on such a scale that it threatened to turn into a civil war. The appalling repression and incompetence of the military regime subsequently could not detract from the fact that Argentina would have degenerated into anarchy if the army had not intervened at the time. Once the fire was out, it is terrible to discover that one's belongings have been soaked by the firemen's hoses; but they could have been destroyed much more comprehensively by the conflagration otherwise.

A third example is Pakistan in 1977. The economy was in tatters, with major ethnic violence also threatening under President Bhutto's regime. Virtually every informed Pakistani heaved a sigh of relief when General Zia ul-Haq staged his military coup. They were to become less certain when he pursued his vendetta against Bhutto to the point of hanging him, and clung firmly to power thereafter (he bore a strong resemblance to Pinochet in his political cunning, ruthlessness, refusal to budge and limited intelligence). But few at the time believed the military intervention was anything but inevitable to forestall chaos. This legitimized Zia's seizure of power.

A fourth example is that of Poland in 1981. General Jaruzelski's take-over was prompted by fears of a Soviet invasion to suppress the country's Solidarity trade union movement and the political and social turmoil accompanying it, which directly challenged communist control of the country. The military authorities concluded that it was preferable for Poles themselves to put their house in order, and moved in to crush Solidarity.

While obviously repressive, the coup could be justified as an attempt to avert the much greater bloodshed and humiliation of a Soviet invasion; moreover, the armed forces moved quickly also to dismantle Poland's incompetent and hated communist leadership, so that the country was arguably closer to shrugging off the totalitarian yoke than it had been before. As ever, the Polish military leadership overstayed any welcome it had enjoyed and Jaruzelski was forced to compromise with a newly resurgent Solidarity in 1989, resulting in the first anti-communist government in the Eastern bloc at a time when the Soviet Union was too weak to intervene.

Thus a common feature of military regimes is that successful seizures of power usually take place only if the climate is right – if establishment and, sometimes, even public opinion, believes that a military government would be preferable to chaos or – as in Poland's case – foreign invasion. Sadly, few military men understand that this support constitutes a mandate in just the same way as an election provides one, and that it can be lost by a bad or incompetent military regime. Shielded from political reality and public opinion, military regimes frequently delude themselves that they retain a mandate when in fact the failure of opposition to make itself felt arises purely out of fear.

Another key characteristic of military regimes is, of course the relegation of all political opponents to the status of enemies. Military training is necessarily carried out in black and white terms. There is your own side, and there is the enemy. Against the enemy, who will try to kill you, anything is permissible. The list of techniques practised by the military to eliminate or suppress opposition is well known: the elimination of political opponents either openly (Bhutto was show-tried and hanged, Allende probably killed in the bombed-out wreck of his palace, while thousands of his supporters were massacred in Santiago's main football stadium) or, as in Argentina, Guatemala and El Salvador, through 'disappearance'. In these countries people have been kidnapped off the streets, in unmarked Ford Falcon cars, and never seen again, victims of army-appointed death squads; imprisonment; routine torture, more to terrorize the opposition than to elicit information; the exile and expulsion of opponents; control of the press and public assembly; and the propagandist creation of a mythical 'enemy'; in Latin America, as elsewhere, this was usually international communism.

In fact, most countries have had minority communist movements, which were the most effective clandestine political operators under military regimes; a number, particularly Argentina and Uruguay and, more recently, Peru, all suffered from terrorism or, in central America, guerrilla threats. Yet in many countries the communist label was used to suppress all political dissidence, from the centre-right to the extreme left.

Although military regimes tend to see even mild critics as enemies, they are not immune from the need for a source of political legitimization, indeed for civilian allies. The inability of generals to run a complex modern economy and state usually causes them to look for partners on the extreme right with simplistic solutions of their own which appeal to simple military minds: in recent times this has consisted of enthusiasm for the Chicago School of monetarist economics preached by Milton Friedman.

However, there is a problem with this solution: the armed forces themselves are a major state institution, consuming, in Latin America's case, a large share of the national wealth. In countries like Argentina and Brazil, moreover, they also traditionally ran a fair-sized chunk of the nations' industries – Fabricaciones Militares in Argentina, Petrobras, the petroleum giant, in Brazil. So free-market solutions to their country's often chaotic economic problems on seizing power must stop short of cutting back on this huge area of state activity; more often than not it is substantially expanded.

The result has been a curious tension between the free-market technicians brought in to run the economy and their military masters which, while usually yielding short-term economic improvements, has resulted in further economic problems in the long term. In some countries, the social classes from which the army was drawn prompted it to behave in a populist, free-spending fashion, even espousing socialism: this was the case for a time in Peru and Ecuador and, also, briefly, in Bolivia.

A further characteristic of military regimes is their vigorous political infighting: while trying to give the impression that they are the unified servants of the nation, in fact, like any human institution, they are often deeply divided politically and corrupted from within. The most obvious division is between the rival services; it is also the easiest to resolve, because the army is almost always the most powerful.

In Buenos Aires on one occasion, the navy tried to press its claim by shelling army positions from the sea; but the army won. In Chile, General Pinochet ignominiously dismissed the air force commander, who had been critical of his dictatorship – and any air force men who might have defended him were quickly convinced by the size of the army units in the streets.

But other divisions are more complex – between rival personalities and generals, between central government and military governors with their local garrisons, between junior officers and senior officers. Some military regimes are characterized by ruthless hierarchy under a single all-powerful figure. Examples of the latter are Chile's Pinochet and Spain's General Franco.

Other armies are characterized by bitter political infighting, resolved only through rotating presidents. In Argentina, Generals Videla, Viola, Galtieri and Bignami followed each other in quick succession, while the frustrated naval chief, Admiral Massera, set himself up as a kind of internal opposition to them. He lacked much popular conviction, as he had presided over the most brutal of the intelligence services.

In Brazil, the problem was solved by institutionalizing change – presidential terms were limited: Generals Castelo Branco, Medici, Geisel and Figueiredo each had a fixed term of office. In Portugal, junior officers disgruntled with the country's colonial ventures succeeded in overthrowing their chiefs in the 1974 coup. If armies are not much good for politics, politics are not much good for armies.

A FINAL FEATURE of most military regimes is that, unlike Cromwell, they do not know when to go. Most such regimes would enjoy considerable popularity if, once they have stepped in to restore order for a year or two, they then would return to the barracks, placing themselves in reserve to intervene again if things go wrong. They would also retain their self-respect. Instead, after the initial emergency is overcome, there seems always to be a continuing peril to be dealt with, subversion to be resisted, the economy to be rescued, and so on. Military rulers deny vehemently that they also enjoy the perks and prestige of running countries and making money out of major industries; but they do.

Because of the climate of repression, it generally takes a fairly long time for opposition to organize itself so strongly that an army has to retreat from office, but it usually does eventually. Intriguingly, appearances to the contrary notwithstanding, armies are not simply brutal repressive machines; they are affected by the general climate of hostility to them, although thick skins take time to penetrate.

In Argentina, it took the unsuccessful and ludicrously misguided Falklands campaign to topple the army. In Brazil, it took the international debt crisis, run up by the military regime and invalidating its claim to responsible economic management as opposed to civilian profligacy and corruption. In Chile, it took a plebiscite into which General Pinochet was unwittingly lured, vainly believing he did indeed enjoy popular support. In Central America it took the loss of American support for the caudillos. In Spain – one of the longest lived of all – it took the death of General Franco, and in Pakistan, that of General Zia (almost certainly assassinated). In Thailand it took the killing of scores of demonstrators in Bangkok, and in Poland, the resurgence of Solidarity and the virtual paralysis of the country when there was no longer any prospect of Soviet invasion. Very few military regimes have voluntarily relinquished power.

This leads to a further characteristic of military rule: when armies leave, they have usually achieved little; as a political and economic crisis generally clears them out of office, the country is often in the same state of chaos that they used to justify their initial intervention. Moreover, the crudeness of their policies often ensures that their civilian supporters are as unpopular as they. Genuine political parties in most countries, being necessarily organized from the bottom upwards, have deep roots that a few years of military rule cannot pull up.

In Argentina, on the army's departure, the Peronists and the Radicals re-emerged; in Chile the Christian Democrats came out into the sunlight smiling; in Turkey, the same Mr Demirel that was deposed all those years ago was the main beneficiary; in Pakistan, it was Mr Bhutto's daughter, commanding the same old Pakistan People's Party.

If there is a moral in all this, it is that military rule is best avoided; indeed frequent military interventions give politicians the excuse to behave irresponsibly in office, while the going is good, in the knowledge that the armed forces will pick up the pieces. Of course, there are occasions when military intervention is justified, even inevitable, or preferable to the alternative. In one respect military government succeeded without qualification, although brutally: the war against terrorism in Argentina and Uruguay was undeniably won. But no one should harbour any illusions about the nastiness, incompetence and transient nature of most military regimes. Putting soldiers in to run a country is like placing a baggage handler in charge of a flight control tower.

Military-backed rule is now confined to a handful of African countries, just two in Latin America – Peru, faced by a collapsing economy and a huge guerrilla threat, and Haiti; and, in Asia, Indonesia. As will be seen, the return to barracks was one of the great victories for democracy and individual expression in the 1980s. But it is far too soon to conclude that the soldiers will remain confined there. Already, in Latin America, they have threatened to break out in coup attempts in Venezuela and Guatemala.

In Russia, and in the Ukraine and Romania as well, military rule remains a much discussed option in the event of social and economic disintegration. The same is true of Africa's civilian governments. In Asia, although the army's influence has been sharply reduced in South Korea, Thailand, the Philippines and even Malaysia, it remains considerable and could re-emerge in an emergency. The countries that have already had a spell of brutal, incompetent military governments are on the whole less enthusiastic about it today and have more of an incentive for avoiding the mistakes that led to the experience than those that have not, like Russia.

CHAPTER FIVE

GOVERNMENT BY ELITE

CAIRO, ON THE FACE OF IT, seems to be a city that cannot possibly work: it can take hours to get from the airport downtown, through one of the ugliest and biggest sprawls of industrial suburbs on the globe, and its inadequate road network is entirely choked by traffic. The centre of the city is another mess, with the exception of some superb examples of Islamic architecture and a picturesque old quarter. The place reeks of pollution, with pedestrians fighting cars for street space. The only peace to be found, away from the clamour of car horns and shouts, is by the banks of the languid, slow-moving Nile.

The government of Egypt seems to work – or not work – along the same chaotic lines: beneath the Sphinx-like imperturbability of the forever slightly smiling President Mubarak, a coalition of interests jostles as best it can for a share in power. No elite is dominant amid the chaos. This is typical of the fourth major source of authority for the modern state, which might loosely be called rule by the establishment. In a host of post-colonial states, in particular, a curious hybrid of powers yields a kind of collective authority usually led by a respected, but not all-powerful figurehead. In many cases this has replaced the glow of charismatic leadership that immediately followed the triumph of liberation movements and the end of the colonial era. This is particularly the case in much of Africa, and in parts of the Arab world.

The main components of this establishment are part of the senior bureaucracy, the armed forces, the political establishment of the (usually) single political party that is permitted to run in the elections that legitimize the system, senior business leaders and, sometimes, government-sponsored trade unions. The system was first and most successfully pioneered in Mexico, where that contradiction in terms, the Institutional Revolutionary Party, continues to wield a largely autocratic power while the rest of the continent has moved on to a functioning multi-party system.

The PRI evolves its leadership through careful consultation and competition between elites; it permits opposition, but through patronage, strong-arm tactics, fraud, corruption and the denial of resources, never permits its rivals to win. The PRI changes president every six years, so personal dictatorship is avoided and the regime never appears stultified. Variations on this system are now practised in a host of other countries.

In Egypt, the charismatic leadership first of Nasser, then of Sadat, has been replaced by the bumbling amiability of Hosni Mubarak, an air force officer whom no one pretends is more than *primus inter pares* in the government, which contains representatives of all the elites. In Algeria, President Houari Boumedienne's leadership was replaced by faceless soldiers and party apparatchiks.

In those African countries which have not slid over to military rule – Uganda, Kenya, Zimbabwe, for example – the leaders, Milton Obote, Daniel arap Moi and Robert Mugabe, are not one-man rulers but pragmatists presiding over establishment coalitions of the dominant interests and tribes. Of two other historic figures in post-independence Africa one, Hastings Banda in Malawi, is now elderly and has lost control of his country and the other, Kenneth Kaunda of Zambia, has been ejected in a democratic election.

Two other countries with a similar alliance of ruling party, armed forces and bureaucracy bear mentioning, although these are slightly different: Iraq and Syria. They each bear the panoply of a single-party socialist state, which to a degree they practise. They each use the armed forces and security services ruthlessly to crush dissent in a manner unthinkable in gentler 'establishment' states like Egypt or Mexico.

They are each personal dictatorships, where the decisions of the ruler – Hafez al-Assad in Syria, Saddam Hussein in Iraq – primarily determines state policy. Both are incredibly tough-minded products of the different varieties of Baathist socialism and both rule through guile and terror – the immediate elimination of political threats, as has invariably happened to scores of challengers in Iraq. It may be too much to hope that Assad and Saddam will eventually be replaced by a gentler, more consensus style of leadership; but it is not impossible.

Finally, a hybrid all of its own. Iran's regime is cited as a unique form of rule today – a theocracy. It is very unusual in that the clergy have an enormous influence within the government. But, following the end of Ayatollah Khomeini's charismatic leadership, the clergy has had a largely subordinate role: real power is shared between the political leadership of the wily President Hashemi Rafsanjani and the increasingly one-party system he presides over: the bazaari middle class; the state apparatus; the armed forces and the revolutionary guards; and the clergy. The last can occasionally pressure the government into policy changes by sudden campaigns against Westernization; but their power has waned and the Iranian system is gradually evolving into an establishment consensus political system of the kind already described.

Such a system derives popular acquiescence primarily through responsiveness and acute political antennae: as rule by an elite, rather than through democractic election, it could easily become unpopular and too remote. But the political front organization exists both to provide the illusion of popular rule, by winning rigged elections, and more importantly, to reflect genuine grievances among ordinary people, so that these can be defused.

The difference with, say, the Communist Party of the Soviet Union is that for a long time this projected itself as the party of the elite, local party officials telling others what to do with dire consequences if they didn't – as during Stalin's rule. A more efficient one-party system acts as a channel to connect the rulers with what people are thinking. In addition, the consensus nature of such rule, through taking into account the various interests that make up the modern state, does make for at least a fairly cautious government – even if sometimes a paralyzed and over-bureaucratic one.

Finally, while the repressive apparatus is always present, it is used as a last resort, rather than a first one. These systems are neither in place through the naked use of force or fear, as military regimes are, or through the exercise of one-man, charismatic personal dictatorship, but through the medium of consensus-building and acceptance among the elites.

They are largely a transitional phenomenon, partly owing to their staggering corruption. As states undergo rapid industrialization, it is highly probable that a gradually larger and more literate political class, and a slightly more prosperous workforce, will seek their own vehicles of political expression to represent their interests, and that it will prove impossible to contain such pressure within the single political party. In Egypt and Algeria, there is a very real fear that any move towards greater political pluralism will result in a victory for Islamic fundamentalists; so it might, because the fundamentalists are benefiting from being the only effective opponents of the regime.

However, it is far from clear that increasingly harsh repression of the fundamentalists is the answer. Rather the ruling elites should cast about for ways of organizing credible parties that could win free elections and rally the interests that would be threatened if the fundamentalists took over. It is a very real dilemma. Zambia has shown that one-party establishment systems can be transformed into functioning multi-party systems, although the Islamic element is lacking there. In countries with substantial middle classes like Egypt it should be possible for Islamic zealots to be beaten at the ballot box, or at least marginalized within wider and more moderate Islamic movements; that – rather than their survival in power – should be the priority of ruling elites in developing countries with regimes of this sort.

CHAPTER SIX

THE NEW AUTHORITARIANS

The Diet building in Tokyo – Japan's Parliament – is a colossal edifice in neo-Gothic mausoleum style, dominating Nagatacho district and close to the tranquillity of the moat which surrounds the Imperial Palace. It sits astride the oasis of public buildings and parkland in Central Tokyo, surrounded by the giant sprawl of the city, with its huge variety of jumbled and colourful high-rises, the glitter of the Ginza shopping district, the pleasant hillside two-storey residential areas, the ostentatious vulgarity of Shinjuku. Across this diverse and dazzling city march millions of salarymen in identical dark suits and white shirts, a giant army of conformity.

The Diet, in its modern baroque bulk, is theoretically the seat of government and power in modern Japan. In practice, it ranks third in the pecking order, behind the enormously powerful bureaucracy and big business, and ahead of the armed forces, astride the ordered hierarchy of society. The system can best be described as Confucianist authoritarianism. Its inventor is Japan, and a number of other Asian countries are following in its footsteps. They include, massively, China, as well as Taiwan, Malaysia and Singapore. In some aspects the system resembles that of the establishment one-party state. But it differs in that it has a philosophical underpinning, is much more formalized and happily coexists with a private enterprise economy.

Japan has evolved into a uniquely sophisticated political system. The main players in the 'iron triangle' of Japanese politics, as recently defined by its mildly reformist former prime minister, Morihiro Hosokawa, are the bureaucracy, the political system it controls and the business interests that penetrate both.

The political system, which ought to be the pinnacle of any society, is the weakest of the three: routinely electing the Liberal

Democratic Party for nearly four decades, from 1955 to 1993, the politicians act as a vote-buying façade to permit the bureaucrats to get on with the job of running Japan: the analogy is with management running a business, while the politicians acted as rather marginal shareholders on the outside. Not only do senior bureaucrats not take any notice of their supposed political masters; in some cases they do not even know their names. As political impotence becomes obvious, so politics degenerates into little more than a grubby game of faction-fighting and vote-buying. At the same time Japan's powerful business interests are engaged in the job of buying both politicians and bureaucrats. A further partner is the armed forces, greatly weakened after the Pacific War, but still a growing force in its own right.

Underpinning the power play at the top is a deference society, built on a remarkable system of indoctrination through the family, schools and business. An individual is taught that he exists only in relation to society and has no rights of his own, just a huge burden of debts to others which must be repaid on his journey through life. Schooling relentlessly curbs independence and original thought, placing a premium on the acquisition of vast numbers of facts and statistics through sheer hard work. The new arrival in a major company goes through a relentless process of indoctrination, chanting company slogans and performing menial work that is reminiscent of early military training.

The system produces an immensely ordered, hard-working, law-abiding, conformist society where self-expression and independent thought are only acquired through seniority. In economic structure, the state plays a large role in underpinning and 'guiding' businesses, which nevertheless competed furiously with each other as giant cartels and on which a huge substructure of Japanese business depends.

The system resembles nothing so much as a kind of competitive utopian communism – only it works. The Japanese have proven that a state-dominated economy, rigorous conformity and an essentially sham political system can function as the best performing economy in the world, in a massive repudiation of two Western values held to be universal – private enterprise and political freedom.

Is the logical conclusion that these values are not universal after all? Pointing to the Soviet bloc, military regimes and third-world one-party establishment states, Westerners have been able to define a society's backwardness by the extent to which it has attained those values. But Japan is something different. In practice, the Japanese model is probably something unique: no people that had not been taught Confucianism and Shintoism for centuries, and had only just emerged from international isolation and immense agrarian overpopulation and backwardness, could probably be made to adopt a system of such rigorous personal submission to the state.

But is the Japanese model at least a local Asian model? Mohammed Mahathir, Malaysia's intolerant and authoritarian Islamic prime minister, certainly believes so, and has expressed that opinion. He says bluntly: 'We should not be the slave of democracy; in Malaysia we accept democracy but we must not be too extreme. Unlimited freedom is dangerous.' Singapore's Lee Kuan Yew, always disposed to press censorship, rigorous central planning and political control, also agrees. But it is the colossus of China itself that seems to be the chief convert to the Japanese model.

It is now no longer possible to consider China a communist country. The country was designated in March 1993 as a 'socialist market economy' operating 'a political economy on the basis of socialist public ownership'. Deng Xiaoping, China's dominant leader for a decade, was once described by Mao as knowing 'nothing about Marxism-Leninism'. Deng has certainly fulfilled his promise, being responsible for forcing the Chinese economy to accept hundreds of thousands of small businesses. He has also accepted a fledgling private education system and permitted the rampant private investment that is already transforming the skyline of Shanghai, as well as in the large hinterland of Hong Kong, which is growing at one of the fastest rates in the world. The state retains control of key major heavy industries; but its share of the economy is already little more than those of Western Europe's mixed economies.

A senior Chinese economist said privately in 1993, 'Socialism is ridiculous. Our only hope is peaceful evolution. Otherwise we die.' Deng has argued, 'the essence of socialism is to liberate and expand the productive forces'. The state now accounts only for around a third of economic output in China, with farming and retailing now quasi-private, although subject to government contracts. In 1991, state companies accounted for only fifty-three per cent of industrial output, against some thirty-six per cent for collectives and eleven per cent for private business.

The transformation is enormously exciting – and exceedingly dangerous. The main opposition to the attempt to open up China's economy comes from the peasants who were the bulk of Mao's own communist movement and the backbone of the Cultural Revolution, when reformists were purged in quite terrifying numbers. The peasantry is restless again, chafing at urban corruption, inflation and widening disparities of wealth, and could strike back. Rural strength is still overwhelming in population terms and within the Communist Party which reflects the rural–urban split quite faithfully.

An eighty-six-page report, written for the Chinese Academy of Sciences in 1993, held out the possibility of disintegration after Deng's passing from the scene. The report claimed: 'It is possible that a situation like post-Tito Yugoslavia will emerge. In ten years, at the soonest, and at the latest between ten and twenty years, the country will move from economic collapse to political breakup, ending with its disintegration.' By the year 2000, state revenue could account for only 11 per cent of GNP, a third of what it was fifteen years earlier. China's central government currently negotiates the amount of tax it raises from the provinces. Another lurch backwards would destroy China's overheated economy and create a xenophobic and suspicious nation. It is too early to say that China's capitalist spurt is irreversible.

Yet if the experiment survives, an extraordinary hybrid will have been created: a state that permits a huge share of the nation's wealth to sit in private hands, yet retains the political repression of a communist regime. There can be little doubt that China's political gulag is awesomely greater than almost everywhere else, now that the Eastern bloc and Latin America have largely made the conversion to democracy. Staggering numbers of political prisoners and forced labour camps remain in existence: China has some 2,000 labour camps with a total population of 10 million. Number Thirteen Labour Reform Detachment, known as Tang-ge-ma farm, has some 20,000 inmates and is seventy kilometres wide, sited in Qinghai province, on the edge of the Gobi desert.

The Tiananmen Square massacre was as brutal a display of repression as anything seen in Chile, Burma or Thailand, rendered all the more shocking because it was unnecessary: the demonstrations there that had surfaced during the Gorbachev visit had dwindled considerably in size. The repression has now slightly eased, in response to adverse overseas publicity. Deng has permitted economic liberalism to evolve alongside the authoritarian, repressive aspects of communism.

The contrast with Russia could not be more obvious: as Russia liberalizes politically, it has found it difficult to do so economically without imposing enormous suffering upon the people. In retrospect it seems that China's Marxist–Leninist uprising was not that at all: it was a crude peasant revolt which invoked communist nostrums to begin with, succeeded in improving the living standards of the peasants at enormous cost, and shook the communist doctrines off when their failure became apparent. Stalinism in Russia was the very reverse – the brutal extinction of the peasant class and their power.

In Russia there was a much greater commitment to the ideology and it was much longer-lasting – seven decades as opposed to four. But the reliance on authoritarianism in China was also commensurately greater. In Russia there was a colossal authoritarian tradition, but also a democratic bourgeois Westernized one, backed up by a large and growing middle class which has now, to a large extent, taken control.

In China the middle class is small, the peasant and urban classes huge, the army extremely powerful in an almost Latin American way, and there is no democratic tradition at all. The danger is of accelerated economic growth whose accentuation of the differences between city and country creates the potential for social explosion. The Chinese view the Soviet experiment with contempt, as that of a politically weak regime trying to liberalize economically and stumbling in the process. But a politically insensitive regime like China's, trying to do the same thing economically, seems much more likely to hit the buffers.

The Chinese have thus largely adopted the Japanese model of Confucianist authoritarianism. They have liberated hundreds of thousands of small businesses, which provide the momentum for the country's remarkable spurt of economic growth. The big state industries remain under careful tutelage, however – rather in the manner of Japan's *keiretsu*. The three-quarters of China's 1.2 billion population that live in the countryside have benefitted from the trickle-down of these new urban riches: the World Bank reckons that the number of Chinese living at subsistence levels in 'absolute poverty' has fallen from 220 million in 1980 to 100 million in 1990 – a staggering improvement.

Nevertheless it is in the countryside that the most active resentment at the corruption and inequalities ushered in by the economic boom can be registered. The peasants form the backbone of Communist Party support and its bosses – still labelled 'village warlords' – the bulk of the party leaders. The tension between town and country will determine China's future. It was these backwoodsmen who insisted that the pro-democracy movement in Beijing be crushed, they who bolstered Deng in his decision that order must be maintained at all costs; the urban intelligentsia demanding a political opening is, by contrast, relatively small.

Thus China has unconsciously emulated Japan's example of economic growth alongside a repressive political system (China's is much more openly repressive than Japan's). This might seem to contradict the widely held view that economic liberalism inevitably brings political pluralism in its wake; but it accords with the view, fashionable in much of the developing world during the 1970s, that political authoritarianism is a necessary accompaniment to rapid economic growth: the view that democratic politicians are too demagogic and corrupt to implement the right economic policies. In this, the Chinese actually considered themselves superior to the Russians: in their view, the latter made the mistake of permitting too much political liberalization and too little economic freedom. It remains to be seen which will prove to be right.

Is Confucianist authoritarianism an ideal system in itself, or merely a transitional model for countries undergoing accelerated development? There is much to suggest the latter. In spite of the rigorous mental conditioning in Japan, there are growing calls for more accountability – as shown in the 1993 election results and the calls for reform of the Liberal Democratic Party, which lost power, probably temporarily. There is a growing recognition that Japan's economic miracle has been at the expense of the workforce and the consumer. There are demands for a more creative educational system. These should not be exaggerated: Japan's political, social and corporate culture remains intensely authoritarian and conformist; but it is possible that in a couple of generations, a more relaxed and affluent Japan will move gradually towards greater accountability.

In China there are those who see the booming coastal provinces adopting more pluralist systems; yet the enormous power of the peasantry remains a drag on political development. The greatest danger is that if China moves too fast towards free markets and democracy, a backlash could develop in some of the remoter provinces which could halt both political and economic development. Global finance, acting on its herd instinct to pour money into China, seems as blind as ever to the political dangers in this unpredictable country. If Confucianist authoritarianism is a largely transitional system, the transition in both China and Japan seems likely to be very long. Liberal democracy is likely to be slow to reach the shores of the two Asian giants.

CHAPTER SEVEN

GOVERNMENT BY TALKING SHOP

THE SIXTH AND fastest spreading political system is liberal democracy. A glance at the past two decades shows that it has been making converts at a truly awesome speed. Its cradle, Western Europe, harboured three dictatorships, Spain, Portugal and Greece in 1973 – all three are now democratic. In Eastern Europe, there were twelve communist autocracies, if the Ukraine and the Baltic Republics are each counted as a separate state, and only one democratic one, Austria. Now all but Greater Serbia have converted to some form of democracy, and it is possible to argue that even the latter is crudely, if unappealingly, representative.

In the Middle East, a democratic desert for so long, Israel has been joined by democratic Turkey, while Yemen, Jordan and Kuwait are inching towards democracy and even the Palestine Liberation Organization is internally pluralist, if not exactly democratic. In the subcontinent, long-democratic India and Sri Lanka (although riven by sectarian strife) have been joined by Pakistan. In the Far East, South Korea, Thailand and Hong Kong have made strides towards full democracy. The huge sprawl of the Soviet Union is now at least half democratic.

In Latin America there were just three democratic states in the subcontinent: Venezuela; Colombia; and Costa Rica in 1976. Now there are sixteen, and only two authoritarian systems – Mexico and Cuba. On a very rough count, 2.5 billion of the world's 5.7 billion people now live under governments which they have helped to elect, compared with proportionately half that number twenty years ago.

What is liberal democracy? How can it be distinguished from a system like Egypt's whose political leaders claim is representative in a different way? What is its special appeal?

The first thing to understand about democracy is that it is a relative term. There is no full democracy anywhere in the world. On the assumption that human nature is imperfect it is probably unachievable.

Full democracy – full freedom – would mean that every individual was fully involved in every decision concerning his or herself. In an ideal, perfect world we would all agree what was in our own interests while not impinging on the interests of others. There would be no need for a parliament, indeed for a state, because we would all agree all the time what was right – a kind of utopian Marxism; indeed, authoritarianism believes it has found the answers on behalf of the people – but, of course, being managed by human beings is wrong much of the time. This of course is a dream. Democrats, acknowledging human imperfection, believe in the free interplay of argument and ideas.

In fact, we need a state to arbitrate between us and to represent us in the outside world. Modern liberal democracy provides a rather imperfect way of controlling that state: we elect representatives every few years, to make the state accountable to us.

A TRIP TO the oldest liberal democracy in the world, Britain's parliament at Westminster, shows just how imperfect this mechanism can be. The ordinary voter, arriving there to meet his Member of Parliament, will be taken to the central lobby, which is rather like a great railway station, where literally hundreds can assemble and lobby their MP. The MP will promise to raise a constituent's grievance with civil servants or local authorities, and sometimes gets matters put right.

Turning to the left under the great Gothic ceilings of Pugin and Barry, the visiting constituent will be led along a corridor to a smaller, even busier lobby, where MPs have the right to buttonhole ministers and lobby on behalf of constituents. Through the swing doors, they can enter Parliament itself: there MPs can express their points of view in speeches in debates, put down Parliamentary questions to ministers designed to elicit information or make a critical point and, twice a week, ask questions of the mightiest figure in the land, the prime minister.

In practice, the 600-odd MPs lack the resources and opportunities to monitor the actions of tens of thousands of civil servants: they can only scratch the surface of the bureaucracy and only the most energetic ministers leave a stamp on their departments. In theory MPs vote on every piece of legislation brought before them in the best interests of their constituents.

In the many votes on any one sitting day, the MPs will do exactly as their party whips tell them to, and vote many times on matters they know nothing about, because the government wants to get the legislation through. Only occasionally, on a matter of purely constituency interest or on a matter where their conscience troubles them will they disobey those instructions. The electorate – watching their representative go through the 'aye' or 'no' lobby at a fast trot, registering his presence, the main job of MPs – may feel this is something of a charade.

How representative is the mother of parliaments? The answer is that the people's will can make itself felt directly just once every few years, and indirectly in a number of ways. The population has the choice – and it is limited to that – to throw out a government they dislike. This is a considerable right, to be able to do so peacefully, without bloodshed or confrontation with an unelected government. In addition, through writing to an MP, and through the unions, professional associations, employers' associations and pressure groups, the voters can hope to influence political issues.

This should not be viewed as a minor right: MPs are acutely sensitive to their constituents, when they can reconcile their demands with the general injunction to follow the party line. However, their power to influence the bureaucracy, while not insubstantial, is not all that large.

What are the main ingredients of liberal democracy – given that it is still very limited? The essentials would seem to include the existence of one or more major parties, and the possibility of ejecting the government from office. It is true that in a number of countries one-party rule has been the norm, even though people are free to vote for other parties – Italy and Japan being the obvious examples. But this does qualify their democracy – Italy's to a lesser extent, because the Christian Democrats up to 1994 had always had to share power with others, Japan to a greater because, until 1993, it seemed virtually impossible to eject the Liberal Democrats from office (and the circumstances of 1993 were a revolt within the ruling party, not an opposition victory).

But in the United States, Britain, France, Germany, Canada, Australia, Sweden, Norway, Spain and Portugal it is possible to throw the rascals out. In each of these countries this has happened in recent history at least once, twice or repeatedly. The right of voters to change their government is perhaps the most fundamental qualification for democracy.

Elections must be free and fair: balloting must be secret, there must be safeguards against intimidation, counting should be scrupulously conducted, freedom of assembly must be guaranteed and party financing must be as even-handed as possible.

Another characteristic is freedom of the press. This is immensely important. There is a danger, even in a developed democracy, of the press being controlled only by a single interest – usually that of big business – because money has the power to acquire newspapers; as soon as choice is stifled, so a country slides towards the one-party option. The same, obviously, is true of broadcasting but the safeguards are usually much clearer there.

Obviously political freedom is essential, in the sense that anyone can express an opinion or organize a party without fear of being arrested, or of indirect retaliation. There is also the need for a whole set of guarantees of individual rights backed up by an independent judiciary. People's personal freedom must be protected from the tyranny of the majority: this means that the police should have no right to enter people's homes without warrants, of detention without trial, of interrogation without lawyers. In a large number of new areas, usually related to worthy popular causes such as health, road safety, the need to protect against crime or to define people as financial or insurance risks, worrying inroads are being made into individual liberties even in countries like Britain (even the Press cannot be absolved). The state has to make the case for encroaching on the freedom of the individual, rather than the individual for defending himself against state authority because, by definition, the state is infinitely more powerful.

Finally, the apparatus of the state, the civil service, should be independent, prepared to serve whatever political master is elected, and at all times prevented from supporting or lending its political offices to supporting a particular political party. These six features are a bare minimum. The democratic ideal is always moving, and needs to develop. Greater decentralization, referenda, different types of electoral system, the possibility of a popular say in targeting taxation, greater participation in choosing political candidates, primaries – all of these are ways of deepening democracy; but the six factors discussed are the least necessary for a country to consider itself a democracy.

To turn to the second question: why is democracy so appealing, why is it spreading? Obviously everyone likes to have a say in their own government, the way they are ruled. Far better to have a government chosen by yourself in some degree than one imposed from above. Yet this was far from being a universal view even in relatively recent times: it was argued that democracy would lead to demagoguery, corruption, populism, the simplification of issues, the tyranny of the majority, the breakdown of authority, extremism. Autocrats throughout the century have argued that rule by the educated, the elite, is better than votes for all. Patrick Kennon's recently published work *The Twilight of Democracy*, arguing that 'only highly trained, anonymous technocrats' can be trusted to run modern countries, shows that the ancient line of thinking is dead.

The fact remains, though, that as a people become better educated and more prosperous they demand nothing less than a say in their own government, and democracy is the system that provides it. Moreover, there seems to be a kind of natural democratic equilibrium: when a system has a large enough middle class and a working class that is reasonably prosperous and not too oppressed, it is remarkable how sensibly people vote.

In a very few cases, populists have won power: Hitler was elected by popular vote – albeit by a third of the people; the ineffectiveness of his opponents allowed him to win absolute power. For the most part, almost every dictator, populist or extremist politician has won power through non-democratic means. Democratic choices have almost invariably been more moderate, stable, less nationalistic and belligerent, less ideological.

To return to the old triangle of powers: democracy provides a means by which ordinary people can peacefully check the power of the modern state – which is a huge and unchanging fact of life. If ordinary people lack the visible power, the rulers can behave as they will and an explosion of the self can quite quickly follow – as has happened in so many countries, from Iran to Poland. In much of the world democracy is necessary to guarantee social peace, not because it is an ideal system.

Elites never give away their power unless they have to: the more intelligent do so because they realize this is the means to guarantee their continuity and social stability. The more sophisticated a society, the more important democracy is as a means of reconciling different interests peacefully, and of securing the acquiescence of the governed to government which, *pace* free market minimalists, is an absolutely central feature of modern life.

The trend towards democracy will continue even in places where it meets with much suspicion, as a challenge to a paternal system of rule, like China and Japan. It is fast becoming the minimum necessary to secure the acquiescence of those at the bottom to a society which necessarily has to be ruled from the top. Democracy is essential in part to defuse the assertion of the self, something which autocrats have long failed to understand.

But the whole happy picture of a world moving inexorably towards democracy out of enlightened self-interest after the collapse of communism is being grossly and terribly distorted by the possibility that elected governments no longer have the power to decide their own nations' destinies – a subject which we will now consider. It is not much use having the vote if the people you vote for are merely playthings for much larger, unelected, impersonal, directionless forces.

PART THREE

The Nation-Smashers

CHAPTER ONE

TYPHOON

On 16 September 1992, the managers of one of the major economies in Europe, led by one of the most technically competent finance ministers in history, Norman Lamont, awoke to what seemed a routine day. The economy looked in pretty good shape. Inflation was low and falling. A policy of rigorous financial orthodoxy and perhaps needlessly prolonged recession continued, but there were slight signs of economic movement in spite of still high real interest rates, running well ahead of inflation.

On other counts, Britain was performing well: its wage costs had been held down without industrial trouble. Industry was leaner and fitter than it had been for years. The budget deficit was under control, although social security costs were beginning to spiral. Direct taxation was low, following the orthodoxy of 'supply-side' economic theorists. The extraordinary prudence of Lamont could not but be applauded by the international banking community, the OECD and the other central banks, as well as the IMF. Britain even had Walter Mittyish hopes of replacing its rival, Germany, as Europe's major reserve currency because of its reputation for single-mindedness and responsibility.

Above all, a general election had just taken place which the Conservative Party had won for the fourth time running – a postwar record. This confirmed the country's new political stability: the sick man of Europe was no more: strikes, absentee-ism, trade union militancy, nationalization threats, constant changes of government – these were things of the past. The people had just spoken, and had plumped for caution.

There had long been mutterings that the pound was over-valued: that it had entered the Exchange Rate Mechanism of the European Monetary System at too high a level – it is said that the Prime Minister, Margaret Thatcher, had insisted upon this, overriding her chancellor, John Major, as the price of adhering to a system she deeply opposed. Whether she was acting for reasons of national pride, or because she knew the level was unsustainable, and was likely to bring discredit on the system itself, can only be surmised. For all that, the impact of British membership of the ERM, at a time when German interest rates were high in order to stifle domestic inflation, was a highly disciplinary one for the British economy.

Within a few minutes of the exchanges opening on 16 September, pandemonium had broken out. A massive wave of selling of sterling had begun and seemed to gather momentum every minute. Panic set in: the market was going to force sterling to devalue: thus, whoever started it – and the initial selling of sterling may have been quite small – other major funds had to join the rush in order to secure their position. To stay in sterling when it was about to be devalued would have left their investors with billions of pounds' worth of losses. The lament of the speculator – that while many do it for profit, others do it to avoid losses – is thus half true.

That this movement had nothing whatever to do with normal economics was beside the point. That Britain's economy was working, highly competitively, unaffected by trade union militancy and with a newly elected Conservative Government counted for nothing beside the simple fear of devaluation that dominated the financial markets.

'You cannot buck the market' was the common refrain of the free-market economists which held sway through most of the 1980s; another such refrain was that the market is always right. If your economy is healthy and free enterprise oriented, you will be rewarded; if not, you will be in trouble. Britain's healthy, only a little too rigidly policed economy in 1992 was smashed by a wave of speculation followed by a wave of panic selling that had nothing to do with the country's fundamental economic health. You couldn't buck the market because of its sheer size – a straightforward truism.

Only a few days earlier a massive European safety barrier had been arranged for sterling; when the tide first rose past danger levels, Lamont attempted to erect hasty defences, raising interest rates first by two per cent and then by a further two per cent. If this policy had succeeded, Britain's fragile economic recovery would have been completely crushed. But the tidal wave was so great – some $700 billion – that it swept all before it.

Britain withdrew from the ERM, floating the pound to permit it to bob back to a natural level in the wake of the wave, rather than let it be anchored and swamped altogether. This was announced by Lamont at 7.45 in the evening. An economic hurricane had struck, leaving devastation in its wake.

ALL OF THIS might seem merely a parable on the futility of fixed exchange rates. But it was also a cautionary tale about the new power of international speculation, the so-called 'market'. It was simultaneously repeated with the Italian lira, the Irish pound and the Swedish krona, and later with the Spanish peseta and the French franc – which had to be shored up with immense difficulty by the apparent villain of the piece, the deutschmark. Not only were national central bank reserves proved wholly inadequate as a defence against speculation; so were such European funds as existed to prevent currencies being overwhelmed in this way.

There was a predictable chorus of outrage on the iniquities of the ERM, which was partially justified. But currencies outside the ERM would have been even more vulnerable: in fact the lesson was precisely the reverse of the one proclaimed by the Eurosceptics: only a single currency, fully implemented, would have had the strength to withstand such a wave.

Yet the real issue was different: it was the power of international money, the sheer size of the flows, and the caprices that governed those flows. Some $300 billion cross the currency dealing rooms of the City on an average day. 'Hot money' similarly flows in and out of bond and equity markets across the globe, with seriously destabilizing effects – as was evident in Latin America in January 1995. In 1991, the financial derivatives market, a kind of gamble on future money, currency and stock market prices, alone saw transactions of no less than $7 trillion; this rose to $12 trillion in 1994. The collapse in February 1994 of Baring Brothers, the City's oldest merchant bank, as a result of investment on the derivative market by just one Singapore-based employee showed the urgent need for proper regulation of these markets.

The franc crisis of 1993 saw Germany, France, Belgium, Denmark, Holland, Spain and Portugal spend some $17 billion between them – a drop in the ocean – to support the franc, the Dutch kroner, the Belgian franc, the Spanish peseta and the Portuguese escudo. France, Belgium, Denmark and Portugal all had well-managed economies following orthodox policies. The analogy was again with the sea. Even large, well-steered ships like the British economy could be engulfed by currency movements as big as any previously experienced in the world.

What were the consequences for the British economy of this storm? What was the origin of this massive flow? Did it respond to economic logic? Did 'the market' – like Nanny – know best?

The answer to this last question has already been touched upon. The market 'knew' that the pound was overvalued. It probably was; many economists could not see the sense in keeping sterling at a rate of exchange that only served to make British exports dearer and imports cheaper; even if this is slightly inflationary, it always makes more sense for a currency to be undervalued rather than overvalued, as there is nowhere to go but up and it improves competitive advantage.

In orthodox economic terms, the pound was at a perfectly acceptable level, justified by reduced interest rates and the health of the British economy. However, the market's guess proved self-fulfilling: if enough currency dealers can be persuaded that the pound will be devalued, a run will start, and logical economics can take a running jump. The pound will be devalued solely because enough people fear that it will. The market decides, but not for reasons other than its own overwhelming size, certainly not for orthodox economic reasons, as traditional free-marketeers would have it.

The Times journalist, Anatole Kaletsky, brilliantly dissected the underlying irrationality of the markets in September 1994 when he pointed out that American investors at the time were panicking at the failure of interest rates to affect inflation over a two- to three-month period, when orthodox economics showed there was a time lag of two to three years between the two; that the market's latest fad was in believing that interest rates and inflation would automatically rise in line with economic growth – whereas inflation has usually tended to fall until the last two years of the growth cycle. Finally, he believed the market, correctly this time, also panics not because it fears a rise in inflation, but because it assumes central banks will raise interest rates because they fear a rise in inflation – thus compounding the errors of the central banks and making them self-fulfilling.

> It is for this reason that bond markets invariably fall when central banks tighten monetary policy despite the supposed improvement in anti-inflationary credibility that is supposed to follow such responsible moves. That is why long-term interest rates, as well as 'inflationary expectations' are higher today in Britain than they were before Mr George (the Governor of the Bank of England) made his 'pre-emptive' strike against inflation. And that is why it is often possible to go on making money in the financial markets by being stupid. As Keynes said, 'the successful speculator does not try to be clever, he merely tries to anticipate the stupidity of the market as a whole'.

To return to the second question: the origin remains obscure: it is now realized that major currency dealers like George Soros made as much as $1 billion by selling pounds early enough, and he seems to have accepted some of the status of 'lead' speculator; there were others, and there will be many more. At the time of the sterling crisis, there was speculation, particularly in Europe, that the Americans, and possibly the Japanese, were involved in a 'plot' to destroy the ERM, in order to weaken the whole process of European integration, viewed as hostile to their interests.

In February 1993, the German Chancellor, Helmut Kohl, alleged that unnamed forces were seeking to 'torpedo' the principle of a single European currency through market speculation. After the attack on the franc in August 1993, Karl Lamers, foreign policy spokesman for the Christian Democrats, suggested that the assault on the franc had been planned in 'government offices'. Kohl's aides privately suggested that the British government had encouraged the City and Wall Street to attack the franc.

Even the Belgian foreign minister, Willy Claes, suggested that the crisis had been the result of an 'Anglo-Saxon' plot to keep Europe divided and 'condemned to play a secondary role in the great economic debate'. France's prime minister, Eduard Balladur, denounced 'unjustified speculative movements and major upheaval in the financial markets' and called for measures to prevent rapid currency falls. However, a report by the Bank for International Settlements said that Europeans were responsible for nine-tenths of the funds crossing currency markets in the franc crisis.

The Americans pointed to their relatively small share of the speculative wave. However, as already argued, it does not take a huge sum to start the wave; once the perception of an imminent devaluation is under way, the currency traders have an obligation to their customers to join in on a massive scale. The possibility of American or Japanese 'triggers' cannot be discounted, a point which will be returned to: traditionally, neither country has shown much restraint in seeking competitive economic advantage.

As far as domestic economic policy was concerned, the impact on Britain, at least, was entirely to knock off course the policies on which the general election had just been won, and to substitute others – as it happens, rather good ones: a steady reduction in interest rates and a competitive upsurge stemming from the low rate of sterling – which got the rather sluggish British economy moving and even partly reduced inflation further. Yet these policies were the reverse of the ones thought sensible by central bankers and orthodox free-market theorists. The market had in fact stood orthodoxy on its head. In the process it had also comprehensively thwarted the will of the British people just expressed at a general election for the government to continue following prudent policies.

If the international currency market does not behave in an orthodox free-market manner, if it does not reward the virtuous and punish the spendthrift, what in fact does determine its sudden outbursts of pique and turbulence? The world has now experienced well over a decade of increasingly massive currency flows, and it is possible to draw some conclusions about the market's behaviour. Certainly economic virtue counts pretty low on the list of reasons for staying with a currency, even if the central banks, the IMF and the OECD set such a store by this.

The market is a dedicated follower of fashion. In a world always uncertain precisely which mix of economic policies is the right one – if there were a right one, everyone would pursue it – certain things are fashionable at certain times. In the 1970s rigid orthodoxy, corseted by stern monetary targets, was indeed fashionable: currency traders would buy currencies that conformed to certain orthodox prescriptions – low public borrowing, low inflation, low taxes, high interest rates, etc.

By the late 1970s and early 1980s, petro-currencies were all the rage. Britain suffered one of the stiffest doses of deflation in its history in the early 1980s, the consequence of a soaring pound caused by currency inflows, attracted by its North Sea oil wealth: British products became enormously difficult to sell abroad at inflated prices, bankrupting thousands of otherwise perfectly solvent companies.

Stephen Dorrell, now a Conservative treasury minister, published a devastatingly effective pamphlet at the time entitled *North Sea Oil: Black Gold or Black Death?* which argued this passionately: but he was running against the prevailing orthodoxy, later abandoned by Mrs Thatcher, that on no account must the government interfere in exchange rate policy. Towards the mid-1980s, interest rates seemed to be all that the market was interested in: money flowed to countries with the highest rates, whatever the actual economic health of the economies behind those currencies.

The first to take advantage of this on a grand scale was the United States in the mid-1980s, which by any orthodox economic analysis was in dire straits, with a massive and growing budget deficit, caused by a sharp, ideologically motivated reduction in taxes coupled with no corresponding decrease in spending – in fact a huge increase in defence outlays – as well as a huge trade deficit. In order to fuel the budget deficit, American real interest rates were raised to unprecedented levels, attracting vast currency inflows. America was able to get away with this because of its sheer size: if a medium-sized economy had practised such policies, it would have been accused of profligacy and a run on the currency would have ended in devaluation (although high interest rates might have stemmed this, leading to domestic recession).

Then, in Germany in the 1990s high interest rates set in order to control the inflation unleashed by the huge costs of German reunification resulted in a rush towards that currency. In both cases, the effect was highly negative and deflationary on weaker currencies which, in order to maintain themselves, had to raise their own interest rates and stifle domestic economic growth. The answer for those currencies would have been to devalue, and undermine the American and German bullies; but that is where national pride steps in.

The speculation against European currencies that started with 'Black Wednesday' has been of a more anarchic sort. There was not much wrong with British interest rates or economic policy, save that it was too cautious, but the currency was probably overvalued; the lira was more obviously fragile, with Italy's chronic budget deficit and political instability; but the currency was, if anything, undervalued. The franc, which soon came under intense pressure, was probably at about the right rate and should have been boosted by the return of a conservative government. Thus Britain, Italy, Ireland, Sweden, Portugal and France were each successively forced into devaluations.

The president of the European Commission, Jacques Delors, suggested that 'the time has come to study ways of limiting short-term money movements . . . Money movements are complex, but we should have an international agreement to enable us to establish the rules of the game'. Given the size of the flows, this seemed a tall order: the difficulty of differentiating between speculative and legitimate patterns of international financial movement seemed almost insuperable. Still, the issue of what was behind these huge, seemingly random flows was being addressed for the first time.

In immediate European terms, the danger inherent in the collapse of the ERM was not that each country would go its own way – a suicidal course – but that its revival, after a decent interval, by the core EEC currencies, particularly the mark and the franc, but not including perfidious sterling, would transform Europe into a fast- and a slow-lane community, with the latter denied the kind of currency support that the fast would enjoy, becoming liable to be picked off at the currency market's whim.

George Soros, the currency speculator, is engagingly candid about the benefits of monetary union: 'In my opinion, freely floating exchange rates would destroy the Common Market because in this climate floating exchange rates are cumulatively destabilizing. The more they fluctuate, the greater the relative importance of speculation. Speculation tends to be trend-following and the excesses it produces can be self-validating . . . Since all exchange rate systems are flawed, it is best not to have one at all, but to have a common currency. The fact that it would put speculators like me out of business is one of its merits.'

Yet the central issue was more fundamental even than that: the size of international financial flows had successively demolished one country's economic policy after another in a seemingly capricious way. Thus, in a crucial area of economic policy, national governments even of large industrialized countries like Britain and France had lost much of their power. Around the world there might be greater democracy than ever before: voters might feel they had the ability to influence events. Yet in practice the economic policies of the governments they elected could be altered at a moment's notice by huge, impersonal, apparently directionless and illogical forces, colossal currency transactions and speculators.

Of course, the process had been under way for some time, with the growth of the offshore Eurodollar market, effectively setting up a reserve currency that escaped national financial regulation, and with the acceleration of the speed and extent of currency trading made possible by modern technology. Taken together with the liberalization of capital and financial markets, all of which resulted in the creation of a massive backwash of capital that could move within moments around the financial and equity markets of the world, this was scant consolation for the nations so affected.

'Black Wednesday' was the most dramatic example yet of the new phenomenon – the globalization of capitalism – which is changing the shape of the world and which, in fact, is fast eroding the authority of nations, and the ability of ordinary people, through the votes cast in new and old democratic entities, to influence their own destinies. It is not much use being allowed to choose your representatives and government if, in fact, they are powerless.

There are those who argue that this is desirable – that voters are poor judges of economic choices. But this has been the argument of authoritarians and autocrats throughout the ages, and runs counter to all political evolution and the spread of liberal democracy around the world. The new economic elitism has not been the subject of proper debate in the Western democracies and is both wrong – people are better judges of their own interests than experts and markets – and profoundly dangerous, threatening to ignite popular anger.

Exactly the same phenomenon of globalization is taking place in a whole variety of other areas. The flow of international bank lending was the crisis of the 1980s, just as the flow of speculative currency and equity transactions was that of the 1990s. The spread of the multinationals was the crisis of the 1960s and 1970s. In addition to these three, trade flows have become vastly more complex and less subject to control by individual countries. Both the latter phenomena have important implications for the shrinking of national sovereignty. Each of these three further features of the globalization of capitalism must now be taken in turn.

CHAPTER TWO

BLACK HOLE

THE INTERNATIONAL banking crisis of the late 1970s and most of the 1980s was perhaps the most foreseeable, irresponsible and destructive economic whirlwind to hit the global economy in modern times. It was foreseeable in that anyone on the ground could tell what was happening as early as the late 1970s; it was irresponsible in that those who should have known better – principally the commercial banks, but also central banks, governments and international financial regulators – turned a blind eye not just to the catastrophic effects upon the countries concerned, but also to the interests of their own countries and banking customers. It was destructive in the impact not just upon the economies of the countries concerned, but also upon the major banks involved – although there at least catastrophe was avoided amid much self-congratulation, even if just a little foresight would have averted the danger in the first place.

I hope readers will forgive my inserting a personal note, not because I was anything but a minor observer of these events, but just to show how myopic and callous the attitude of the 'experts' in charge of the banking system was at the time. I travelled to Brazil in May 1980, before there seemed any threat of an international debt crisis, and was horrified by what I found. I reported at the time in *The Economist* that:

> Foreign bankers should pay close attention to the thinking on the subject of the foreign debt that is taking place among the moderate opposition leaders who may be brought into a government of national unity before 1982, or may have a majority in parliament afterwards. Senator Tancredo Neves (later Brazil's first democratic president in two decades) insists that 'Brazil has always paid its debts and always will.'

Yet another senior opposition leader, who preferred not to be named because of the sensitiveness of the subject, told your correspondent that he believes the government should go to the country's creditors and point out to them that the country is now borrowing not to finance its development, which would make Brazil an acceptable credit risk, but merely to service its debt. The government, he says, should then point to the political dangers of exacting impossible sacrifices from Brazil in order to pay for its foreign debt, and should ask for the terms of repayment to be substantially extended and the rates of interest to be sharply reduced.

The most vivid political danger, for a government that appears to be inflicting further hardship on Brazilians already living on the breadline in order to service the foreign debt, is that it provides a ready platform for that most traditional of Brazilian political animals, the populist nationalist. No one has yet emerged from the opposition's ranks to urge Brazil to tear up its debts and expel the exploiting multinationals.

So far the main nationalist drumbeats have come from within the army, where the right-wing officer in charge of recruitment, General Andrada Serpa, was fired for attacking the 'savage capitalism' of the multinationals. The present army chief of staff, General Ernani Ayrosa, is thought to share much the same view. It is the fear that some such figure will stage a coup that is keeping the opposition so quiet at the moment.

Brazil is no Jamaica, Peru or even Turkey. The very size of its foreign debt gives it a form of muscle. Mr Delfim Netto (Brazil's economic supremo) knows that western bankers have so much to lose should anything go seriously wrong with Brazil politically that they must put up the money in the end. For if Brazil were to default on its foreign debt, there are few effective sanctions that could be brought to bear. Mr Delfim Netto insists that nothing could be further from his thoughts than the idea that overborrowed developing countries should ask their creditors to write off part of their debt.

If pressure from the nationalists in the army or in the opposition threatens to topple the government, Mr Delfim

> Netto may (next year?) have to go to Brazil's creditors (or the International Monetary Fund?) with a penitent smile and point out that, unless they soften the terms of the debt, a fire-breathing nationalist may end up in his place. Either way, the international banking system should start girding its loins for the possibility that it may never again see some of the money it has splashed out to Brazil.

This, written well in advance of the debt crisis, created a furore, with the vice-president of one of the biggest American banks exposed in Latin America flying out from New York specially to protest to my editor in London that 'irresponsible' speculation of this kind was not only inaccurate but – a directly contradictory argument – damaging to the stability of the international banking system (surely if there was no danger, my article could do no harm?). Three years later I predicted in *The Economist*, reiterating the tentative sentence at the end of my Brazil article, that 'most of the loans [to Latin America] are now irrecoverably lost'. The debts could never be repaid anything like in full, and the banks' main effort over the next few years would consist in attempting to find a suitable and respectable cover to mask their retreat and write off a large part of the money.

The Mexican debt crisis quickly followed, and a decade of financial turmoil ensued in which the banks, eventually recognizing that most of the loans were lost, tried to stage as dignified and ingenious a retreat as possible, selling debt at a discount, swapping debt for equity, renegotiating the debt on less and less favourable terms to themselves, always maintaining the fiction that they were hanging tough with the irresponsible borrowing nations, that the international banking system was working smoothly, that this was merely a 'technical' problem – a fiction exposed later by the huge losses of the banks themselves.

The retreat was something of a success, in that the write-offs were accepted gradually and without the collapse of any major part of the world banking system. Its main sequence was: an attempt by a major debtor to renegotiate its debt; then, after talking tough, insistence by the commercial banks that the IMF enforce a harsh austerity programme, which would improve things in the short run, but provide no long-term answer; and finally, conditional on that programme and accompanied by a great deal of lecturing by the irresponsible banks on the irresponsibility of the Third World, a write-off in real terms of part of the debt which was usually insufficient to prevent the same crisis recurring a few years later. There would be congratulations all around in international banking circles, huge losses for their shareholders and customers, and appalling suffering among the peoples of the underdeveloped borrowing countries.

A brief look at the origins of the crisis is in order, as it was the biggest and most spectacular demonstration to date of the insouciance with which global capitalism could treat not just nations, but whole continents.

THE CAST IS the same, although the backdrop varies in the little scenes of human anguish being played out along the 3,000-mile length of Latin America. The toddlers are invariably barefooted with grubby faces, chubby yet undernourished, bearing earnest, puzzled expressions as they wipe their hands on cloth shorts or crinkly paper-thin skirts. The teenagers, their eyes burning with spare energy, hang around in the doorways of the local bars, poolrooms and fast-tortillas-and-beans joints, without the money to play, drink or eat.

The resigned, slack-shouldered men, middle-aged at twenty-five, chat in groups, at a loss what else to do, missing their work more even than the pay. The old women, plump and short, swathed in peasant black or in shapeless blouses and slacks, caw ceaselessly at each other. The teenage girls are usually indoors, helping their mothers make the most of the little they have: interminably washing clothes, because there are too few for washing to be allowed to pile up.

The just-above-the-breadline poverty looks much the same in the *cerros* (hills) surrounding Mexico City, where terrace upon terrace of no-cost housing made of cardboard, hardboard, old planks and rusty iron sheeting gaze sad-eyed over low-cost, rapidly deteriorating municipal units on the edge of town.

Much the same in Lima, where the poorest 40 per cent of

the population is crammed into dusty, mud-brick slums. They appear to contain fair-sized houses until you peer into a doorway and realize it gives on to a miniature cobbled street with a single drain down the middle, overlooked by two rows of single-roomed houses, resembling nothing so much as pigsties in design. Much the same in Santiago, where to the south of the city, camouflaged by trees and brush, lie acre upon acre of tatty, jerrybuilt shacks in which, perhaps, 15 per cent of the population live.

The situation is similar in Rio de Janeiro, where conditions in the picturesque and precarious *favelas* that cling to the rocky hillsides compare favourably only with those on the bleak government-built housing blocks to the west of the city, where drainage, refuse and repair facilities were things of a fleeting past. And much the same in the stilt slums of Guayaquil, where a slip can be fatal for a three-year-old child negotiating the catwalks above putrid sewer-marshes that offer the only available building sites for families without money.

Latin America's bottom third are by no means the poorest of the third world's poor; they are better fed, housed and clothed than their counterparts in Africa or on the Indian subcontinent. But they were offered the hope of something better, and have seen that hope recede into the distance over the past two decades. That, probably, is worse than if they had never been offered any hope at all. It is no consolation that these people are the victims not, as they often believe they are, of *los ricos*, *las multinacionales* or *los gringos* but a world economic mega-accident which no one of those categories quite seems to know what to do about.

It should be no consolation for the West, either, that Latin America's once modern industrial structure is becoming obsolescent as investment declines; Latin America's political institutions are being undermined, possibly to the point of revolution; and the result of growing political unpredictability there could be seriously to weaken the West's financial structure.

*

EXTERNAL DEBT first piled up in Latin America in order to cope with the yawning balance-of-payments surpluses caused by the first oil price shock. Brazil's rose from $10 billion in 1973 to $47 billion by 1979; Argentina's from $3.5 billion to $11 billion; Colombia's from $2.7 billion to $5.5 billion; Peru's from $2.4 billion to $8 billion; Chile's, more modestly, from $3.4 billion to $5.5 billion. Even petro-plutocratic Mexico and Venezuela fed at the same trough. Mexico's external debt rose from $7.2 billion to $37 billion; Venezuela's from $2 billion to $10 billion. The debt increases, said the planners, were comfortably in line with world inflation and nothing to worry about.

They probably weren't – until the second oil price shock of 1979–80, which did three things to Latin America. It punctured the self-confidence of the non-oil-producing Latin American economies by imposing an almost intolerable strain on their balance of payments. Simultaneously, because the immediate response of the developed world to the second oil shock was medium to massive deflation, world money markets were saturated with petrodollars in search of a home. Latin America's third problem was that, owing to depressed demand in the developed countries, the bottom fell out of the markets for the commodities that the continent produced.

The response of the non-oil-producing Latin American countries was to borrow to cover their growing trade deficits. The response of the oil-producing countries was to borrow because the money was there for the asking and, what the hell, they had oil, the best of securities, to borrow against anyhow. By the end of 1982, the Latin American debt total stood at around $300 billion, with Brazil owing some $90 billion, Mexico $80 billion, Argentina $38 billion, Venezuela $32 billion, Chile $22 billion and Peru $10 billion.

This much is history. The response of the international banks and, behind them, the central banks of the developed world was to send for the local sheriff, the International Monetary Fund, to tell that saloonful of free-spending Latinos to sober up. The trouble was that at least five of those countries – Brazil, Mexico, Venezuela, Chile and Peru – found it extremely hard to service their debts and afford the imports that they needed to fuel economic growth. Economic recovery in America and some parts of Europe was a help; but recovery alone was not sufficient to deal with the scale of Latin America's debts.

Enforcing laws against borrowers is hard. Any bank offering a loan usually wants to be sure that the debtor will put the money where it will yield a return that will pay off the interest and eventually the debt; and that it has a security that the bank can grab in case something goes wrong. In lending to sovereign countries there is no such security, except a country's concern to preserve its creditworthiness (banks can lay their hands on a country's financial assets only when much of these are held abroad, as was the case with Iran in 1979).

Creditworthiness is a limited asset: there can come a moment when the cost of borrowing can outweigh a country's wish to be able to go on borrowing more. So a lot depends on the bankers' sense in lending money where there is some prospect of real return denominated in dollars, not in local currency. That means that borrowed money needs to be invested to boost exports or to save on imports. In the crazy world of 1980–81, where sober-suited bankers were chasing scapegrace adventurers in Latin America, there was never any prospect of a return on much of the debt. The money went:

> ON NEW GOVERNMENT SPENDING. Brazil's hard-pressed government, wincing from the grumbles provoked by the country's 1979–80 recession, sighed with relief when it gained access to new foreign borrowing just in time for a pre-election year. The minimum wages of those the Brazilian government had most to fear from, the employed urban working class, could be promptly underwritten. The financing was there to polish off a host of projects, ranging from the São Paulo underground to the Itaipu hydro-electric scheme.
>
> The Mexicans, themselves in a pre-phoney-election year, poured money into construction (up twelve per cent in 1980–81), mining (up ten per cent) and electricity generation (up ten per cent). Even battered Mexican

manufacturing registered six per cent growth. In Chile, General Pinochet eased his spartan economic disciplines to give workers real wage increases of fourteen per cent, and splashed out $700 million on improving Santiago's underground.

ON PURE SPECULATION. The worst examples of this were in Argentina and Chile, where a plethora of *financieras* – barely regulated financial holding companies – were set up to channel money largely into booming property markets. It was possible at one time for a more or less penniless *financiera* to borrow $1 million to buy a property in downtown Santiago and sell it for $2 million after a few months. That was all right for some, but when the boom came to a stop a lot of people found themselves stuck with properties they had borrowed to pay for at grossly inflated prices.

Quarter-occupied luxury hotels and office blocks are the lingering monuments to the loan boom. Most Latin American countries enjoyed a short-lived construction boom: total value added by construction in Latin America jumped by some $8 billion between 1978 and 1981. In Argentina and Chile, many of the *financieras* and property companies went down with a resounding crash in 1981–82.

STRAIGHT OUT AGAIN. Many Latin American countries had no exchange controls; where they existed, they could be evaded fairly easily. Western bankers reckon that maybe as much as $100 billion was recycled back in 1981–82 from Latin America to the United States and Western Europe. Mexicans were reckoned to hold some $40 billion in assets abroad, Venezuelans some $18 billion. At least $12 billion left Brazil in 1981. Even in an economy as small as Chile's the capital flight in 1981 was around $1 billion.

Most of the loans were irrecoverably lost, but did it make much sense for the bankers to try to stretch the Latin American economies on the rack to recover their losses?

In one sense, of course, it did. The IMF's arrival on the scene brought a healthy dose of sound financial sense to economies whose direction was for long dictated by local politics. The IMF's three main macroeconomic prescriptions for the Latin American countries were admirable. They were: a reduction in government budget deficits; limits to money supply growth in order to bring inflation down; and a policy of currency depreciation to achieve balance-of-trade improvements without contributing too much to inflation.

Yet if the IMF viewed its role as being that of restoring the Latin American economy to solvency, or seeing that the interest on the Latin American debt got paid anything like on time, or that the debt was repaid in full at all, it was condemned to frustration. The hope of some Western bankers, that the Latin American economies, taken in hand, could take advantage of a United States recovery to climb back to solvency, was a forlorn one.

There was a limit to the extent the Latin American economies could be squeezed. The Brazilians, for example, throttled domestic demand; imposed virtually prohibitive tariff barriers on imports (running a considerable risk of retaliation); and cut oil consumption (by guzzling alcohol and raising petrol taxes) substantially to some 795,000 barrels a day in 1982. A battery of incentives was installed to promote exports. Yet Brazil achieved only a modest trade surplus.

The Mexicans and the Venezuelans had more fat to cut; but their real oil revenues plummeted as the OPEC price cracked. The Argentinians had the biggest scope for a balance-of-payments turnaround. The country's ability to switch a huge deficit into surplus overnight merely by consuming less meat and grain and exporting more of both abroad was displayed in the mid-1970s, when a $1.3 billion current account deficit in 1975 was transformed to a $1.3 billion surplus two years later.

The Chilean economy, after seven years' hard labour and one year's respite, was squeezed hard again, but only yielded the very narrowest of trade surpluses. The Peruvians, after a prolonged spell under IMF tutelage between 1976 and 1978, did convert a $1 billion current account deficit into a $600 million surplus, but the improvement was short-lived and secured only at a huge social cost.

A revival of the economy of the United States would certainly boost raw material prices. It would provide new markets for Latin American goods only if the Americans lowered their non-tariff drawbridges against most Latin American products. Mexican textile manufacturers moaned that their slimmed-down, export-oriented businesses were denied access to American markets until approval of the NAFTA package in 1993. The Latin American scrabble to boost exports and reduce imports contributed to a sharp contraction in trade between Latin American countries.

Latin Americans pruned their public spending, under IMF pressure. But the pruning came largely from investment budgets, not current spending. Indeed, current spending rose in most Latin American countries, as governments tried to keep their restless people in a minimum of food and work. The state was no longer, however, fulfilling its traditional role as the locomotive of investment and modernization.

The private sector, starved of profits by the slump in manufacturing, was in no shape to take on that role. Borrowing from abroad for new investment in industry and capital projects, rather than for rolling over old debts, virtually dried up. Even in conditions of global recovery would more international money be available for private sector and project financing? Not necessarily: Latin American countries, with their dubious credit ratings, would have to compete with a revival in demand for credit from American and European and, now, Eastern European borrowers. The one part of the Latin American economy that ought to be most encouraged – private-sector manufacturing – suffered worst from the slump in export markets and in domestic demand.

The main burden on most countries' balance of payments was the cost of servicing the debt itself – even now that American interest rates were fairly low. Moreover, the problem, in the words of one Brazilian economist, 'does not have a mathematical solution'. Whatever, in fact, happens to interest rates or to Latin American trade, the debt is now so huge that it devours all improvement, requiring a still bigger improvement the following year. 'The debt is a black hole growing larger on the money it absorbs', remarks another Brazilian economist, with a little poetic licence.

From being the main symptom of the Latin American malaise, the debt became the malaise itself, as a look at some case histories shows.

THE MEXICAN economy, after speeding rather dangerously along the *autopista* of growth during the 1970s, spun wildly out of control in 1980–82, and crashed. The two main causes of Mexico's economic mishap were a huge increase in public spending after 1978 by the government of President Jose Lopez Portillo; and his decision to keep the peso overvalued in order to dampen down the inflationary effect of all this spending. The result was large trade deficits.

Borrowing soared to pay for the government spending and the trade deficits. By 1981, the public-sector debt had reached $53 billion, a 56 per cent increase on the year before. Short-term borrowing as a percentage of the Mexican public debt rose that year from 4 per cent to 20 per cent.

Only when the flow of borrowing began to dry up did the government take belated action. In February 1982, the peso was devalued by 40 per cent. The government promptly wiped out much of the benefit of the devaluation by raising wages by the same amount. In April the government drew up a seventeen-point emergency programme, which it then failed to implement. Public spending, which was supposed to come down from 14.5 per cent of GDP in 1981 to 11.5 per cent in 1982, instead went up to 16.5 per cent. In June, Mexico obtained a syndicated loan of $2.5 billion with considerable difficulty.

In August, the government was forced to devalue further: a rate of fifty pesos to the dollar was decreed for the payment of external debt (otherwise the domestic cost of servicing Mexico's dollar borrowings, 91 per cent of the total, would have multiplied), while the rate for most other transactions was allowed to float down, eventually, to 150 pesos a dollar. The United States rushed to the rescue, providing more than $3 billion in loans, while the Mexicans announced that they would start talking to the IMF about a restructuring of the country's debt following a three-month moratorium on all payments.

In September, the retiring President Lopez Portillo delivered a parting blow: he nationalized private banks and imposed exchange controls banning the import or export of currency. The loony intention behind the second measure was to trap private capital from leaving Mexico, while being able to keep interest rates low. But capital continued to soak out of Mexico, while domestic savings collapsed because of the negative real interest rates.

In November Mexico's treasury minister, Jesus Silva Herzog, announced that Mexico had signed a letter of intent with the IMF allowing it to draw on credit of some $3.9 billion. This opened the way for a postponement in repayment of some $20 billion in debt falling due in 1982 and 1983, and to a $5 billion commercial bank credit, which was tied down the following March.

Under the IMF letter, the Mexican government agreed to slash the public sector deficit from 16.5 per cent of GDP to 8.5 per cent in 1983 to 5.5 per cent in 1985 and to 3.5 per cent in 1985. The Mexican government agreed to phase out the country's by now triple exchange rate system and to allow interest rates to rise to realistic levels. The Mexicans promised to achieve a trade surplus of some $8 billion–$10 billion and to get inflation down from nearly 100 per cent to less than 70 per cent.

The Mexican economic and social landscape meanwhile looked as though a hurricane had swept through it. Hundreds of firms went bankrupt every month. Private investment declined some 15 per cent in 1982. Unemployment jumped from 8 per cent to around 13 per cent in the space of a few months, in an economy in which under-employment anyway probably stood at around 45 per cent. This, in a country where a motor mechanic earning $12 a month was considered employed.

Real industrial wages, hitherto the Alamo of the trade

union wing of Mexico's ruling Institutional Revolutionary Party, fell fast. Mexico's economy stagnated, in a country whose population was growing by some 3 per cent a year. After a decade in which growth rates averaged some 9 per cent a year, ordinary people got a shock. Yet by the end of 1983, Mexico owed some $87 billion and was paying nearly $12 billion in interest.

Unless American recovery was spectacular, sustained, import-led (two-thirds of Mexico's trade each way is with the United States) and succeeded in driving up the price of oil again, there was no obvious respite in sight. Meanwhile, Mexico was paying nearly $12 billion a year in interest. At the end of 1984, the $20 billion in postponed loan repayment fell due, along with a pile of medium-term debt.

CONSIDER A MORE cautious borrower: Brazil. Many of the problems of South America's giant arose from the increase in the price of oil. Brazil's borrowing grew much more slowly and responsibly than Mexico's, to around $90 billion in 1983. Much of the cash that was not compensating for the trade deficit was going into projects with some economic justification. The Brazilians also went through a dose of IMF-type deflation in 1979–80, before the temporary reprieve of 1981 and the disaster year of 1982.

'I am worried that Brazil has not taken the decision to postpone payment of a large part of its debt, but is surviving from month to month', said one of the architects of Mexico's debt renegotiation. It was in Brazil that the difficulty of escaping the debt trap became clearest. The relatively modest growth in the Brazilian debt by $10 billion in 1980–81 took place firstly to service the existing debt, and secondly to finance a small pre-election boom. This brought the debt up to more than $80 billion, according to the IMF, or $90 billion, according to most Brazilians.

The world credit drought drove Brazil to the IMF. In February, the fund agreed to lend Brazil $5.4 billion, opening the way for commercial bank lending of $4.4 billion and a postponement of debt repayment of $4.7 billion. Brazil also managed to get $9 billion in short-term debt rolled over.

The interest picture was bad enough; the repayment profile for Brazil's medium- and long-term debt was awful. On IMF calculations, debt repayment rose from $7.2 billion in 1983 quite sharply through to $15.9 billion in 1987. Thus, by 1987, Brazil had to shell out some $26.4 billion on service payments on its medium- and long-term debt alone – and that was only on the lowest possible projections of likely future borrowing.

Only by squeezing living standards savagely was the target hit. In 1981 Brazil's GDP fell by around 3.5 per cent. In 1982 it stagnated; in 1983 it fell by as much as 3 per cent. With Brazil's population growing by around 2.2 per cent a year, this amounted to an effective fall of GDP per capita of about 12 per cent in three years.

Unemployment was reckoned to have shot up among the industrial labour force from around 11 per cent in the mid-1970s to around 20 per cent (about one million of São Paulo's four-million-strong workforce were without jobs). Underemployment was around 30 to 35 per cent. There were no social security payments to the jobless. Fearing labour trouble, the Brazilian government protected the purchasing power of the lowest paid while cutting back on salaries for skilled workers and the middle classes.

Impoverished Brazilians without jobs trekked back to the countryside, where they found that any prospect of a job was gone, thanks to some long overdue improvements in Brazil's agricultural efficiency. Brazil's industry meanwhile rusted; productive investment plummeted, while capital goods imports into Brazil fell by 16 per cent in 1981 and a further 10 per cent in 1982.

ARGENTINA IS A country much too rich for its own good. The country goes on wild spending sprees, ends up in a dosshouse, is set up in business again, and almost immediately returns to its bad habits.

The much-abused military government that took power in

1976 did in fact do a good job, to begin with, of clearing up the mess left by Mrs Isabelita Perón's mayhem of a government. By 1979 the government had turned a whopping trade deficit into a whopping surplus, had reduced inflation from a towering 600 per cent to around 50 per cent a year, and had cut the state sector deficit from around 17 per cent of GDP to 3 per cent. However, the then economics minister, Mr José Alfredo Martinez de Hoz, was told by the army not to squeeze as hard as he would have wished to, and to begin raising public spending again.

By 1980, things started to go badly wrong. The armed forces were becoming increasingly unpopular and tried to buy back appeal by inflating. The country joined in the general Latin American borrowing boom, its foreign debt rising from $11 billion in 1979 to $39 billion by 1982. The government spending, and the new money, caused inflation to rise again: the government tried to hold this by revaluing the peso, thus reducing import prices. The trade deficit grew.

Argentina's soldiers belatedly tried to do something about it all by squeezing the economy savagely in 1982. GDP fell by an unheard-of 5 per cent, causing unemployment to rise from its level of 3 per cent in 1978 to 13 per cent. Real incomes fell by around 20 per cent. Demonstrations against the military government became more frequent, as the trade union and political parties became bolder. The junta tried to distract the attention of Argentinians from the mess by invading the Falklands in April 1982, but lost the war there and added the heavy cost of the military campaign to public spending.

Argentina trudged to the IMF after the Falklands débâcle, reaching agreement on a letter of intent in November. In January 1983, a $2.2 billion IMF loan was arranged in principle, payment of some $12 billion in short-term debt postponed, and the commercial banks agreed to provide $1.5 billion. The Argentinians agreed to cut their budget deficit from 14 per cent of GDP to 8 per cent in 1983 and 5 per cent in 1984. Targets were also set for a continuing improvement in the balance of payments, which had already improved in 1982. After a long period of suffering under President Alfonsin,

Argentina's economy began to grow again under President Menem.

If Latin American countries had followed more sensible economic policies, would they have got into the quagmire of debt? This question can best be answered by looking at two medium-sized Latin American countries, Chile and Peru, which each pursued free-market economic policies during the late 1970s. Chile, under the stern eye of President Pinochet, provided laboratory conditions for a prolonged experiment by Mr Milton Friedman's disciples. Peru, which floundered into an economic bog in the mid-1970s, followed policies thereafter largely dictated by the IMF itself.

Chile at first became another economic disaster. The 'Chicago boys' went grey watching their achievements – a decline in inflation from 600 per cent under Salvador Allende's left-wing government to around 33 per cent in 1979, GDP growing by around 5 per cent a year, having fallen 12 per cent in 1975 – slowly wasting away. The Chicago boys were to some extent prisoners of their own ideology. In their dedication to the free market, they would not regulate the flow of private-sector borrowing from abroad, even though public-sector borrowing stayed at relatively sensible levels.

By 1983, the foreign debt had soared to $22 billion, most of it private. The inflow of foreign capital in a small economy jerked inflation up to around 50 per cent. The money washing in allowed Chileans to buy a multitude of imports across the country's newly lowered (to 10 per cent or so) tariff walls. The number of imported cars, for example, jumped by 700 per cent in 1980. Traditionally protected domestic industries went bust, but a boom in the construction industry kept their workers off the streets.

The reckoning came the following year; the tidal wave of foreign capital subsided; a lot of Chilean intermediaries between foreign lenders and local borrowers went bankrupt; and the price of copper, Chile's main export, tumbled. Real wages fell by sixteen per cent. The construction industry collapsed, tossing workers out. Unemployment rose to 21 per cent, and the number of those on *empleo minimo* – the $20 a month minimum wage – rose to around 13 per cent of the population.

Chile's plight was all the worse because, in 1979, the government pegged the exchange rate, partly out of fear of adding to the domestic burden of servicing the foreign debt, 44 per cent of which was dollar-denominated. For ministers who believed in free markets, their attachment to a fixed exchange rate was bizarre – and damaging. Imports flooded in, exporters were demoralized, and Chileans took advantage of the relative lack of exchange controls to pile up their savings abroad. The current account deficit, and the debt to finance it, both soared.

After the dismissal of Chile's arch-monetarist, Mr Sergio de Castro, in 1982, President Pinochet went through three cabinets in search of a return to the economic calm of 1979. It was a salutary lesson for bankers that even a country with fixed monetary targets and a government budget surplus of around 5 per cent of GDP in 1980 could not survive the borrowing wave of 1980–81.

By 1982, as the Chilean government was forced to step in to rescue private companies, it was running a modest budget deficit of 4 per cent of GDP. In January 1983, the Chileans secured a $550 million IMF loan, on condition they reduced the budget deficit to less than 2 per cent of GDP this year. With targets missed, international reserves plummeting and the country lurching from crisis to crisis, the IMF loan did not automatically open the way to new credits.

If Chile's undoing was sad, Peru's was tragic. After an economic spree under left-wing generals in 1968–77, Peru went through two years under IMF supervision, during which it slashed its public sector deficit to 1.2 per cent of GDP and secured a current account surplus of more than $600 million, although it failed to get inflation below 67 per cent. When a democratic government took over in 1980, these orthodox economic policies were continued. Peru's tariff walls were even lowered, from an average of 155 per cent to 35 per cent. Despite these policies, a balance-of-payments deficit, caused by the plunging price of copper, drove the country to the IMF in 1982.

Peru got $740 million from the IMF. In 1987 they went back and, with the IMF's blessing, secured $2 billion in loans rolled over and $880 million in new commercial bank loans at over-the-odds interest rates. The condition for the loans was that Peru slashed several tolerably sensible investment projects by $1 billion ($700 million to be spent on jet fighter aircraft was, of course, politically untouchable) and that they squeezed the economy further to get imports down (imports had already fallen by 25 per cent in 1982).

THE DEBT CRISIS began in Latin America, and the biggest loans were made there. By 1991 Brazil's debt had risen to $116 billion, Mexico's to $102 billion, Argentina's to $64 billion, Venezuela's to $34 billion, Peru's to $21 billion and Chile's had fallen to $18 billion.

But even more intractable and wretched, if possible, was the plight of African countries with little industry, primarily dependent on low-priced commodity exports. Between 1973 and 1983 Africa's debt increased at 22 per cent a year to a total debt of at least $80 billion, and possibly as much as $150 billion. The debt-service ratio – that is the proportion of interest and payments on the debt as a percentage of exports – exceeded 50 per cent, and in some countries a 100 per cent; if those nations tried to meet their obligations, they would have to hand over their total export income and import nothing!

The UN secretary general, Boutros Boutros Ghali, said recently that 'external debt is a millstone around the neck of Africa . . . easing the continent's debt burden must be a priority for the international community'. In Latin America foreign debt amounted to 37 per cent of GNP in 1993. In Africa, foreign debt was more than 100 per cent of GNP on average. Mozambique's debt was 400 per cent of GNP. Only a fraction of scheduled debt is paid in sub-Saharan Africa, so the debt has steadily increased to $183 billion in 1993.

Meanwhile, crucially, because of the debt hanging over them and the fear of default, no one would lend any of those countries any new money: new lending to Africa fell by nearly half between 1980 and 1983. This was a consequence of the banks' refusal to accept a once-for-all write-off, which would have lifted the dangers of default by those countries, and made it possible to lend to them again, much more modestly and sensibly. But the banks needed their face-savers, their fig-leaves, their covers for retreat so as not to offend their depositors, now having to pay up for the banks' initial mistakes. The result was financial famine in Africa, as in Latin America, with a desperate shortage of new money even for very viable projects.

The IMF, as in Latin America, imposed its heavy-footed regime: trade surpluses, balanced budgets and inflation targets had to be met before IMF lending would be granted – which was pretty expensive, but would catalyse much larger amounts of bank lending and debt rescheduling. These programmes, while deepening the suffering of the very poorest in underdeveloped Africa, permitted the banks to maintain the pretence that repayments were being made and staved off financial disaster. Britain's chancellor, Nigel Lawson, imaginatively proposed forgiving a number of African countries their debts to developed country governments in the mid-1980s; but the banks showed no such magnanimity with the larger commercial debt.

By 1985 debt service payments for Africa were around $10–$11 billion; a staggering amount for a desperately impoverished continent. The IMF, which applied its usual prescriptions, proved a mixed blessing. Between 1979 and 1983 IMF lending to Africa tripled. By 1985, payments to the IMF were between a half and three-quarters of debt service paid. A confidential report by one of the World Bank's senior economists at the time concluded bleakly and succinctly:

> Official debt renegotiation takes place at the Paris Club. This is the name given to an *ad hoc* group of western creditor governments which meets in Paris. However, the Paris Club

> mechanism has not been effective in easing Africa's debt difficulties. The relief provided has been too little and too costly. The procedures are designed to keep the debtors on a short leash. This is accomplished by placing strict limits on the definition of the debt eligible for relief and by providing relief on a small part of the debt. This has resulted in repeated reschedulings and an increased debt burden. The rescheduling of debt at the Paris Club has also not had a catalytic effect in mobilizing additional aid, nor has it helped to restore short-term trade financing arrangements.

A country like Kenya, whose politics and economics are relatively stable, showed a decline in real wages of around a fifth between 1981 and 1983 and an increase in stunted children under five through malnutrition from 24 per cent to 28 per cent, reversing the gains of previous years, during the period of IMF tutelage. In Kenya, as in most African countries, the price of basic commodity exports was far more important to their economies than their domestic policies, however good or bad these might be. President Nyerere of Tanzania put it rather plaintively in 1986:

> This year the rains in Tanzania were quite good. The peasants in our major cotton growing regions have more than doubled their crop compared with that of last year. We are desperately short of foreign exchange with which to buy essential imports, and cotton is one of our major exports; we were therefore pleased about this big output increase. But the price of cotton dropped from sixty-eight cents to thirty-four cents a pound on a single day in July this year. The result for our economy – and the income of the peasants – is similar to that of a natural disaster: half our crop, and therefore of our income, is lost. Our peasants – and our nation – have made the effort, but the country is not earning a single extra cent in foreign exchange.

By then around 60 per cent of the country's foreign export earnings were being devoured by debt service.

Zaire's debt by the mid-1980s had risen to some $6 billion,

in spite of the Mobutu regime's total corruption and bankruptcy. Susan George, in her book *A Fate Worse Than Debt*, eloquently outlined some of the projects that contributed to the debt:

> The ONAFITEX (national textile enterprise) in 1973 purchased thirty ultra-modern cotton-treating plants in the USA for $7.5 million. The Zairian delegation that made the deal got $450,000 worth of commissions. None of the plants has ever functioned. One was set up at Gandijika, but the high-tech electronic control system was omitted, so nothing worked. The rest of the material has been lost, stolen, dispersed or has deteriorated, so that no complete plant now has a prayer of getting built.
>
> Immediately after the runway at the Kisangani airport had been completely repaired and lengthened, a second runway was undertaken (the airport serves five flights a day maximum) at a cost equal to a year's income for the region. A worker in Kisangani would need several months' wages just to pay a taxi to the airport, but, once there, he could put his bags on an automatic conveyor belt and enjoy air-conditioned comfort. Total cost: $36 million.
>
> The twenty-two-storey tower of the Kinshasha International Trade Centre is virtually deserted. You wouldn't want to work there either – there are no windows, and the air-conditioning, supplied by a French firm, broke down a month after the supplier's guarantee lapsed.
>
> The TV-communications complex for the 'Voice of Zaire' (Cité de la Voix du Zaire), at $110 million, was a really good buy – surely far better than paying 165,000 primary school teachers for five years, which is another thing one could have done with that amount of money. In December 1980 the system was declared completed. The French manufacturer announced that Zaire was now 'one of the first countries in the world to possess its own domestic satellite communications network'. In any event, the fancy infrastructure for La Voix du Zaire broke down almost immediately. There is rarely any retransmission towards the interior of the country because the

relay stations seldom work. Anyway, most Zairians live, as Kwitny points out, 'a day or more's hard travel from the nearest electricity. Most have never seen a telephone. So they don't need the ultrasophisticated communications system'. But foreign enterprises do.

Foreign enterprises, in this case American, are also deeply involved in the Inga-Shaba power project. The total cost of the project is over $1 billion, Belgian sources say (Kwitny says $1.5 billion) or about twenty per cent of Zaire's foreign debt. Zairian researchers note that the country could pay 290,000 Zairian teachers or nurses for twenty years with that kind of money.

Any serious energy policy for Zaire would have chosen to exploit the huge local reserves of hydro-electric power and build a series of small dams.

The Inga-Shaba power line is supposed to furnish electricity to a copper refinery and an iron and steel complex. The Maluku steel plant has never operated at more than ten per cent of its capacity; the 'steel' it produces is of poor quality and costs three or four times as much as imported steel. It employs 1,000 people instead of the 10,000 promised. The copper refinery has not, so far, produced a single pound of copper. What the project is *not* supposed to do is to furnish power for any of the Zairian villages along its 1,100-mile stretch. In fact, 'an engineering technique was intentionally employed making it difficult or impossible for any electricity to be siphoned from the line before it gets to Shaba.

THE THIRD WORLD debt crisis, both in Africa and Latin America, came to global attention when Mexico declared its moratorium in August 1982, and a banking collapse was narrowly avoided after a frantic negotiation. As the decade proceeded, it was reckoned that, by 1985, there was a net transfer of some $26 billion a year from the poorer parts of the world to the richer, reversing the pattern of decades. Investment in Latin America as a whole fell by a third between 1980 and 1985, a case of the developing world becoming the undeveloping world. Latin America lost some $22 billion, sub-Saharan Africa some $2 billion, and Asia a more modest $2 billion.

In 1985 American treasury secretary James Baker launched the 'Baker initiative', which proposed reducing the value of the dollar, partly in order to diminish the size of the debt, which was largely dollar-denominated, to encourage growth policies for the fifteen largest debtors, to provide another $29 billion in extra financing and to try to encourage private banks to adopt a more positive approach to rescheduling. The plan at least recognized the size of the problem for the countries concerned: but very little new finance in fact followed for countries like Brazil.

An influential and devastating report by the influential British Parliamentary Group on Overseas Development, under the chairmanship of two heavyweights, Bowen Wells and Jim Lester, concluded sombrely:

> First, that in 1987, the Third World's debt problem seems no closer to resolution than it did in 1982 (when the crisis broke) or in 1984 (when the major international institutions predicted an upturn). Since 1983, in fact, developing countries' net capital transfers have turned negative. They are, moreover, now paying more interest than principal repayments. Net bank lending to most lesser-developed countries has stopped, the expected spontaneous revival of lending has not materialized, and the 'Baker Plan' and the innovations of the late-1986 Mexico deal have not altered that overall pattern. Adjustment and retrenchment have not of themselves brought a return to creditworthiness.
>
> Second, that so long as the debt burden cripples the performance of so many developing countries, it stifles the growth potential of the world economy – in particular world trade growth, but also the market for credit. Thus, economic and social costs are borne by us all in an apparent endeavour to satisfy some creditors' financial requirements. Senator Bradley told us how US exports to Latin America had fallen by twenty-five per cent between 1981 and 1985; over the same period, the World Bank calculates Latin American and

> Caribbean imports from all countries have fallen by forty per cent.

With a little foresight by the banks, usually shown in the excessive prudence with which they treat ordinary borrowers, the crisis and suffering need not have happened at all. It had been a global economic mega-accident for which the careless driver surely had greater responsibility than the beggar that had stepped into his headlights.

WHAT CONCLUSIONS are to be drawn from the debt crisis? They are pretty bleak. Allowing for normal human error, they involved probably the worst, most unnecessary hardship to affect the largest swathe of humanity for the longest time in modern economic history: droughts, famines, natural disasters and so on, although beginning to be avoidable by man's efforts, are part of the natural order of things. The debt crisis was entirely artificial from beginning to end; it affected an enormous number of people, and was entirely avoidable.

Not that many people actually died as a result of the debt crisis, although some did: but hundreds of millions were kept on a marginal existence, many dying prematurely of malnutrition, disease and poverty, while, for hundreds of millions the progress of the previous three decades was dashed because of an entirely avoidable, technical, global macroeconomic problem. There had been no precedent for it, except for the mistakes that led to the Great Depression – and the recovery from that was much quicker; the depression in the developing world has been deeper than that of the 1930s for the industrialized nations.

The economic betterment of the Third World has been replaced by its deterioration – particularly in the poorest part. Much of the developing world has become the undeveloping world. A decade of progress has already been lost, and another threatens to be. The poorest are getting poorer for no reason other than sheer short-sightedness, not malevolence, or even greed. The world of career managers meeting specific lending targets in order to ascend to their next job was not equipped with the long-term vision to ask whether the lending itself was safe; repayment would be somebody else's headache.

What kind of development, how to feed people in resource-starved countries when there is a surplus of food in developed countries, how to wean countries away from dependency on aid without leaving them to starve, does foreign aid inherently lead to dependency? – these are all complex and genuine issues. The foreign debt problem, which has been on a much bigger scale and far more damaging in the long run, allows no such ambiguity: it is the product of stupidity, and has created untold suffering. It is the greatest and most terrible consequence of the unchecked, unregulated globalization of capitalism.

It is necessary to point the finger of blame, to avoid further such catastrophe. One element was a chance one, for which no one could have allowed: the oil price increase which first sucked liquidity out of the Third World and then, through the recycling of petrodollars in the form of loans through the international banking system, put it back in a massively expensive form. From then on, three parties shared the blame: the governments and central banks that encouraged the commercial banks to lend for fear of a liquidity crisis in the Third World (a good motive, at least); the commercial banks themselves; and the borrowing governments.

To take each in turn: there can be no doubt that usually sensible Western governments and central banks actually encouraged the commercial banks to put up the loans; there was much self-congratulation at the time about the recycling of petrodollars. Banks later quite justifiably say they were summoned to meetings with central bankers at which they were virtually ordered to play their part in rescuing the Third World.

The borrowing governments must also accept a major share of the blame: it was possible to watch with fascination as, for example, Brazil's finance minister, Delfim Netto, would turn up in London for yet another round to borrow millions of dollars for projects that were entirely mythical – they went into balance of payments support – to keep the country operating for another few months. No one in Brazil pretended that anything else was happening.

As it turned out, the money could not have been used more irresponsibly, for instance: for speculative ventures, amassing large fortunes, capital flight and so on. The bankers exercised no control, splashing out to crooks in corrupt developing countries with no questions asked in a manner they would never have dreamt of with sober clients in their own countries; the banks positively chased customers with money.

The bulk of the blame must rest with those that lent the money, the banks. It was always something of a fantasy to believe that 'sovereign' lending was copper-bottomed: a nation cannot be any more responsible than an individual, although it does invariably borrow much more. The United States in the late nineteenth century had funded part of its industrial development through defaulting on loans from British banks. Many of the projects for the Third World loans were transparently bogus. In many cases bankers competed with each other to lend, arriving in Latin America with their surplus funds, literally begging local governments and investors to take their money. The purpose was to dump their surplus liquidity, which the bankers' own governments feared would create inflation back home. There was no altruism in this: bank profits depended on their being able to get the money off their hands and into loans.

Proper examination of the projects into which the lending was going was not carried out. None was volunteered by the lenders. In Venezuela, I learnt of a major German company which, in collaboration with the bankers, sold obsolescent steel mills to a country which had little experience of its own in the field, which paid for the deal with money put up by the West German bankers. In this case the banks were conniving in a loan they knew to be bad in order to do a favour to one of their domestic industries! There were many other examples of this kind of thing: the banks displayed knavery, as well as naïvety, in their lending.

Responsibility was never to be attached to individuals: provided managers met or exceeded their lending targets, they were promoted; other executives were in charge when the bills came in and the banks proved unable to recover their debts.

The success of the banks during the lending rush of the late 1970s was judged by the number of loans they had made, not by whether they were likely to be repaid: short-term results were everything.

One of the most depressing aspects of the affair was that the men who made the decisions rarely had to pay for them. Those most intimately involved in the lending, such as Walter Wriston, chairman of Citibank, had retired before the problem became too acute. The overall perspective was lacking even at the top, as banks were judged by monthly, quarterly and annual results. How big is the spread? How much return do we get on a loan? This was the perspective of the bankers, while on the borrowers' side, a little more or less in interest rates was neither here nor there provided the money could be obtained and then used for whatever short-term purpose the borrower intended – sometimes just rushed out of the country to buy property abroad.

This non-responsibility has been one of the key and depressing features not just of banking but of major corporations. There was no intentional effort to wreck the economies of the industrialized Third World. It stemmed from huge mistakes made by people incapable of any overarching judgement. It does not take a genius to work out that if money is put into ill-managed countries to fund a mass of bogus projects, a crisis will result. Once the false premise was accepted – that there is no risk in sovereign lending – the banks were begging takers to borrow their money.

Dollops of righteous indignation have been heaped upon the corruption and economic mismanagement of debtor nations: yet all these things were plain enough before the lending rush began: it was the bankers' job to ensure that the credit risk was an acceptable one, not the borrowers' responsibility to restrain themselves when money was being offered with no conditions attached. Who is to blame: the crook, accepting the money, or the sober-suited banker, with the suitcase full of money that ultimately belongs to his depositors, who is offering it to the crook?

When the enormity of the crisis became apparent, and the banks realized they would not get much of their money back, they were forced to resort to ever more imaginative ways of writing off their losses and squeezing money to pay for these out of their depositors. British bank debt paid in 1991, largely as a result of the debt crisis, was staggering. Bank profits, for example, fell by a third to £533 million, after bad debt provision of some £1.75 billion. The main high street banks set aside more than $6 billion for bad debts in 1991. In the late 1980s some $9 billion had to be written off the Third World debt by Britain alone, with the result that 20,000 jobs were lost at Barclays, Lloyds and Nat West in 1991, many as a result of closing small provincial banks which had no responsibility in the matter, helping to prolong the recession.

Nat West's chairman, Lord Alexander, commented primly that 'there were undoubtedly some departures from the principles of sound banking', while Barclays' Sir John Quinton, even more nauseatingly, argued that many of the losses, 'even with hindsight', were made 'according to good banking principles'. The then deputy governor of the Bank of England, Eddie George, remarked that 'both now tend to blame the authorities for allowing, or even encouraging, the party to get out of hand, though I seem to remember they rather enjoyed it at the time'.

It is worth asking whether the British banks' desperate drive for business and increased credit in the mid-1980s was not prompted by the need to offset their losses on Third World debt. In addition, the huge expansion of personal credit, based on the security offered by soaring property values that created the inflationary boom of the period, helped to yield the funds to write-off Third World debt; in turn this boom had to be dampened down by the prolonged recession of the late 1980s.

High interest rates, coupled with a continuing sharp expansion of credit were an unusual feature of that crisis, but one of great assistance to banks strapped for cash. High interest rates, wheeled in invariably as the orthodox solution to inflation, themselves in the short run help inflation, not just because they increase production costs for businesses and customers, but because they increase returns to the banks on a vast number of ordinary deposit accounts, on which no interest is paid at all.

This increased liquidity helped to write off Third World

debt, and also increased the incentive for banks to extend credit further, even at a time of high interest rates and, later, recession. Customers were still being offered credit and services at a time when interest rates were so high it seemed unlikely that they would be able to pay them back. On a smaller scale (although in the United States quite a large scale) the banks' hard-line drive to lend caused similar problems in the developed countries during the 1980s to those of the developing countries in the 1970s.

CHAPTER THREE

LAND OF THE GIANTS

THE GLOBALIZATION of capitalism represented by the coming of the multinationals was, in its time, the subject of much alarm, now largely ridiculed. A famous tract by the French politician Jean-Jacques Servan-Schreiber, *Le Défi Américain* (the American Challenge), portrayed a Europe threatened with take-over from American multinationals acting in their country's interests.

Subsequently, the threat seemed overblown. American multinationals like IBM and Ford were careful to act in a reasonably responsible way to avoid antagonizing host countries: they were seen as bringing work to Europe, providing a boost to local economies and conferring the benefits of technology on the host country. In fact, governments and local authorities began to compete with each other to attract major foreign companies. In exchange the multinationals acquired access to European markets and the benefit, in some countries like Spain, of a cheaper workforce.

In addition, as time passed, the Europeans joined in the game themselves, with major companies like Volkswagen and Fiat investing heavily in, for example, Latin America. The British, for their part, engaged in an astonishing transAtlantic assault on American assets, buying them at a rate that left Britain only just behind the United States and Japan in terms of global foreign investment. No one in America viewed this British acquisition of assets as a threat.

The tale of foreign investment, it seemed, had a happy ending. In the Third World there continued to be protests at the way the multinationals exploited cheap labour and raw materials, as well as the dangerous influence they wielded over local governments. But by and large, foreign investment, and the role of the multinationals, is perceived to be positive – and infinitely more so than the alternative method of capital export – debt. As between the extreme advocates and detractors of foreign investment, Norman Macrae and Tony Benn, the former seems decisively to have won.

The picture is indeed rosier than many people feared was at first the case. But this should not obscure certain real consequences of multinational control, size and foreign ownership. In the first phase this has been creative and beneficial: indeed local branches of the multinationals have been given substantial authority by their parent companies, and their boards and chief executives were often recruited from the host country: this was true for example, of IBM UK and Rupert Murdoch's media conglomerate, News International; they thus became truly multinational, not American companies based in Britain – although ultimate control rested with the parent company.

The problems arise not in times of expansion, but in times of difficulty. Failure in one country may lead to retrenchment or a change in the role of the multinational in another country which is not justified by conditions there or local performance. Volkswagen's retrenchment in Spain in 1993, with the possible loss of 10,000 jobs at its Seat factory in Barcelona, has been caused by the company's global problems, as well as local ones. IBM's massive worldwide losses in the early 1990s have led to pressures for cutbacks at its efficient British offshoot, IBM UK. News International's risky borrowings at the end of the 1980s had to be financed by the profits of such profitable outlets as its British newspapers, the *Sunday Times* and the *Sun*, even though these should have been using the fruits of their success to finance their own further growth. When plants close, because of difficulties in overseas parent companies, this leads to justifiable anger locally.

In addition, there is the hard-to-define issue of the political influence of the multinationals. A major employer, anywhere, has a great deal of clout with local authorities and governments which are eager to retain investment and jobs. If that employer is an overseas one, local authorities, government and the unions will be anxious to keep it happy; as with the issue of currency flows, the right of ordinary people to share in their own destiny will be curtailed. A local authority may be elected that believes strongly in environmental control. That authority may, however, have to tailor its views to the interests of an environmentally unfriendly foreign-owned multinational.

Multinationals pick and choose locations for investment according to what they believe to be the economic and political stability of the country concerned, the benefits offered and so on: this is entirely understandable. But it is a buyer's market for them: countries have to tailor their policies to retain them. It is not uncommon for multinationals to pull out of a particular country because they disapprove of the political or industrial relations conditions there and to relocate elsewhere. Again, this is not unreasonable: but it does represent a diminution in the power of the nation state, and therefore of popular choice. A nation could regulate and control its own industries in the past; it must negotiate and even yield to the multinationals if it wishes to keep them.

A further development has been the growth of predatory international takeovers. One company, for example, buys another to suppress a competitor in the international marketplace, or simply to strip it of its assets. On a national level these actions are usually subject to regulation; on an international level, they are much more difficult to police. Who can prove the real intentions of the predator? It has to be said that these practices, for the most part emanating from America, have sometimes had very negative competitive effects: far from representing the glories of free trade, the intention has been speculative, to get rich quick. Viable industries have been pillaged with sometimes openly monopolistic and anti-competitive motives. The British President of the Board of Trade, Michael Heseltine, has eloquently outlined the dangers:

> We are in a game of snakes and ladders – or, rather, in hundreds of simultaneous games – in which our competitors' rules allow them (but not us) to climb up the snakes, while we (but not they) find that the ladders mostly lead downwards.
>
> This is nowhere truer than in the arena of take-overs and

mergers, where the habits of investors have left British companies riper for plucking than any others in Europe. Our European colleagues do not have a history of takeover battles fought by distant shareholders; they tend to talk through the advantages, take a longer-term view and negotiate in the interests of the company. They see the British advocacy of the unfettered market as focused on the short term, exploiting today at the expense of tomorrow. This is a view shared by capitalist Japan; although companies are more freely available, the sheer scale of their larger companies effectively precludes most hostile bids, while vigilance in the Pentagon and Congress keeps a protective shield around their high technology industries.

Most quoted companies in Britain are vulnerable to takeover. Their owners have few effective forums within which to gather when under threat and to reach a collective judgement; and the advisers to individual shareholders are often in a position of fiduciary trust where anything but acceptance of an enticing offer leaves them vulnerable to legal remedy . . . Suffice it to say that Britain is the predator's natural hunting-ground. Not only is virtually everything for sale but there are few centres where specialist skills in the management of disposals and acquisitions are so highly developed as in London . . .

The logic of a single market must be that any considerations of monopoly and public interest are made first in the context of all Europe, not in that of a single national sector. If we are to bring together the resources of all twelve economies, it makes no sense to start by defining a British company's market share with reference to Britain alone. A proposed merger which combined, say, 50 per cent of the UK market, might command no more than 5 per cent of the European market. The former might be against the public interest by tending to monopoly; the latter hardly so. National governments cannot administer such policies, since each would take the most self-interested view. Imagine a French takeover bid for a British company where it fell to the French to determine whether it was in Europe's interest or not, or vice versa!

There is a balance to be struck: mergers below a certain scale should remain in national hands and those above should be considered by the European Commission . . . At the moment Britain is taking too innocent a view of the takeover climate . . . Sometimes a takeover provides a corrective remedy, achieves necessary rationalization or serves as a discipline to otherwise lax management. But it carries with it dangers that decisions turn on short-term maximization of profit at the expense of the expenditure on research, training or investment on which long-term health and the greatest rewards depend.

If British companies are more available for acquisition than others, it is they that will be converted into branch offices of overseas companies. Some take the view that this does not matter, indeed that further investment will then follow. In the production line and assembly sectors of industry this may be true; but a company owned in Britain will almost certainly have its head office there, and head offices not only have control but also attract a range of service industries around them. British-owned companies will locate their research facilities close to British universities and colleges whenever possible. The spin-off is usually seen locally: innovation grows close to the innovator. When rationalization comes, in recession or under competition, it is the distant factory or branch office which tends to be first in the firing line. No one should expect companies to take unwise commercial decisions in the name of patriotism but nor should anyone assume that company directors are detached from a sense of national obligation. Nor are our fellow Europeans, or other countries anxious to see their companies move into Europe, under any obligation to play by British rules. When only one soldier in a squad is out of step, he is wise to assume that he is the one who is wrong. There is need for a new sophistication in Britain's approach to the ownership of her industrial assets if they are not to be acquired in growing numbers by our rivals as pieces in the game of restructuring European industry.

*

A FINAL TWIST in the saga of the multinationals and overseas capital flows has been the advent of the 'screwdriver' assembly plant, pioneered by Japan. Unlike the major American investors in Europe, these plants are said by their detractors to be for the basic assembly of parts manufactured in Japan, endowing the minimum in technology transfer, providing only low-skilled local jobs and retaining a corporate leadership that consists almost exclusively of Japanese whose loyalty to the parent company and authority is never in doubt. The purpose of such operations is to take advantage of local incentives, cheap labour and, above all, to duck under protectionist fences and gain access to local markets.

The claims may be exaggerated, but there is certainly some truth in them, as also to the argument that, by under-cutting local producers, they may in fact be destroying more jobs than they are creating. If this stimulates inefficient local producers to be more productive, it may be a good thing. In Japan's case, industry has been assisted by a mass of uncompetitive practices that make it open to doubt that their success stems from greater efficiency alone: for example, the close relationship between Japanese industry and the banks permits it to benefit from much lower costs of financing than a Western competitor: bank lending to industry was characterized in Japan by virtually non-existent interest rates for a long time.

Japan's investment policy abroad bears this out: the establishment of Japanese local plants overseas began in direct response to protectionism. For example, the Voluntary Restriction Agreement on Japanese car exports to the USA stimulated the setting up of major assembly plants in America by Honda in 1984, Mazda in 1986, Mitsubishi in 1989 and Nissan in 1987, as well as the Toyota–General Motors joint venture. These 'voluntary' agreements limited Japan's sale of imported cars to some 2.3 million in the United States in 1987; the Japanese went for high-priced cars to circumvent this. The average price of American cars rose by $1,300 as a result.

In Europe the restrictions were much tougher. Compared to Japanese penetration of some 23 per cent in the United States,

Britain limited protection to some 10 to 12 per cent of the market, France to 3 per cent, and Italy to just 2,750 cars and 750 four-wheel-drive vehicles. In addition, the EC resorted to more justifiable protection against dumping, imposing duties on a wide range of goods from outboard motors to ball-bearings, electronic typewriters and photocopiers.

Protectionism has been sharply on the rise: in 1975 only 8 per cent of American imports received some form of protection. By 1984 the figure had risen to 21 per cent, and by 1986 to 25 per cent. Japan initially had very small interests overseas: only 2 per cent of its manufacturing output was offshore in 1983, rising to just 5 per cent in 1986, before mushrooming. The Japanese strategy to begin with was to start up wholly-owned manufacturing subsidiaries using non-union labour in government-supported greenfield sites in economically deprived areas. Komatsu's purpose in having a $12.5 million assembly plant in Britain was clearly to avoid 26.6 per cent anti-dumping tariffs on imported excavators. Toshiba's $1.2 million video recorder plant in Britain was to dodge import surcharges; and so on.

There were initially only a small number of Japanese acquisitions of plant (as opposed to acquisitions of real estate, which was on a much larger scale); those accelerated sharply in the late 1980s to 95 totalling $9 billion. Many of the acquisitions were in the firms supplying materials to the car plants – for example, Kawasaki Steel purchased 50 per cent of California Steel, and Nippon Kokan took a 50 per cent stake in Wheeling, Pittsburgh. The Japanese companies have introduced radical innovation in the management technology techniques they use in the West, which has seriously undercut local products. Among these were computer-integrated manufacturing, incorporating flexible manufacturing systems, computer-aided design and computer-aided engineering, robotics, numerically-controlled machine tools, sensors and telecommunications, which allowed smaller batch sizes in continuous flow to be produced, without large inventories of components and huge stocks of finished product. One observer, Barrie James argues that:

> The 'new' manufacturing not only allows companies to monitor the flow of materials but also the flow of information needed to manage production from delivery of raw materials, through to shipping out finished products. This helps firms to operate in smaller manufacturing plants and increasingly to customize product ranges through small production runs. At the same time they can reduce their breakeven point and lower their unit costs. Labour in these highly automated systems has become a far less important component of cost.
>
> Japanese companies have been quick to spot the advantages of the 'new' manufacturing and to adopt these new techniques, which allow them to move away from countries with low labour costs to the developed consuming markets without the old penalty of incurring higher labour costs. Japanese companies have also pioneered totally new approaches to manufacturing – for example, 'mechatronics', which combines mechanics and electronics to eliminate mechanical parts by replacing them with electronic components. This has not only eased manufacturing complexity, but also provided better precision, more reliability, lower costs and led to better customer features.

In addition, backing the new overseas companies, is Japan's enormous financial muscle: Sumitomo Bank, for example, is the largest banking company in the world. Six of the world's top eleven banks and fifteen of the top twenty-five are in Japan: these can give a major boost to Japanese companies abroad that undercuts local competition, which is forced to rely on more conservative methods of financing: drawing on unlimited credit, Japanese companies can produce cheaper goods in order to gain market share.

The Japanese have also been notoriously tough about driving hard bargains in the countries where they settle. By going to depressed areas, they secure non-union agreements and workers at below union rates (as for example Mazda in Detroit, which negotiated with the United Auto Workers' Union). Energy, raw materials, land and labour are all more cheaply available abroad than in Japan. One Japanese company operating an assembly plant for robotics in Britain imports all its engineered spare parts, thus ensuring the least transfer of technology and the least training for the British workforce, whose jobs are limited to simple functions, in a virtually colonial style of manufacturing.

The Japanese newcomers have provided thousands of jobs; but they have also caused thousands to be lost. For example, Ford and Vauxhall announced redundancies of 2,400 jobs early in 1992 because of 'significant challenges' from the Japanese. The cuts were designed to reduce Ford's workforce to 4,500 producing some 45,000 cars a year; this is to be compared with Nissan's workforce of 4,500 at Sunderland, producing 270,000 cars a year, and Toyota's workforce of 3,300, producing 200,000 cars. By the mid-1990s Japanese car makers were expected to produce some 600,000 cars a year in Britain. Output per head in the British plants is roughly a quarter below that of Japanese plants.

There can be no doubt that Japan's attitude to inward investment remains rigorously restricted. Foreign companies have only some 2 per cent or 3 per cent of shares in Japan, compared with ten per cent in America and some 20 per cent in West Germany, France and Britain. James argues, convincingly, that the employment generated by the new plants is likely to do no more than compensate for a part of the employment lost by local manufacturers, as a result of increased Japanese sales. In his view, 'To many critics Japanese manufacturing investments in the West are synonymous with exporting low value-added metal-bashing and assembly operations which offer marginal if any quality in investment.' He goes on:

> Japanese companies have long practised market subsidisation using the cash flows generated in Japan, a high-priced market heavily protected from Western competition, to subsidize the penetration of Western markets. Both the US and the EEC regard cross-market subsidization or 'dumping' as unfair competition and have imposed fines, duties, tariffs and restraint agreements to protect local companies.
>
> In the current climate of increasing protectionism and high yen values export price subsidization has lost much of its

> viability. However, the new globalized approach of Japanese companies offers indirect opportunities to maintain cash-flow subsidization. With highly developed networks sourcing, shipping, producing and assembling on a global scale, Japanese offshore units became part of a complex logistics system. This provides the opportunity to leverage the flow of raw materials, semi-processed and finished materials, components, subassemblies and even finished products between the various manufacturing, assembly and sales operations in different countries. The permutations to continue cross-subsidization of country market share battles with global cash flows, to support product positions, are almost endless given the complexity of global logistics systems – and almost impossible to identify.

What this means is that on a global scale it is possible to practise the kind of market manipulation that the *zaibatsu*, and then the *keiretsu*, have long since carried out at home. Further, the Japanese are adept at exploiting local subsidies in depressed areas in the West: There are no guidelines in the US or EEC which limit the incentives available to investors. So Japanese companies find themselves the targets of different communities outbidding each other to draw them in. For example, Britain's Department of Trade and Industry is believed to have increased its subsidy from £2 million to around £7 million in an effort to attract a new NEC plant to Telford instead of to Hanover in West Germany.

Such incentives are escalating: in 1982 Honda was given grants of around $16 million to build a plant in Ohio, while Toyota was given some $125 million in incentives for its car plant in Kentucky in 1985. The West in fact has huge potential bargaining power with Japan: America and Europe consume more than nine-tenths of its trade surplus between them. Thus Western governments would be wise to insist that potential investors persuade them of the real value of their investments. In fact, this has happened in much of Asia, where Japan is treated warily.

The solution is for much tougher controls to be imposed on

Japanese inward investment. Incentives can be linked to the level of local content and paid after a period to ensure that the company complies. Training grants could be made available only for programmes which create or upgrade genuine skills. Or the level of grants could be linked to the level accorded to foreign firms in Japan. This would require massive Western co-ordination. It seems obvious that this approach is preferable to gut protectionism or exclusion, which can only create inefficiency, would anger the Japanese, and reduce world trade.

It can hardly be clearer that the Japanese are determined to maintain an ever-increasing overseas investment strategy. The Economic Planning Agency stated baldly in its programme for the year 2000 that:

> In a long-term view of the future of the economy, it is inevitable that Japan will take the route from being a major trading partner to being a major power in direct investment. There are a number of forces at work, including the relatively rapid increase in international standing of Japanese companies in terms of financial, technological and management strength, and the difficulty of acceptance of trade from a single point for those major export items in which Japan has established a leading position. The increase in real incomes from Japan's relatively high rate of economic growth (a rise in wage and service prices), the possibility of a sustained increase in the yen exchange rate, and the relative increase in production costs in Japan, will be the forces making for overseas direct investment henceforth.

In 1989, Japan's direct investment abroad had grown from just $8 billion in 1975 to $154 billion, placing it third in the world foreign investment league, behind the United States with $373 billion and Britain with $192 billion. Of this, the bulk was in America and Europe. In 1990, for example, Japan invested $27 billion in North America, $14 billion in Europe, $7 billion in Asia and some $4 billion in Latin America. However, the bulk of foreign manpower employed by overseas Japanese firms was in Asia – some 474,000, compared with 354,000 in North America, 120,000 in Europe and 114,000 in Latin America.

WHERE ARE the multinationals going today, and is their impact likely to be as trouble-free as in the first two or three decades of their operations? Their role, while more parochial and less dominant than once predicted, has been quite formidable. Their principal attraction stems from the fact that the Third World was so devastated and shell-shocked by its first major encounter with global capitalism – the debt crisis – that it turned in despair to multinational investment as a saviour.

Without such investment, there would be precious little capital at all for the Third World. In a sense, the debt crisis softened up the previously proudly nationalistic and independent developing countries into abandoning their hostile attitude towards the multinationals.

Howard Perlmutter's dire predictions that by now 200–300 companies would control four-fifths of the non-communist world's productive assets has fallen far short of the mark. It is reckoned that some 35,000 multinationals – on a broad definition of the term – exist around the world, controlling some 170,000 affiliates. Of these, the top 400 multinationals account for some $3 trillion of world assets. Anything up to half of all cross-border assets are controlled by the top 100. *The Economist*'s editor, Bill Emmott, calculates that the top 100 control about 16 per cent of the world's productive assets, and the top 300 around a quarter (although I would put it at closer to a third). This, as he remarks, is not dominance.

But it does represent colossal global power. For just 300 global corporate oligarchies between them to control more than 25 per cent of the productive wealth of the entire world is astonishing, leaving them dwarfing many nation states in wealth. Japan's *keiretsu*, which control around a third of Japanese business, nevertheless dominate Japan's business scene. As proved there, when smaller firms are fragmented and often act as suppliers of the big boys, the domination of the latter is quite secure.

The table opposite gives a list of the top fifty – among them monsters like General Motors, with total assets of $180 billion, Exxon and IBM with $88 billion apiece, Mitsubishi with $74 billion, Toyota with $56 billion and Siemens with $50 billion.

In October 1993, a $33 billion merger between the Bell Atlantic Telephone Company and Tele-Communications (TCI), America's largest cable corporation, was announced. The new company is America's sixteenth largest with $60 billion in assets and $16 billion in revenues, reaching more than 40 per cent of American homes. 'Baby Bell' has in effect swallowed America's largest cable company.

Just by comparison, the total production of a medium-sized economic power like Britain was $960 billion in 1991 and the size of its state sector was $180 billion. For the biggest developing economy, Brazil, the figures were $450 billion and $65 billion respectively, and for a medium-sized developing country like Thailand, they were $180 billion and $9 billion respectively. Thus the assets of General Motors are two times greater than the entire annual production of Thailand, a fifth of the annual production of Britain, and as great as its entire public sector. That is power indeed.

The unelected, anonymous, self-appointed bosses of General Motors, Ford, General Electric and Royal Dutch can and do look upon the great majority of world political leaders patronizingly, *de haut en bas*, because they serve larger enterprises (although of course the politicians represent many more people).

Even within the UN's 35,000 multinationals, there is considerable concentration. Half are based in America, Japan, Germany and Switzerland. Further, as much as a third of all world trade is concentrated within multinational companies. By 1991, the European community countries, including Sweden and Switzerland, were the world's biggest global investors, with stock totalling $634 billion, more than Canada's total gross national product.

One striking feature of the multinationals has been the way their investment moved away from the developing countries during the 1970s debt boom, and into the developed countries. Recently the bias has been the reverse. The multinationals

The top 25 . . .

Largest non-financial multinationals 1990, ranked by foreign assets*

Rank		Industry	Country	Foreign assets $bn	Total assets $bn	Foreign sales $bn	% of total sales
1	Royal Dutch/Shell	Oil	Britain/Holland	n.a.	106.3	56.0†	49
2	Ford Motor	Cars and trucks	United States	55.2	173.7	47.3	48
3	General Motors	Cars and trucks	United States	52.6	180.2	37.3	31
4	Exxon	Oil	United States	51.6	87.7	90.5	86
5	IBM	Computers	United States	45.7	87.6	41.9	61
6	British Petroleum	Oil	Britain	39.7	59.3	46.6	79
7	Nestlé	Food	Switzerland	n.a.	27.9	33.0	98
8	Unilever	Food	Britain/Holland	n.a.	24.8	16.7†	42
9	Asea Brown Boveri	Electrical	Switzerland/ Sweden	n.a.	30.2	22.7‡	85
10	Philips Electronics	Electronics	Holland	n.a.	30.6	28.6‡	93
11	Alcatel Alsthom	Telecoms	France	n.a.	38.2	17.7	67
12	Mobil	Oil	United States	22.3	41.7	44.3	77
13	Fiat	Cars and trucks	Italy	19.5	66.3	15.8	33
14	Siemens	Electrical	Germany	n.a.	50.1	15.1‡	40
15	Hanson	Diversified	Britain	n.a.	27.7	5.6	46
16	Volkswagen	Cars and trucks	Germany	n.a.	41.9	27.5‡	65
17	Elf Aquitaine	Oil	France	17.0	42.6	12.2	38
18	Mitsubishi	Trading	Japan	16.7	73.8	41.2	32
19	General Electric	Diversified	United States	16.5	153.9	8.3	14
20	Mitsui	Trading	Japan	15.0	60.8	43.6	32
21	Matsushita Electric Industrial	Electronics	Japan	n.a.	59.1	16.6	40
22	News Corp.	Publishing	Australia	14.6	20.7	5.3	78
23	Ferruzzi/Montedison	Diversified	Italy	13.5	30.8	9.1	59
24	Bayer	Chemicals	Germany	n.a.	25.4	21.8	84
25	Roche Holding	Drugs	Switzerland	n.a.	17.9	68.8‡	96

Source: United Nations   * where not available, foreign assets have been estimated for ranking   † outside Europe   ‡ including export sales

. . . and the next 25

Largest non-financial multinationals 1990, ranked by foreign assets*

Rank		Industry	Country	Foreign assets $bn	Total assets $bn	Foreign sales $bn	% of total sales
26	Toyota Motor	Cars and trucks	Japan	n.a.	55.5	26.3	42
27	Daimler-Benz	Cars and trucks	Germany	n.a.	48.8	32.7‡	61
28	Pechiney	Metals	France	n.a.	14.3	9.2	65
29	Philip Morris	Food	United States	12.5	46.6	15.2	3
30	Rhône-Poulenc	Chemicals	France	12.2	21.4	10.4	72
31	E.I. Du Pont de Nemours	Chemicals	United States	11.9	38.1	17.4	43
32	Hoechst	Chemicals	Germany	n.a.	23.8	14.1‡	50
33	Michelin	Tyres	France	n.a.	14.9	9.1	79
34	Dow Chemical	Chemicals	United States	10.9	24.0	10.3	52
35	Total	Oil	France	n.a.	20.8	18.2	77
36	Thomson	Electronics	France	n.a.	20.7	10.4‡	75
37	Amoco	Oil	United States	10.6	32.2	8.5	30
38	Saint-Gobain	Construction	France	9.9	17.6	8.3	65
39	ENI	Chemicals	Italy	n.a.	60.5	7.9	19
40	Electrolux	Electrical	Sweden	n.a.	11.7	12.5‡	89
41	Petrofina	Oil	Belgium	n.a.	12.3	5.7	33
42	Générale des Eaux	Miscellaneous	France	n.a.	27.9	5.9	29
43	Hitachi	Electronics	Japan	n.a.	49.3	10.5‡	21
44	Chevron	Oil	United States	8.4	35.1	9.8	25
45	Sandoz	Chemicals	Switzerland	n.a.	10.1	6.3‡	70
46	C. Itoh	Trading	Japan	n.a.	47.8	19.1	13
47	Toshiba	Electronics	Japan	n.a.	32.7	8.5	29
48	Xerox	Office machinery	United States	8.0	31.5	7.5	42
49	Stora	Paper	Sweden	n.a.	15.0	8.9‡	84
50	Texaco	Oil	United States	7.8	26.0	18.0	44

Source: United Nations   * where not available, foreign assets have been estimated for ranking   † outside Europe   ‡ including export sales

behave like the imperial powers in targeting their investment into four geographical regions. Thus, while there are major flows between America and Europe, and from Japan into America and Europe – with little going back into Japan – each of the three giants has its 'clusters'.

For America, the satellites are Latin America (with the exception of Brazil), Bangladesh, Pakistan and the Philippines in Asia, and Papua New Guinea and Saudi Arabia elsewhere. The Europeans prefer Chad and Morocco in Africa, Brazil in Latin America, India, Sri Lanka and Vietnam in Asia and a clutch of Eastern European countries. Japanese favourites in Asia are South Korea, Singapore, Taiwan, Thailand and Fiji. The tendency of the multinationals is to dominate a handful of preferred countries.

Broadly, of course, they invest in those with a favourable economic climate: openness to investment, incentives and orthodoxy in economics and politics. The multinationals are in a buyer's market: they can pick and choose locations favourable to them, which pursue the economic policies they like.

ANOTHER MAJOR trend among modern multinationals is the propensity to form alliances – joint ventures, supply deals, research groups and licensing agreements: this suggests that the trend is towards a cartel system, with firms exchanging favours for each other and mapping out turf rather than competing for the benefit of the customer. Such alliances are particularly prevalent in biotechnology and information technology, and are prompted by the expense of research and innovation, the need to gain access to markets, or to carve up a market.

Bill Emmott of *The Economist* argues that this is probably no more than a trend: 'Like anything else, international business is prone to fads and fashions. Unsure of what to do, many simply follow the herd, and in recent years the stampede has been towards the alliance – which is almost always called "strategic" in order to make it appear long-lasting, serious and vital. Nobody ever calls its alliances tactical.'

But the phenomenon is more than a passing one. In a classic

free market, a firm arrives in a new market, competes with existing firms and thus improves the range and quality of goods and lowers prices for the consumer. This still sometimes happens, particularly with the arrival of Japanese firms, who use aggressive pricing and production to drive local firms out of business. But in most countries it is far easier for a major foreign firm to enter a deal with a major local one, in which each tacitly accepts what their market is going to be than for them to engage in a furious price war which serves neither of their interests (although it might serve the consumer).

In such alliances, the consumer and the free market will be the loser. While it suits the big firms to preach the virtues of the free market, it is in their interests to practise cartelization. That is what is happening on a global scale now. If this seems something less than monopoly – the classic adversary to free market thinking – it is not all that far off.

In terms of direct control, moreover, in a number of key sectors, there is an astonishing domination by just a handful of companies. Only five companies sell nearly 70 per cent of the world's total supply of consumer durables. A similar number of companies carve up 60 per cent of world air travel; five aerospace companies control over half the world's production of aircraft while the same tiny number dominate its electric components industries; five in excess of half its electronic and electrical equipment industries; five at least half of world personal computer production; five over 40 per cent of the global media; five a third of world chemical production; and five some 30 per cent of world insurance.

These are staggering concentrations of control which, spread across the globe, far eclipse the powers of national regulators to control them. In addition, Boeing and Airbus dominate civil airline production, General Electric, Rolls-Royce, Pratt and Whitney and SNECMA carve up aero-engine production between them, and Intel and Motorola the production of microprocessors.

It would be naïve not to imagine that these colossi are going to maximize their profits in their own interests, whether through domination of the markets or alliances to carve up the market, although occasionally relations will degenerate into a ferocious war over turf or prices which might benefit the consumer. Of course, other tough-minded companies often try to break the hold of the giants, and occasionally tunnel through; for example Laker and Richard Branson's Virgin Airways confronted British Airways' dominance in Britain. Laker lost, while Branson survived British Airways' avowedly underhand attempts to crowd him out. Only the very toughest can hope to prevail against the huge power of the big corporations using their bureaucratic, monopolistic and anti-competitive practices to dominate.

Just because no obvious political backlash to the power of the multinationals has yet emerged, it would be wrong to believe that the lid had been raised from this particular pressure cooker. The developing world eased its old takeovers of multinational corporations, which peaked in the early 1970s, because this was so obviously counterproductive. In money-starved developing economies, debt was the alternative way of raising capital from abroad; they had no choice but to go cap in hand to the multinationals, and, indeed, invite them in by, for example, privatizing and selling off state assets. IMF conditionality made this necessary and emphasized the need for balanced budgets and reduced state intervention.

Huge swathes of admittedly badly run state industry were bought up by the multinationals at knockdown prices: in 1990 alone more than seventy countries had privatization programmes and had sold assets of $185 billion. The need to improve efficiency and raise capital is powering this move, and it is proceeding more successfully than the doomsday theorists predicted. But that does not rule out a potential backlash against the sale of national assets, pollution, the exploitation of resources, the corruption of local politicians or simply pushing around local governments.

That may yet be to come. Even the United States is beginning to talk in angry terms about, for example, Japanese ownership of such assets as Columbia Pictures and the Rockefeller Center. The Third World seems unlikely to ignore such a lead, which is far more appropriate to their own predicament. True, the multinationals are less obviously bullying, less concentrated, more sensitive to local needs and have expanded more slowly around the world than expected by a few soothsayers. But still the trend has been unmistakable, and the political reaction, although much slower, may occur in a very dangerous form from countries already experiencing intense suffering as a result of the debt crisis.

CHAPTER FOUR

THE FIGHT FOR MARKETS

THE FOURTH AREA in which the world economy is becoming globalized is, of course, trade. The explosion in world trade since the Second World War has brought enormous benefits in terms of global economic growth, expanding the range of products available to consumers throughout the world and improving competitiveness to the benefit of the consumer. From this it is easy to draw the iron conclusion that free trade is a good thing, as virtuous as being against sin. The obverse of free trade is protectionism, which helped to lead to the world slump of the 1930s and which, by excluding foreign products, limits consumer choice. Protectionism hampers economic growth and permits the erection of inefficient industries behind high tariff walls, which allow a country to slip behind its competitors, and, when an economy has to compete in the global marketplace, ultimately leads to impoverishment and industrial collapse.

The one cornerstone of free-market economics that has never been dislodged is the faith in free trade – justifiably so. What, however, the theory does not touch upon is what to do in conditions of imperfect free trade: that is, when some countries do not abide by the rules. The classical theory of free trade is also flawed in one respect: it is in fact possible, and may even be necessary, for a newly industrialised nation to build up highly competitive industries behind tariff walls. The argument here is that a country, in order to develop its major industries, needs them to have a large share of the domestic market: this is unlikely to happen if already efficient external competitors are pouring in goods which local industries are only just beginning to manufacture.

In fact, this has been the pattern for virtually every major country in the early stages of industrialization: Britain, as the first, had no need to be protected and became, unsurprisingly, an ardent advocate of free trade for its own products. Germany and France both built up their domestic industries from behind tariff walls, as did the United States, all of which opened up their economies and themselves became proponents of free trade as they became more confident they could compete abroad. Exactly the same technique has been practised by Japan and the Far Eastern countries over the period since the 1950s, as well as by Brazil. One of the world's foremost free-market theorists, Brazil's former finance minister Roberto Campos, told me in 1994 that tariff protection was permissible in the early stages of industrialization – provided that it was export-driven, and therefore local goods were competitive with overseas products. Indeed, a cycle occurs in which a country embarks upon a highly competitive export drive from behind tariff walls, which goes unnoticed for a while, then leads to demands for less protectionism by countries at the receiving end of the exports; in turn this leads to an opening up by the newly industrialized country's economy and, usually, a conversion of that country to the free trade camp.

With Japan, however, something rather different has happened, and is threatening to throw the whole theory of beneficial free trade into disarray. First, Japan has been repeatedly accused of maintaining hidden barriers towards imports and foreign investment – which seems to be borne out by the relatively small penetration of either into Japan. The Japanese retort that the problem is simply that ordinary Japanese – who are, it is true, somewhat xenophobic – shun foreign goods. Their competitors reply that there exists a whole network of barriers – from cartels, to a loaded distribution system, to a refusal to accept foreigners on company boards – that discriminate against them.

The second charge is that Japan's economy is rigged to promote exports in a way no other Asian economy is, for example, through links between banking and industry which permit Japanese goods to be sold at a very low price or even below the cost of production for a time, with the banks absorbing the risks, in order to see off the competition. Both of these are formidable charges. With the Japanese retorting that they have no substance, a remarkable thing has occurred: the Japanese are now the world's prime advocates of free trade, while its old proselytizers, America and Europe, are increasingly dubious about its virtues.

In America, free trade is no longer the totem it once was. Robert Heilbroner, a leading economic historian at the New School for Social Research in New York, argued that 'all trading nations' will go down the path 'of some form of managed trade'. Clyde Prestowitz, the former American trade negotiator, has been blunter still.

> It is not unfair for other countries to have a different view of industrial or antitrust policy than the United States. If the Europeans want to subsidize Airbus, and if the Japanese want to target supercomputers, that is their business. Lambasting them as unfair will only poison relations. The United States should, however, be prepared to offset the negative effects of their policies on its own industry.
>
> Americans should always be willing to negotiate, but they must be prepared to act unilaterally with countervailing subsidies or other measures – not out of moral outrage, but for self-preservation.
>
> The same holds for structural asymmetries. That the Japanese, for example, have a different market structure is not wrong. Americans should not blame them or insist that they become more like Americans. At the same time, the way the Japanese (and others) do business does sometimes put important US industries at an unacceptable disadvantage.
>
> The long-term solution to this problem is, of course, structural convergence. Since it will not come quickly, however, Americans must reconcile themselves to a certain amount of trade management with Japan.

The more extreme argument brought to bear against free trade today is that because of accelerated global transactions the rich become poorer while the poor suffer massive dislocations. In rich countries, competition with low-wage economies has forced wages and benefits down and caused huge trade imbalances. In America recently more and more families have been forced to rely on two incomes, while insurance for workers has been reduced and pension funds have often been raided in the course of corporate mergers. As the American commentator William Pfaff observes:

> High tariffs certainly contributed to the Great Depression of the 1930s. But it is equally clear that low tariffs are contributing to the great recession of our times – the competitive austerity and disinflation, and competitive unemployment and 'social dumping' of the 1990s. Industrial specialization in the poor countries has too often tended to turn them into low-wage suppliers of goods that they remain too poor to consume, while weakening or destroying their agricultural self-sufficiency and undermining their social stability.
>
> The French-British financier and sometime corporate raider Sir James Goldsmith, whom no one has ever accused of bleeding-heart liberalism, recently published (in the Paris newspaper, *Le Figaro*) a powerful social as well as economic argument against further GATT tariff liberalizations. Writing for a European audience, he said that Europe is essentially self-sufficient in economic terms, and added: 'Let us recognize, once and for all, that economic growth is valuable only to the extent that it reinforces the stability of our societies and augments the well-being of our people.'

Sir James further asserts that the impact of free trade has been 'to impoverish and destabilize the industrial world at the same time that it cruelly ravages the Third World'. John Gray, an Oxford academic, argues against 'the quasi-religious devotion to securing a GATT agreement'.

> GATT is designed to create a global free market in all goods and services, including agricultural products. Such a global free market can only enhance the destructive radicalism of

> market institutions, which is the principal danger of the post-socialist age. The globalization of market forces has already undermined local and regional ways of life in many parts of the world. For the Third World, global free trade means the destruction of agrarian communities and peasant traditions, as local farming practices are undercut by mechanized Western agribusiness. This in turn means the accelerated migration of impoverished agricultural workers to swollen mega-cities whose social and economic sustainability is questionable. The prospect of over a billion ruined peasants being peacefully absorbed into the cities of the Third World will be taken seriously only by those whose support for market institutions is fundamentalist in character.
>
> In truth, the GATT agreement promises to complete, under the auspices of *laisser-faire* liberalism, the desolation of peasant life wreaked by communist governments throughout the world. For the developed world, global free trade means a massive increase in structural unemployment as workers try vainly to compete with the low-wage economies of the newly industrializing countries. In both Third and First worlds the GATT proposals are a recipe for social upheaval and political instability on a vast scale. The world envisaged by the GATT proposals is, in fact, a fantasy of economic rationalism, as utopian and as dangerous as its mirror image in Marxism.

Against this have to be set the staggering benefits of free trade: in the last forty years exports of manufactured goods have risen more than twenty-five times, the volume of trade has increased twelve times and world output has jumped six times.

The United States has indeed moved sharply in the direction of protectionism, passing the Omnibus Trade and Competitiveness Act in August 1988, 'a wide-open door for protectionist legislation', according to Martin Feldstein, a former chairman of the President's Council of Economic Advisors. The share of American imports subject to quotas or official restraints has risen from 10 per cent to 25 per cent. The emphasis has now been placed in Washington on 'fair' rather than 'free' trade.

In 1991, President Bush paid a visit to Japan and a deal was sought by which the Japanese agreed to limit their exports to the United States in certain key areas: this represented a step towards 'managed' trade – barter – which could leave third parties like Europe at a disadvantage and violate the customer's right to buy goods from across the world as he wishes. It was denounced as such by the European Commissioner responsible for trade, Sir Leon Brittan. European restraints on Japanese exports, such as cars, remain high, with Europe demanding 'reciprocity' in trade.

There are also increasing signs of a trade war between Europe and America, with the 1988 European ban on $150 million worth of American hormone-fed meat imports, and in 1992 the row over American restraints on steel exports. Charges of 'Fortress Europe' have been flying about. In official pronouncements, the virtues of free trade remain paramount.

Both America and Europe believe Japan is flouting the rules. The Americans are retaliating through managed trade, thereby flouting the rules themselves, and the Europeans are likely to retaliate in the one area where free trade remains a reality – European–American trade. There is no need to be too pessimistic about this: handled with firmness and flexibility, these huge frictions need not degenerate into catastrophic trade wars. But the ideal of genuine free trade remains very far from being realized.

The globalization of trade, of course, has had an immense effect on the autonomy of individual countries. On the one hand it can lead to improved competitiveness in a country subject to foreign imports; on the other to the decline of domestic industries and the loss of jobs. The flows of money that accompany it are also important: a large Japanese trade surplus, for example, serves as a brake on growth in the rest of the world economy, particularly if the rest of the money is not put to increase Japanese demand for goods produced abroad. If the money instead flows out to fund Japanese purchases of foreign assets abroad – as it has – this greatly increases Japan's hidden 'power' in other countries.

The purchase of American treasury bills to fund the US

budget deficit gives Japan huge leverage in any argument about trade with America. Certainly, this leverage has to be used carefully: a sudden major withdrawal of Japanese money would lower the value of the dollar and diminish the value of the rest tied up in bonds and property. But it places a major weapon at Japan's disposal should the American administration get too angry about the trade deficit. As with every other example of the globalization of the world economy, the power of national governments to impose their will upon events is steadily diminishing.

CHAPTER FIVE

THE END OF SOVEREIGNTY

Two huge consequences flow from the transcendence of the power of the nation state by these huge economic forces. To the ordinary person, the forces that control his destiny seem bigger and more impersonal than ever. He can vote for the party he wants: but governments are increasingly forced to follow much the same policies, and are inevitably buffeted by larger external economic forces. In other words, just as the principles of free enterprise, personal rights and liberal democracy are making steady strides forward, they are being eroded by much larger forces that elected governments have very little control over – a directly contradictory phenomenon. It is not much use having the right to vote, and to be an entrepreneur, if your government has no freedom of action, or you cannot in practice compete against the big boys.

The second consequence goes back to the basic tripod political theory outlined earlier based upon the individual, the strong and government. The latter, in a properly balanced democracy, exists to prevent the powerful depriving the ordinary man of his freedom – while permitting the strong enough freedom to help create the wealth of the nation. In a global marketplace and economy, the powerful corporations have escaped the control of governments, endowed with legitimacy by popular mandate: in other words, we are back to the state of nature which, as Hobbes argued, was less libertarian than any for the ordinary individual – if not for the strong.

To some free-market theorists, this is entirely desirable (very few recognize the inherent contradiction in arguing passionately for the freedom of the individual, while espousing a world in which his electoral choice counts for less and less). There is a thread running through much free-market theory which asserts that central banks should be independent of governments, which decide things for 'political' reasons and that technical economic decisions are far too important to be left to corrupt and ignorant party hacks, interested only in grubbing for votes. The government that governs best governs least. The market is self-regulating with an ingenious mathematical equilibrium that irons out every distortion. Governments only damage delicate natural mechanisms if they interfere; leave the market alone and it will look after itself.

Pure free-market economics is the mirror image of communist economics – the reason why it is so attractive to so many of the old proponents of the latter, seeking another perfect mathematical formula to fit pseudo-scientific theories. Both display spectacular ignorance of human nature: the self plays no part in their calculations. To communist theorists the state had to have control of everything and history fitted a pattern of scientific inevitability; to free-market theorists, economics will automatically determine the best order of things if left alone.

In fact free-market theorists perform much the same role for the power system they justify – the big corporations – that communist economists performed for the all-powerful state. While communism represented the perversion of the power of the state to its zenith, free-market economics represents an idealization of the power of the strong. Set the strong – the large industrial and economic conglomerates, the banks and financial institutions – free of irksome government interference (which in communist countries was deeply inefficient and unproductive, while in democratic societies represented the valid concerns of ordinary electors) and wealth would be maximized.

In the world economy the strong have already been set free because they largely escape government regulation – except for that of the three global superstates swirling together: the Americas; Europe; and Eastern Asia. These giants, in fact, are fast becoming the strongest of the strong and are thus best placed to secure their own interests in the international state of nature, where there is no supreme state authority. For behind the ideal global free market lies the reality that it best serves the interests of those who are strongest.

For a long time after the Second World War, this was the

United States, the prime advocate of free-market economics. With America's relative decline, its passion for free trade, at least, has sharply declined, while the enthusiasm for this in Japan, previously one of the most protected economies in the world, has grown commensurately. Meanwhile, weaker countries have had to look after themselves as best they could.

When, in the 1980s, the United States wanted to expand its defence budget while cutting taxes (a 'supply side' economic theory at some variance with personal motivation), it was able to increase its budget deficit and raise interest rates to attract funds, crippling its smaller European partners – simply because, in the jungle of the money markets, it was the biggest animal. European countries had to follow the rise in American interest rates to avoid a run on their currencies. This had nothing to do with classical free-market theory – that exchange rates set themselves at the levels justified by the state of the economies concerned – it just had to do with the largest economy throwing its weight about and the rest proving too small to resist.

On a smaller scale, German interest rates recently surged absurdly high for slightly more defensible domestic political reasons and smaller Western European economies, from the cautious to the profligate, suffered accordingly. The currency markets are increasingly flawed judges of a country's economic viability. Interest rates are the main determinant of currency flows and these bear only an indirect relevance to the state of an economy: for example, high German interest rates may have actually done damage to that country; in Britain, the perception of a 'petro-economy' early in the 1980s contributed to an unusually strong pound – unreflected by the real economy – that helped to bankrupt thousands of enterprises.

The upshot of all these developments is the same: the old nation-state has been bypassed, and no longer controls the huge flows of international trade, investment and finance that determine the fate of nations today. Nation-states are increasingly democratic and responsible to the people: the giant interests that manage these flows are not, and are more powerful. A world in which people, far from gaining control over their own destinies through the spread of liberal democracy, are in fact losing it through the globalization of non-responsible economic forces is surely one moving in a dangerous direction. In fact, it is in the very same direction that the communists moved for more than seventy years. As ordinary people become more aware that the governments they elect exercise no real power, but merely stage a sham political theatre while being buffeted by larger economic forces, resentment may explode – in the form of political anger, such as demands for trade protection or the exclusion of foreign investors.

THE ISSUE OF the transcendence of politics has to be addressed. To some free-market theorists, as noted, it is eminently desirable that the old nation state should have increasingly less power in the face of giant economic forces and that politicians' choices should be restricted and even frustrated by the wider economic forces they face. On this theory, although absolute state interference is worst of all, even limited state intervention is bad, determined by 'crowd-pleasing' and populism and grubbing for votes rather than the necessary technical adjustments imposed by the markets. In Latin America, in particular, the 1970s was the decade of the 'technocrats', men who believed that authoritarian military regimes would permit the sometimes unpopular policies of economic liberalization necessary for economic growth and stability.

The emphasis on monetary policy and taking central banks out of political control is another example: by handing one of the key institutions of economic control to the 'experts', the temptation by politicians to inflate will be reduced. And so what if the globalization of economics removes economic policy from the hands of elected governments? If governments are increasingly forced to follow prudent economic policies because to do anything else would result in financial disaster, what is the harm in that? If an incoming Democratic administration, like Bill Clinton's in America, or a possible Labour government in Britain is quietly forced to renege on its election promises and follow policies not unlike those of its Conservative predecessors, is this not a good thing?

This argument is flawed in most of its key aspects. To begin with it must be recognized as an essentially authoritarian, anti-democratic argument. Just as communists argued that they only saw what was in the true interests of the people – the latter were too ignorant to know – so the technocrats argue that they alone enshrine economic wisdom which ordinary people are too stupid to understand for themselves; the voter does not know his own true interests.

The argument also asserts that the market is pure and all-knowing. As we have seen, the market is certainly a formidable force, but it obeys rules all of its own, which sometimes are no more than the fashions of the day: there is no such thing as an objectively 'correct' economic policy, as the enduring arguments on the subject attest. We may be groping towards greater understanding, objectivity and judgement, but we do not have all the answers. An economist or central bank governor is just as likely to be flawed in his judgement as a voter.

Further, this theory of expertise obscures the key point that economics is about priorities and choices. It is certainly true that there is an objective body of economic laws that seems to hold true in most economic situations. For example, if a country's money supply expands faster than its productive capacity, or if wages are allowed to rise much faster than output, or if the government increases public spending but does not raise taxes, inflation will result.

But that may reflect a conscious choice on the part of voters: if a Labour government is elected after a long period of Conservative rule it may be because voters are now more concerned with the quality of public services or the fall in real wages than they are about inflation. Conservatives would try and convince them otherwise, arguing that inflation will in the long run make them worse off. But if the voters have a different set of priorities, they cannot be forced to change them. Or if voters prefer high taxes and high public spending to low taxes and low public spending, a Conservative can argue against this; but, again, it is a matter of the voters' own perceived self-interest. If voters prefer to spend money on social services rather than defence, a

Conservative politician's job is to try and persuade them of the importance of the latter; but he cannot impose his choice.

In a democratic society, we respect the choice of ordinary voters, even if we believe it to be wrong, and seek to persuade them through argument. If crowd-pleasing is so bad, why not do away with the whole tiresome business of democratic elections, and let the experts get on with running the show? The theory that the gentlemen in Whitehall know best has much more in common with classical socialist theory than with the free market, and leads inexorably towards totalitarianism: a free society is founded on the free rights of the people, including the right to make wrong choices.

A tyranny which disregards the rights of the people may in theory make wiser decisions, but precedent is not encouraging: usually authoritarian governments simply impose the choices of the clique in power upon the people. In an authoritarian society people may be told to do the 'right' thing (although the authorities, as often as not, get it wrong), but it is not the people's own preference; hence the sense of alienation from government that, throughout the centuries, has resulted in an explosive assertion of the self. Liberal democracy in its present form is not an ideal system; but it is increasingly the only form of government that can persuade people to give their peaceful assent to state policies and actions.

Leaving matters to the 'experts' can seriously distort matters. In 1990, Germany's democratically elected government, for electoral purposes, promised a one-for-one exchange of good West German marks for worthless East German ones. In the absence of high taxes this was highly inflationary, and the independent expert, the Bundesbank, had to raise interest rates to squeeze inflation out of the system.

Was that the right policy? Possibly, although it might have made more sense to permit a modest degree of inflation to cope with the once-and-for-all phenomenon of German unification rather than strangle Germany's economic recovery, and most of the rest of Europe's as well. The Bundesbank should not be blamed: its job was to maintain the value of the currency, and it did exactly that. But its independence reduced the flexibility of German economic policy. It was really up to the elected government to decide whether to permit a degree of inflation as part of the price of reunification. Instead, it was able to wash its hands of responsibility for the policy of high interest rates, and blame the Bundesbank.

To the expert central banker, inflation is viewed as an unmitigated evil in quasi-religious tones – this is understandable, as his job is to prevent the currency being debased. Yet inflation is in its own way no more than a form of disguised – some would say dishonest – taxation. The German government's mark-for-mark policy was in reality a tax upon West Germany to subsidize the East: that would have been the most honest way of presenting it.

To argue that experts should be left to run economic policy in a democratic society is like saying that foreign affairs should be left to the diplomats. The purpose of diplomacy is to negotiate between nations, to avoid war, and to lubricate the sometimes rough edges of national interests as they grate against each other. By making concessions, just about any war can be avoided. But a political judgement must be imposed to say, thus far and no further; this is wrong, the people will not stand for it; even war is preferable to the further surrender of national interest, or of justice to aggression. Similarly, the level of inflation, taxation or health spending people will stand for is a political choice which technocrats are singularly ill-equipped to judge, because most of them have very little contact with any but the most restricted circle.

CHAPTER SIX

APOLOGISTS OF MIGHT

AT THIS STAGE it bears noticing that historically a great deal of economic theory has been an authentication, or justification, of political choices. After the Second World War there was a surge of support for welfare policies which benefited left-of-centre political parties with the rationale provided for this by the economic theories of Keynes and his disciples. With the free-market reaction against this in the 1980s, orthodox economic theories were trotted out to press for such things as lower taxes, lower spending on the social services and low inflation.

There was something to be said for each set of policies at its particular moment in history. But economic laws, unlike scientific ones (although even these are increasingly seen in terms of probability) are not subject to iron rules of cause and effect, and economics is really the art of rationalizing and justifying particular political choices. Economics also involves analyzing a constantly innovating and changing economic environment: who could have foreseen the credit boom that followed financial deregulation and the house price boom of the late-1980s?

A quick glance at the history of economic theory bears this out. John Kenneth Galbraith argues persuasively that the wealthy throughout the ages have needed theoretical justification for their being better off than their fellow men – particularly in view of Christianity's essentially egalitarian message – and that economists have for the most part been employed to provide this.

A first foundation of economic thought was that with the introduction of real money, coins of fixed weight and purity in place of weighed amounts of metal, it was morally incumbent on governments not to debase the value of the metal, otherwise they would be guilty of nothing less than fraud. 'Who then would trust the prince who would diminish the weight or fineness of money bearing his own stamp?', asked the first theorist of monetarism, Nicholas Oresme. Indeed, some of the moral indignation of today's monetarists can be traced back to this fundamentally puritanical attitude towards money.

With industrialization, which in place of unchanging rural stagnation and poverty offered the possibility of escape and improved living standards – although for most this took a long time to materialize – further theories were required to justify the differences in living standards between factory owner and worker. Adam Smith, however, was justly accorded his later fame because he was no mere apologist for the factory owners but an independent, impartial observer in the early stages of Britain's Industrial Revolution.

An Inquiry into the Nature and Cause of the Wealth of Nations was published in 1776 and, although rambling, was a brilliant work. On the one hand it legitimized the force of self-interest as the prime mover in the creation of wealth:

> It is not from the benevolence of the butcher, the brewer, or the baker that we expect our dinner, but from their regard to their own interest. We address ourselves, not to their humanity but to their self-love . . . [The individual] is in this as in any other cases, led by an invisible hand to promote an end which was no part of his intention . . . I have never known much good done by those who affected to trade for the public good. It is an affectation, indeed, not very common among merchants, and very few words need to be employed in dissuading them from it.

He was also fairly hard-nosed in his attitude towards pay: this was merely the cost of bringing a worker into the workforce and keeping him in his job. Smith was a passionate advocate of freedom of internal and international trade, based on his observation that the specialization on which the Industrial Revolution depended would be impossible if they were not free. Every worker would otherwise have to concentrate inefficiently on duplicating separate products; instead, each should specialize in making what he could do best, purchasing from another what he could do best through the market.

For Smith the division of labour, and hence economic efficiency, was limited by the size of the market. The wider the market, the greater the division of labour, and the greater economic efficiency. As industry transcends crude specialization, and as markets grow to vast size, this clearly does not apply today – which has not stopped some ardent admirers of Smith still believing it. Here he can be faulted, rather unjustly as his powers were not divine, of not foreseeing the distant future.

Smith goes on brilliantly to attack mercantilism – the idea of protection to ensure a country's stock of precious metals. He asserts, almost incontrovertibly, that a nation's wealth should not be measured in its stock of silver and gold. Instead national wealth is:

> The annual labour of every nation [that] is the fund which originally supplies it with all the necessaries and conveniences of life . . . wealth is created by the skills, dexterity and judgement with which its labour is generally applied; and secondly, by the proportion between the number of those who are employed in useful labour and that of those who are not so employed.

He vigorously criticized two of the restrictive practices of his times – colonial preference and monopolistic practices. He observed caustically that:

> People of the same trade seldom meet together, even for merriment or diversion, than the conversation ends in a conspiracy against the public, or in some contrivance to raise prices. It is impossible . . . to prevent such meetings, by any law which either could be executed, or would be consistent with liberty and justice. But though the law cannot hinder people of the same trade from sometimes assembling together, it ought to do nothing to facilitate such assemblies, much less to render them necessary.

He loathed the professionally managed company in words which resonate down to the big corporations of today:

> Being the managers rather of other people's money than of their own, it cannot be well expected, that they should watch over it with the same anxious vigilance with which the partners of a private company frequently watch over their own . . . Negligence and profusion, therefore, must always prevail, more or less, in the management of the affairs of such a company.

Smith was truly a revolutionary, and the popularizer of the new individualists, anxious to justify their new fortunes.

The era of the professional economist now began. Jean-Baptiste Say, at the beginning of the nineteenth century, argued, with terrible consequences for later economics, that demand was inevitably exactly equal to supply: if goods are produced, the return in wages, profit, interest or rent is sufficient to buy that product. Even if money is saved, it will eventually find its way back into the system to balance the economy.

This theoretically attractive but nonsensical view was to be the orthodoxy for more than a century, and was later to return to haunt the late twentieth century. It was the father of the view that, since the economy automatically balances itself, nothing must be done by government to interfere with the market. The elegant equations of economics would balance themselves. It is easy to see how seductive this view was to nineteenth-century capitalists seeking to minimize the calls for their regulation: all intervention is damaging.

This argument ran directly counter to the economic evidence that from the earliest stages of the industrial revolution, cycles of boom and bust began to repeat themselves. At some moments there was too much demand in the system, at others too little; governments actually had to take action, otherwise the economy would overheat or suffer serious slump.

Another baleful economic influence was Thomas Malthus, who argued that the lower classes' insatiable appetite for procreation was the source of their misery. As they bred without control, the only thing that would keep their numbers down was hunger and starvation. So employers and governments were ill-advised to help the poor: all that would happen would be even more breeding, and more misery: it was *laissez-faire* with a vengeance. The existence of such grim theorists, to justify the most callous and brutal of capitalist attitudes towards those who helped to create their wealth through their work, was a remarkable feature of the Industrial Revolution. As Galbraith comments:

> Among the many who sought to put the poverty of the poor on the shoulders of the poor – or remove it from those of the more affluent – none did so more completely than Malthus.
>
> David Ricardo, the other economic guru of the age, argued that the amount of labour used to produce a product decided its worth. He went on to say that wages 'are the price which is necessary to enable the labourers, one with another, to subsist and to perpetuate the race, without increase or diminution'.

Thus, just as chillingly as Malthus, he argued against a benevolent employer or government improving the conditions of the workers, because this would merely increase their numbers.

However, by urging that the amount of work involved would decide the value of a good (which is actually not true: the value of a precious stone has nothing to do with the labour involved in its extraction) Galbraith was an unwitting forerunner of Marxism: for why should anyone not doing any work benefit from any profit over and above his 'Iron Law of Wages' and 'Labour Theory of Volume'? Other exponents of the classical school were three Austrian economists: Ludwig von Mises; Friedrik von Hayek; and Fritz Machlup; who, in understandable revulsion against the communists at the very gates of their country, took the view that all state intervention was a compromise with socialism.

*

HOWEVER, BY THE late nineteenth century, both in Britain and Germany, there was a growing concern among the better-off about the impact of industrial capitalism upon the huge new working class. In Germany, Bismarck decreed laws to provide for accident, sickness and old age. In Britain people like Robert Owen, George Bernard Shaw, the Webbs, the trade union movement as a whole and, above all, Lloyd George in 1911, pushed through schemes for unemployment insurance and sickness pay. None of this had anything to do with economic theory: it was the response of people disgusted with the plight of the working class – and in great measure it improved their lives without the dire consequences predicted by arid economists.

These straightforward measures to bolster the conditions of the working class were given a further boost, and their first theoretical justification, with the Depression of the 1930s. When this occurred it became impossible to argue, as the classical economists had, that supply and demand inevitably balanced each other. Perhaps they did in the end, but there were huge time lags, and meanwhile terrible economic recession in which workers lost their jobs and lived on the breadline. 'In the long term,' as John Maynard Keynes wryly observed, 'we are all dead.'

Keynes was the economist who discovered the obvious: he argued in essence that the modern industrial economy did not find its equilibrium with full employment; it could live with unemployment. There could be a shortage of demand, and government had an obligation to step in to prevent this – even if this involved excess spending. In fact his views were extremely cautious, and were elaborated in response to the virtual collapse of classical economic theory. Keynes argued more boldly in favour of government stimulation of the economy – something then happening only in Germany and Sweden – as a substitute for the collapse of domestic demand, through the reluctance of savers to invest their money in a productive economy.

In this he was surely right: the major problem in any slump is to find a reason for those with money to put it back into the system either by spending – which many are reluctant to do at a time of insecurity and uncertainty – through investing in enterprises which seem likely to generate profits, or, if interest rates are high enough, investing in bonds. Keynes argued that governments should subsidize the economy with public works programmes if private investment was sluggish, a standpoint which was widely denounced as socialist, in some way merging with left-wing calls for greater public spending on social security and state control of the economy. This was almost certainly the reason why America, at least, emerged from the recession under Roosevelt. Keynes, on the contrary, believed he was saving capitalism from its own destruction: he was a committed believer in the capitalist system. His right-wing critics believed he was bent on destroying it.

He turned out to be right in the 1930s; and in the 1950s, with the introduction of the welfare state in much of Europe and to a lesser extent in America, the pendulum appeared to move decisively his way. In fact, the 1950s in Britain could be described as economically the most successful period of modern times; although accompanied by the usual hiccups, labelled 'stop-go', the economy grew steadily while both unemployment and public spending were kept at historically low levels. Derailment was to occur when the Labour government of Harold Wilson added a major new twist to public spending at just the moment when it should, probably, have been brought under control. The result was diminishing productivity and higher inflation, which in turn resulted in a backlash, a reversion by Conservative governments in the 1980s to the economic orthodoxies of the century before.

THE PROPHET of the new order, an economist every bit as important as Keynes, was the Chicago economist Milton Friedman, who preached that, allowing for time lags, prices were entirely dependent on the supply of money in an economy. Control that, and you controlled everything. Friedman also clung to the reductionist view of the state and did not believe government intervention, either positive or negative, achieved anything. The theory was as mathematically ingenious as it was crude in human terms, and represented a reversion to the *laissez-faire* philosophies of Say, Malthus and Ricardo. Let business get on with it, let government keep out, the market will inevitably and miraculously work things out for the best – provided the supply of money is controlled.

It is, of course, a truism, that if there is less money in the economy, there will be lower inflation; but this completely obscures the more fundamental problems in an economy, such as the power of certain groups to secure a greater share of the available money – employers and unions alike. Moreover, monetarism was incredibly crude as an instrument, permitting governments to hand over power to financial managers and central banks. Finally it was overwhelmed by the inability of the market – in particular in exchange-control-free economies – to control the money supply, in an age of international financial flows and booming credit.

By the late 1980s, Friedmanite monetarism had been rendered obsolete by the very force it had set free – financial liberalization. Moreover, far from being a solution to all ills, the creed soon became a kind of abdication of responsibility, abandoned by even its most ardent practitioners, such as Britain's Mrs Thatcher in about 1987. Galbraith has written an eloquent passage on the subject in *The Culture of Contentment*:

> No tax increases would be necessary nor any curtailment of public expenditure. Nor would there be any enlargement of government function; all monetarist policy could be accomplished by the central bank, in the United States the Federal Reserve System, with only a negligible staff.
>
> For some, monetary policy had (and has) another, even greater, appeal, which was curiously, even unforgivably, overlooked among economists: it is not socially neutral. It operates against inflation by raising interest rates, which, in turn, inhibit bank lending and resulting deposit – that is, money – creation. High interest rates are wholly agreeable to people and institutions that have money to lend, and these normally have more money than those who have no money to lend or, with many exceptions, those who borrow money. An

unduly evident truth, as sufficiently emphasized already. In so favoring the individually and institutionally affluent, a restrictive monetary policy is in sharp contrast with a restrictive fiscal policy, which, relying as it does on increased personal and corporate income taxes, adversely affects the rich.

Conservatives in the industrial countries, especially in Britain and the United States, have given strong support to monetary policy. Their instinct in this matter has been far better than that of the economists, who, along with the public at large, have assumed its social neutrality. The applause for Professor Friedman from the conservative affluent, which has been great, has been far from unearned.

As the 1970s passed, inflation persisted. High taxes, lower public expenditures, direct intervention on wages and prices, were all ruled out as remedies. As sufficiently observed, only monetary policy remained. So in the latter part of the decade, by the ostensibly liberal administration of President Jimmy Carter in the United States and the avowedly conservative government of Prime Minister Margaret Thatcher in Britain, strong monetarist action was initiated. The Keynesian Revolution was folded in. In the history of economics the age of John Maynard Keynes gave way to the age of Milton Friedman.

Supply-side economics, judged by results, should be entirely discredited today. Federal spending grew from 21 per cent of national income in 1980 to around 23.5 per cent in 1990. The federal budget deficit grew from 1.8 per cent to 3.6 per cent. Government borrowing caused net national savings to be halved, from 7 per cent to 3.5 per cent of GNP over the period. Government spending rose during the Reagan administration, although the median marginal tax rate fell from 24 per cent to 15 per cent. It is reckoned that America's capital stock was some 7 per cent below what it would have been without supply-side economics, according to a report prepared by the Federal Reserve Bank of New York. In 1990, America's capacity to produce goods and services was some 3 per cent lower ($165 billion) what it would have been without supply-side economics. In almost every sphere the impact of supply-side economics was the reverse of that intended.

The most immediately damaging aspect of all this was, in Galbraith's view, the creation of an underclass with little stake in the economy. In the past, he argues, the well-off were in the minority and were constantly uneasy about the plight of the majority, whom they feared might turn against them. Now the very wealthy are still in the minority, but the great majority beneath them are comfortably off and share a common interest in such things as low taxes, high interest rates on invested income and so on. The great majority have no interest in the fate of the class beneath them, from which they perceive no threat, believing they are secure precisely because they are the majority.

The pattern then is of a new globalization of capitalism that is making a mockery of the decisions of elected governments, save in the very biggest units – the United States, Japan, the European Union – whose views can make themselves felt by virtue of their size. Capitalism is becoming not just remote and non-responsible to ordinary people, but to whole nations. It is escaping the bounds of control and regulation, leaping across frontiers with equanimity. In this unregulated world, the new global jungle, Hobbes's state of nature has returned.

Large industrial plants are closed and moved if conditions in the host country become unsatisfactory; News International buys newspapers and influences foreign governments; chocolate factories launch bids for rival companies in order to close them down; banks pour money into non-performing loans, bankrupting whole countries and hence starving them of funds; currency speculators destroy the policies of democratically elected governments overnight. If this brave new world seems brutal and anarchic, that is because it is, and increasingly so. As with the great issue of international security after the Cold War, the framework for regulating the new international economic order is not in place. Fortunately, there is much that can be done, a subject which will be returned to in the last section of the book.

CHAPTER SEVEN

THE NEW PRINCES

THERE IS ANOTHER major factor that is alienating the greatest wealth-creating machine in human history, the free-enterprise system, from its roots, from the very people it exists to serve: and that is the evolving structure of the modern corporation. The changeover, starting in the eighteenth century, from the one-man entrepreneurial business – which still occasionally re-emerges – to the limited liability company, managed by professional managers on behalf of shareholders, marked a turning point. Western business has tended to raise capital largely from the stock market (and a little from the banks), with short-term financial results as the most important factor. In practice, unless there are a few dominant stockholders, most major businesses have been run by the management as self-perpetuating oligarchies.

Within these oligarchies there have been tremendous battles for territory: for example, the old domination of the industrial managers often gave way to that of the marketing men, and then to that of the financial and legal departments, as management buy-outs and asset-stripping became the fashion. Almost certainly, this has been an unhealthy trend. Both in America and Europe, the prime purpose of much corporate raiding has been to strip assets off an undervalued company, or in some cases to crush a competitor, rather than to improve performance, and the main response has been to make a firm as unattractive – as unprofitable – as possible to a raider. None of this has anything to do with a company's real performance.

The other main 'players' – the employee and the consumer – remain very much the underclass: in very few Western companies do the workers have any form of management participation, and their underlying strength lies in threatening some form of union militancy. Consumer rights have vastly increased in recent years, particularly in America, which has a healthy tradition of anti-trust legislation. Yet their real bargaining power remains light, particularly in certain sectors dominated by cartels.

In fact, the average Western company is an autocratic, self-perpetuating institution, which is fine, indeed inevitable, for small firms competing vigorously, but more disturbing for giant conglomerates in the global market-place. In their secretive management culture, their often immensely bureaucratic way of doing things, the penchant for promotion by protégé, their anonymity, their *de haut en bas* seniority systems (nowadays often disguised behind a common corporate culture which refers to all employees by their first names and permits them to eat in the same canteens), the giant international company of today in fact resembles nothing so much as its defeated communist adversary.

Of course, there is one massive difference: the capitalist giant is subject to the disciplines of the marketplace. If his products don't sell, he goes under, whereas a communist enterprise had a captive market. The difference is more apparent than real: when one looks at any of the strategies adopted by big firms – cutting up markets between them, cartelism, undercutting small competitors, then raising prices when the market is secured – many resort to tactics that are plainly anti-competitive, and can get away with it just because they are so large. In the 'state of nature', as in the jungle, it is size and strength that count for survival rather than the production of inherently better or more competitive products. Of course, the difference still counts enormously: a truly uncompetitive player, as were most of the major industries of the Soviet Union, will go under in the global marketplace. But that is as far as responsibility to anyone stretches.

This should not be seen as too condemnatory: virtually any autocracy, from feudalism to a military regime, to communism, is usually led by well-meaning oligarchs and responsible elders who believe they are doing the best for the people beneath them: large capitalist corporations are no exception. Some degree of authority, as stressed at the beginning of this book, is necessary. This chapter seeks to examine these issues.

THE MODERN corporation is distinguished by its size. In Japan the concentration of capitalism into a handful of giant *keiretsu* – cartels – is becoming increasingly observed by the outside world: vast traditional concerns like Mitsui and Mitsubishi, have been joined by a number of new companies – Sony, Sharp, Canon and so on – expressly groomed for their role by government, with their own banking, marketing and trading groups. These big corporations run a staggering third of the Japanese economy, and dominate another third through their hold on, for instance, much smaller supply firms and retail outlets. Through their privileged access to finance, as well as the government support they enjoy, the *keiretsu* are today being singled out by Western governments for criticism as monopolistic, cartelistic and anti-competitive.

Yet on a smaller scale Western companies are also sinners. In West Germany, the relationship between banking and the big industrial groups, although less close, gives cause for concern, as does the concentration of industry. In France the ties between major industries, a traditionally *dirigiste* central government and banking are worrying. In Britain there is more of a commitment to a free market and a distinction between banking and industry, as well as a much more developed stock market and financial markets in the City. However, in certain areas such as supermarket prices and, above all, in the over-concentrated banking sector, it is hard not to believe that cartelism and price-fixing operate, albeit unofficially, and never on the wrong side of the law.

In America, home of free enterprise, the economic concentration and clout of the major corporations may come as a surprise. In the 1930s it was established that the 200 largest non-banking corporations possessed about one-half of all non-banking corporate wealth, or a quarter of total national wealth. It is now reckoned that the largest 500 non-banking firms in the

United States are responsible for sixty per cent of all production there.

An ideal world of thrusting middle-sized firms conjured up by free enterprise enthusiasts sadly does not exist. Cartelism, price-fixing, big firms using their clout in the market to secure their interests – these are the main features of markets around the world. Of course there also exists a large medium-sized sector, and many hundreds of thousands of small firms alongside the giants. But the latter usually get their own way when they want.

Size confers a tremendous advantage. The classical economies of scale are well known. In addition, in terms of corporate strategy, size confers power. To take two basic examples: a major supermarket chain that decides to slash its prices can do so for quite a while without running into trouble because of its stock of capital and creditworthiness; a smaller competitor, without these advantages, can be forced out of business. Or again, a major firm faced with troublesome competition from a smaller one, can expand its range of products in a manner that the smaller one cannot, thereby becoming more attractive to customers at a stroke.

A typical case was that of the battle between Honda and the Japanese motor-cycle company Yamaha. Honda dominated the Japanese motor-cycle market in the late 1950s through the classic Japanese strategy of borrowing massively from the banks in an effort to undercut its competitors' market share. The leader in the field at the time was Tohatsu, a conservatively-managed group with double Honda's after-tax profits and a debt-to-equity ratio about five times lower. Because of Honda's aggressive strategy, within four years Tohatsu's market share fell from 22 per cent to 4 per cent, while Honda's soared from 20 per cent to 44 per cent. Tohatsu was all but defeated and made huge losses. By February 1964, it had gone bankrupt.

In 1967 Honda decided to enter the automobile market at a time when the market itself was terrified of the new wave of international competition; finance, technical capability and the best managers were directed towards the new venture. Yamaha, a relatively new entrant into the motor-cycle field, saw its chance to stage an ambush while Honda's attention was elsewhere; Yamaha's President Koike claimed that: 'At Honda sales attention is focused on four-wheel vehicles. Most of their best people in motor-cycles have been transferred. Compared to them, our specialty at Yamaha is mainly motor-cycle production . . . If only we had enough capacity we could beat Honda.'

Honda's share of the market had fallen from 65 per cent in the late 1960s to just 40 per cent in 1981; Yamaha had increased its sales from ten per cent to 35 per cent over the same period. In offering new models, Yamaha had also begun to pull ahead of Honda. In 1981, Yamaha announced plans to build a factory that would allow it to double its production of motor-cycles. Koike declared triumphantly: 'The difference between us and Honda is in our ability to supply. As primarily a motor-cycle producer, you cannot expect us to remain in our present number two position forever . . . In one year we will be the domestic leader. And in two years, we will be number one in the world.'

The following year Honda's President Kawashima told his shareholders without delicacy, 'Yamaha has not only stepped on the tail of a tiger, it has ground it into the earth. We will crush Yamaha!' The two methods adopted were massive price cuts of around a third on their motor-cycles, and the introduction of a huge new range of models – more than eighty, while Yamaha could only produce thirty-four – in the space of eighteen months: both companies had only produced around sixty models altogether before that. Yamaha sales collapsed by around half; the company soon had a year's sales of motor-cycles on the stocks; it struggled furiously to stay afloat, not to expand as Honda had done, and its debt to equity ratio shot up from three to one to seven to one in 1983.

In January of that year, Koike surrendered: 'We cannot match Honda's product development and sales strength . . . I would like to end the Honda–Yamaha war . . . From now on I want to move cautiously and ensure Yamaha's relative position (as second to Honda).' He was replaced, dividends were slashed, employees dismissed and production plummeted from a projected four million units at the height of Yamaha's ambitions to just 1.5 million. Desperately, the new Yamaha management begged for mercy, as Honda ruthlessly continued to grow by producing thirty-nine new models compared with Yamaha's twenty-three: 'Since Yamaha is considered responsible for the present market situation, I would first like to study our position and develop a more co-operative stance towards other companies . . . Of course, there will still be competition . . . but I intend it to be based on mutual recognition of our relative positions.'

The main reason for Yamaha's humiliation had been that Honda had carefully waited until its rival was at its most exposed – having invested heavily in a new plant that was not yet producing – before striking. Japanese companies were geared not just to producing goods but to fighting each other in almost a military fashion. Yamaha had dared to challenge the natural hierarchy of the motor-cycle industry and was massacred by the bigger company. That is one of the keys to Japanese efficiency – intense competition beneath the overall constraints of government planning.

A NON-JAPANESE example of big companies crushing competition was the price war raging in Britain's quality newspaper market. Rupert Murdoch's decision in 1994 to slash the cover price of *The Times* – with no change in quality – possibly funded by his other operations caught his competitors on the hop. The slightly less liquid *Telegraph* group was forced to follow suit, while the much smaller *Independent* teetered on the verge of drowning, kept afloat by a Mirror Group lifeline.

Major companies are divided into three types – single-product, conglomerate and diversified. The first speaks for itself; the second, after the recent merger mania sweeping America and Europe, is increasingly common; a collection of random companies brought together to maximize the profit of the controlling group. A diversified company is one consisting of closely interrelated industries which fertilize each other through, for example, common research and development or the manufacture of common components. That is the pattern in Japan, and it appears to be gaining ground in the West.

A further feature of the large corporation is its lack of a competitive character – except towards those aspiring to take its place. The marketplace, far from consisting of a host of furiously competing enterprises, is itself characterized by big companies that by mutual understanding do not stray on to each other's turf, preferring negotiated deals on territory and prices to wars that may be injurious to both: better to conspire against the customer with higher agreed prices than battle each other to lower them on his behalf. Of course, this is not always the case: wars do break out (for example, the British newspaper war), aggressive smaller companies break through to the big league; but it is the standard position.

The modern big corporation is not responsible to anyone but itself. There are four possible sources of accountability for the capitalist organization: the owners – those who put up the capital for a venture; the customers, to whom the product must appeal or the company will go bankrupt; the workforce – those who actually make the product; or the management. In practice, the only one that counts is the last.

According to classical economic theory, the managers were primarily responsible to the owners – the shareholders – and their purpose was to maximize profits. But a famous study by Adolf Berle and Gardiner Means, *The Modern Corporation and Private Property*, established the point, as far back as 1932, that the shareholders had very little influence in most major companies. The management for the most part was responsible for informing the board of directors, which supposedly represented the shareholders. The latter, who stood at one remove from the affairs of the company on the stock market, tended to be uninterested in the daily management of the firm provided the share price went up and dividends were maximized. The stockbroker, acting for the shareholder, would investigate companies to assess their viability, but that was often the limit of accountability. Annual general meetings of shareholders were usually pure formalities.

This has been the position in the United States and Britain, countries with highly developed capital markets. In Japan, and to a lesser extent Germany, the prime suppliers of capital were the banks, rather than shareholders; in addition, government, which stood behind the banks, had a major say. Kenichi Ohmae, Japan's best known management strategist, outlines this quite frankly:

> In the immediate postwar era, capital was very short. The Japanese people were and are assiduous savers, but the future of most corporations was then so uncertain that they lacked the confidence to invest their savings in private enterprise. Instead, they put it into the banks, which enjoyed infallible credibility. It was through the banks that corporations with dynamic growth plans borrowed money. Freed from the need to justify complex growth plans to individual stockholders or prospective investors and from the need to worry about keeping the stock price high, corporate executives could devote all their energies to business: people, production and products. They were convinced that by doing a superb job on these three P's they would earn the fourth P – profit – needed to repay the debt. And they were right. Had they been obliged to worry about making their financial performance look better in order to get the financing, they would have fallen into the vicious cycle of cosmetic financial management, opting for short-term profit maximization and neglecting long-term investment.
>
> Again, sequencing was critical. Thanks to the integrative Japanese management style and governmental system, these corporations were not forced to perform before they were ready.
>
> Another big helping hand in corporate finance came from the Japanese government's foreign capital phobia. The Ministry of Finance (MOF) and MITI, for example, in their determination to keep foreign capital from acquiring massive chunks of Japanese corporate stocks on the Tokyo Stock Exchange, did their best to encourage institutional stockholding. Although this stance is now gradually being relaxed, nearly seventy per cent of Japanese corporate shares are still

> institutionally held. This helped Japanese companies tremendously, not only because stock prices were less affected by the transactions of individual stockholders but also because these institutional owners were, like the banks, much more understanding of the long-term strategies of the companies in which they invested. And mutual holdings within a group of companies made it impossible to exercise short-term buying and selling options.

Thus, the distribution of power is slightly different in Japan. The banks and institutional investors do indeed have a more powerful role than the thousands of individual investors who make up the owners and capital providers of major companies in Britain and America, because they are large commercial interests with more clout. However, the banks, while providing the bulk of the money, do not actually own the company, and as Japanese industry evolved, with the major companies accumulating large capital reserves of their own, they became less dependent on the banks. Indeed, with so little of the company's capital put up by shareholders, the management owned the company in all but name.

By the 1980s, the fact of management control of major corporations had become so blatant that, in the United States, a war took place for control of the major companies. On the one hand corporate raiders moved in to buy out passive shareholders, in a bid to seize control of companies; on the other, management fought back through buyouts to secure their position. Both did so by borrowing large sums of money against the corporations themselves, mainly through the issuing of 'junk bonds', themselves of dubious reliability.

In each case huge debts were loaded on to the firm: in some cases management did so deliberately in order to make the firm less attractive to the predator. This channelled funds away from the firm's real objective – developing and selling products in the marketplace. In order to meet these huge debts, the profitable parts of the business were often the first to be sold off. Finally, many of the investors in the junk bonds went bust, while large profits were made by the various legal and financial advisers.

The whole exercise contributed to productive enterprise and competition in some cases, but it did untold damage to the corporations concerned in others. The corporate raiders, left in charge of successfully acquired large companies, tended to sell off parts of the business to maintain their profits. Having no intrinsic loyalty to the company itself, they tended to judge the acquisition purely by short-term financial results, accentuating the worst features of the stock market. The successful management buyers confirmed their role in real control of their own companies and in many cases improved efficiency. But their role was far from disinterested.

In 1980 it was estimated that the chief executives of the biggest 300 American companies had incomes some thirty times as great as those of average manufacturing workers; in 1990 the figure was ninety-three times as big! A survey by Britain's conservative *Sunday Telegraph* in 1993 found that there was no correlation between mushrooming levels of pay for top management, bolstered by lucrative share option schemes and the performance of the company. The survey, undertaken by Professor Graef Crystal, concluded that there was no relationship between company size and performance and boardroom pay, and that the top five bosses in Britain were overpaid by some £7 million between them.

Britain's highest paid executive then was Mr Robert Bauman, chief executive of SmithKline Beecham, who took home nearly £2.8 million in pay and options, although his company's size was a long way short of being the biggest in Britain and its performance, while impressive, was by no means exceptional. Crystal calculated that Bauman's real worth was little more than £500,000. Britain's second highest paid executive, Greg Hutchings of Tomkins, who was paid more than £2.6 million, according to Crystal, was only worth a little less than £1 million to his company. Glaxo's Sir Paul Girolami was paid a touch over £2 million, but should have been paid a little under £700,000.

One of Britain's most successful industrialists, former BTR chairman, Sir Owen Green, commented acidly of the highest paid businessmen, receiving some thirty-eight times more pay than average workers:

> I wonder how many of them honestly believe they are worth that money. For these people are neither showbusiness stars nor entrepreneurs. The true creators of wealth are entitled to reward for their labour . . . It suggests an almost papal separation of the leader from his flock. This distancing means executives lose touch with the people who actually do the work. It is not that the executives are objects of envy, though they may be. What they have lost is respect.

The issue of overpaid management in essentially management-run companies is a potentially explosive one.

IT FOLLOWS THAT the question of whether management is accountable to the workforce can be dismissed quickly. In virtually no enterprise is management other than authoritarian towards the workforce, except in small family enterprises. Sometimes management can be benevolent and paternal, and the more enlightened and self-interested are. Ohmae argues this persuasively:

> If we analyse the characteristics of excellent companies in Japan or elsewhere, we find that what distinguishes them is that they are human. These companies have entered what I call the new era of activated enterprise. The strategy and the organization of such a company are in harmony. Everything is geared to execution. That is how these companies achieve excellent results.
>
> In short, the most successful large corporations today, regardless of nationality or industry, display a number of common characteristics. They offer job security, tenure-based promotion, and internal development of people instead of global recruiting campaigns. They provide endless opportunities for employee participation. They regard their people as members, not mere employees. They promote a common value system. Knowing the critical importance of the corporation's long-term well-being, they display a real commitment to the businesses they are in instead of pursuing

> strictly financial objectives with only the stockholders in mind.
>
> Again, Toyota provides a good example. Toyota's suggestion box is certainly not unique to Japan. Back in the early 1950s, the company's 45,000 employees turned in only a few hundred suggestions annually. Today, Toyota gets 900,000 proposals – twenty per employee on the average – per year, worth $230 million a year in savings. Even for a company the size of Toyota, that's not an insignificant sum.

But the purpose is to secure maximum profits and loyalty to the firm: the workers are in no sense owners of the firm. Such rights as they enjoy are handed down by law, not by companies – protection against unfair dismissal, compulsory redundancy payments and so on. Promotion, consultation and pay are entirely within the firm's discretion: the modern company worker enjoys no greater rights than a paid agricultural labourer on a large estate hundreds of years ago. The system is entirely hierarchical and authoritarian. Promotion can take place because of superior ability, or because a worker gets on with his boss: the mentor–protégé relationship is perhaps the most common in the corporate hierarchy.

With recent industrial relations legislation in Britain, coupled with a decline in the power and membership of trade unions worldwide, the control by management has, if anything, increased. Not that the unions were ever much of a check, or a particularly benevolent one: in a situation where workers had no rights at all, they would band together to form an adversarial relationship with management, based on their power to hurt the company through the withdrawal of labour.

This, of course, was damaging to the company and not exercised with particularly good sense; in many cases unions became politicized, dominated by extremists and themselves undemocratic. But it was entirely natural that unions should form when workers were treated so poorly by management; unfortunately, there are few signs that it has learnt this lesson, and there is a danger that the recent period of union retrenchment is being used to extract more for less from the workforce, leading possibly to greater social unrest and industrial militancy in the future.

FINALLY, THERE is the question of management accountability to the greatest arbiter of them all, the marketplace, the customer. This, above all else, is cited as the main difference between a large capitalist corporation and a large communist one. The communist ones were accountable to government to meet ambitious production targets, with each being allocated resources by central planning.

In practice, it has been hard for a communist corporation to judge whether targets are being met or to estimate the right distribution of resources; shortages, bottlenecks, corruption and mismanagement develop as mistakes are made. In addition, without the discipline of balancing one's cash flow week by week, a communist corporation can lapse into self-satisfied sluggishness, aware that mismanagement makes little difference to its surival. The contrast between a medium-sized private enterprise and a communist bureaucracy could hardly be more complete.

But a giant private corporation is not so different from its communist equivalent. To begin with it can manipulate the marketplace, as already discussed, so that the benefits of free competition and the disciplines of producing to satisfy a customer may be absent. Further, if a corporation in fact has a captive market – as many major producers of particular goods have – it need not concentrate its attention on diversification, improving or selling its products.

In fact, a corporation's managers can devote themselves increasingly to the business of office politics, power struggles within the organization and maximizing their own pay and perks – just as happened inside the giant communist bureaucracies. Bureaucratic struggles, moreover, are the same in any big corporation, capitalist or communist: they are struggles for control of the largest number of people in the organization, competition for the key jobs and often an attempt to extend empires. The control of men is the key – not any particular ability to produce a product which the marketplace wants. To return to a point made at the beginning of this book, the communist bureaucracies actually modelled themselves on the giant capitalist enterprises, with their strict division of labour and their social hierarchy, which themselves were probably loosely based on a military model.

The prime analyst of the modern organization was Max Weber, who argued that bureaucracy was the dominant form of organization in the twentieth century, whether in a communist or capitalist enterprise. Weber's analysis has never been convincingly challenged, although he was undoubtedly too pessimistic in the grimness of his vision of bureaucracy which reduced men to automatons, and he failed to foresee the greater flexibility of some late-twentieth-century forms of organization, particularly those making use of new technology.

Bureaucracy was dominant, Weber believed, because of its 'purely technical superiority over other forms of organisation'. He was no enthusiast for this: he mourned the loss of the individual freedom of action it entailed and described bureaucracy as an 'iron cage'. He went on to define the fifteen commandments that are common to bureaucratic organizations. First, they are based on specialization. 'Task discontinuity is achieved by functional specialization. Tasks are specific, distinct and done by different formal categories of personnel who specialize in these tasks and not in others. These official tasks would be organized on a continuous regulated basis in order to ensure the smooth flow of work between the discontinuous elements in its organization.'

This specialization required someone to organize and control the various different divisions. So it becomes necessary, second, for action to be authorized within the organization. Third, this leads inevitably to the establishment of hierarchy: someone has to do the authorizing, and be obeyed. Within the organization, people's responsibilities must be defined; so, fourth, relationships must be contractualized.

Fifth, people's positions are determined by their experience and credentials. Sixth, the existence of a structure means that individuals have to climb it, so there is a trend towards careerization. Seventh, to denote one's status, perks and pay are different, so organizations tend to get stratified. Eighth, the organization is clearly divided between superiors and subordinates. Ninth, because of the size of the organization, formal rules have to be established.

To enforce these rules, tenth, there is a tendency towards standardization. Eleventh, in most organizations there is also a tendency towards centralization. Twelfth, action taken on behalf of the organization must be appropriately legitimized. Thirteenth, power belongs to the office, not to the holder: this Weber calls the officialization of organizational action. Fourteenth, because of the same feature, action by the organization tends to become impersonal. Fifteenth, the organization must be run along disciplinary lines.

If all this sounds a little abstract, in fact most or all of these features are visibly present in any bureaucracy, from that of a large corporation, an army, a school to a government department. Weber was over-pessimistic: the best organizations today are flexible, the most rigid and rule-bound less efficient (although this does not apply in every case, particularly in basic assembly operations, for example). Many new companies now structure themselves by handing out franchises, performance-related bonuses and offer independence and freedom of action to motivate individuals. Yet the bulk of big organizations cannot run themselves without these bureaucratic principles, or they fear chaos would ensue.

This poses huge problems for free-market theorists. Friedrich Hayek, the prophet of capitalist organization, bitterly opposed what he took to be the communist bureaucratic model. For him the market was necessarily the best source of 'order' because it brought together the disconnected motives of millions of disconnected individuals – something no planner, he believed, could ever forecast. However, contradictorily, he regarded corporate bureaucracies as acceptable impositions of order and planning because their objective was to secure profit from the market. Adam Smith would surely have shuddered.

Hayek seemed to ignore the point that a huge degree of planning and assumptions about the market are necessary for any large private corporation – which is just as eager as the state to get its own way. Moreover, most private organizations seek to limit the freedom of their employees in much the same way that the state does.

Ordinary workers serve a company for a combination of reasons: pay, recognition, and satisfaction, sometimes loyalty – or even coercion. In a pure free market workers do not need to stay with a company that treats them badly. In practice, in many areas there may be no alternative but to abide with an existing employer, and not just for geographical reasons: many people, for example, professionals, may be in fields where there are only a handful of employers, and if they wish to practice their chosen profession, there may be no other option but to stay with their firm. Again, the insecurity and upheaval involved in changing jobs is often enough to make workers put up with even a difficult employer: psychologically, change is more difficult for most people, particularly as they grow older, than smoothly functioning free markets allow for.

Unskilled or semi-skilled employment may offer a larger variety of opportunities for mobility than jobs in other fields. A secretary or a building worker may, in reasonable market conditions, find another job fairly easily; not so someone in advertising, or a lawyer seeking a partnership, or someone doing a specialized job particular to one industry. Here there is an element of coercion involved; and many employers will not forgive employees who desert them for another firm, who find themselves dissatisfied and then seek to return. Long-accumulated perks and pay schemes may be at stake. In a recession, the difficulty of finding another job may compel a worker to stay with a firm he dislikes.

Loyalty is a better stimulus to stay in a job, but it must be observed to be returned. Pay, while the common reason for holding a worker, or for his changing jobs, is far from being the only stimulus to mobility of labour, and it presupposes a perfect economy where there are plenty of other similar jobs going. In fact, this is the exception rather than the rule: alternative jobs may be hard to get and people usually think very hard about changing them.

Stewart Clegg pinpoints the difficulty free-market theorists have with the giant corporation that actually dominates the capitalist business world:

> In the vast majority of the advanced industrial societies economic transactions take place either in or between organizations. The greatest volume in monetary terms are controlled by the very small number of very large organizations. Given this then the existence of organizations rather than markets as the major *loci* of economic action is a major embarrassment for the economics of neoclassicism. For one thing, where economic action occurs in organizations then the 'freedom' of the market as a solution to malfeasance or mistrust disappears. While one can easily transfer one's action from one horse-trader to another in a country fair or bazaar, it is somewhat more complex (particularly under the labour market conditions of deregulation favoured by neoclassical economists) as easily to reorder one's employment relations or to choose not to buy some essential from some monopoly or oligopoly supplier.

If a major corporation is accountable in only a limited way to the marketplace, barely at all to the shareholders, and not at all to its workforce, who is it accountable to? The answer is to those who control the firm: senior management.

As corporations have evolved over the century, they have developed a set of values and characteristics that set them quite apart from the rest of society; as the giant corporation is as dominant a feature of the contemporary social and economic landscape, it is worth analysing these. I would expand Weber's list of fifteen characteristics of the bureaucratic organization by adding a further eight more modern ones.

First, major corporations now lay a premium, Japanese-style, on collective decision-making. Few managements are bold enough to rely on the single entrepreneurial or management genius. Rather, proposals are made by the driving executives in any company – usually in their forties and early fifties, and duly ratified by the dozen or so senior executives, usually in their late fifties or sixties.

This system has the virtue of diluting responsibility: if a mistake is made, it is everyone's mistake, and a company cannot fire all its senior executives; if the right decision is made, all share the credit and a particular manager does not get too big for his boots. The nominal principle, of course, is that 'two heads are better than one'. The danger of this system is that the need for consensus makes decision-making painfully slow, and can result in corporate paralysis. Most big corporations, far from being dynamic, are extremely cautious.

A second feature of the modern corporation is that they have their own internal logic and 'ideology'. Enormous emphasis is attached to sometimes quite trivial things because companies pride themselves on the professionalism of that particular skill, often obscuring much more important matters. Indeed, people's ascent in the corporate hierarchy often depends on the extent to which they can spot the internal arguments that really matter to their superiors and adopt the 'politically correct' positions on them. In another company the same essentials of dogma might not matter at all, but entirely different ones would.

A third feature of the modern corporation is its system of self-selecting hierarchical promotion. Few modern companies are meritocratic in the sense that pure ability will lead to promotion: it is important to have the best possible qualification on joining the company; and, once employed, a high-flyer will have to identify himself (or herself) with an up-and-coming mentor, preferably one of the firm's senior managers.

The bright young thing will be put through years of experience, sometimes in quite lowly jobs, being rotated from one part of the organization to another, to get to know the business, before being promoted; but he (or she) will have been identified from the beginning, and provided he does not make too many mistakes and always proffers the appropriate degree of respect to the company, his chance will come.

In his climb he will always have to show deference to his

bosses and organization – coupled with a little bit of acceptable cheek, to show he is human after all. It is not hard to see that this system reinforces the tendency of corporation bureaucracies to play safe, to deviate only marginally from orthodoxy, and by the time a high flyer's time has come, he will be unlikely to have much reformist zeal or critical and original thought left in him.

A fourth feature of the modern corporation is its emphasis on secrecy and loyalty. This is usually unashamedly self-serving: human nature decrees that ambitious and forceful people, particularly if talented, while away their spare time filling in job applications to other firms. But the loyal core of management that make up the backbone of a firm convince themselves that this is not so. If evidence is found of a particular person seeking another job or doing down his company or colleagues to an outsider, the punishment can be quite severe. As a result, and to encourage others not to stray, a loss of corporate status may occur, even sometimes loss of the job itself.

A fifth feature of the modern corporation is its cult of anonymity. Top management are rarely flamboyant or interesting personalities in their own right: the tendency has been to subordinate their will to that of the company while pursuing – or appearing to pursue – its interests with a greater determination than their peers. A perfectly serious handbook for senior management advises anyone being promoted to check that he is moving to a department about to produce good results; he will receive the undeserved credit for them; otherwise, the book advises, he should decline the promotion, or he will receive the undeserved blame.

Giant companies, like any bureaucracy, are jealous and suspicious of personalities and success, except on behalf of the company: the fear is that a particular person might have his own interests, rather than the company's, at heart, or that he may be publicizing himself in order to secure employment elsewhere. If an employee does not have a reputation in the outside world, it is less likely that he will be headhunted to another company and he or she will be dependent on, and therefore more controllable by, the company.

The ideal manager is a man well known within his own corporation, but unknown in the outside world. In addition, a person who is too individualist or too independent in thought tends to challenge company orthodoxy: where decisions are usually made by consensus or committee, an individualist may make his peers feel uneasy. In the tired Japanese phrase, 'the nail that sticks out must be hammered down'.

A sixth feature of modern corporations is their obsession with pay, perks and status. In the closed world of a corporate hierarchy, managers often seem to forget that a world exists outside their own. One major multinational has a pay grid containing more than a hundred grades, with three possible levels of remuneration within each grade; it resembles nothing so much as a school hierarchy of promotion by merits and demerits. The bureaucracy involved in promoting a man was staggering.

In most large modern companies, there is scrupulous attention given to such matters as the sizes of offices and indeed the desks in them and the proximity to the boss's office. Whether or not an employee has a secretary, a company car, an expenses-paid holiday and is invited to weekends in a country house hotel with management are also important matters of status.

Another key badge of status is access. The modern company generally makes much of the boss's accessibility to all, and in the better-run companies the boss will not just know the names of many of his employees, but will give them a friendly nod and smile as he passes. In the most badly run companies, the boss reserves his smiles for those he considers most senior or most worthy and ignores or frowns at the rest. Yet in all firms, any junior who makes too many demands on the time of his boss, or who importunes him at an inappropriate time, or fails to observe the courtesies, is unlikely to go far.

A seventh major feature of the modern corporation – a relatively recent innovation – is the growing tendency to what might be called 'Victorian values', if not outright priggishness and puritanism. A large variety of things, even a culture, are present here. Most companies invariably demand that their employees are well-dressed – which in dealing with outside customers is wholly reasonable; they prefer members of staff to be married; they frown on philandering or homosexuality – particularly between members of the staff; and they increasingly dislike smoking and frown upon drinking – both of which are actually banned in many premises and canteens.

Jollity of the right kind is permitted, but not over-boisterousness, or poking fun at the company itself – not within earshot of a manager, anyway. Understandably, a premium is placed on punctuality, cheerfulness, willingness to do the job, long hours and so on, regardless of the ability or otherwise of the individual concerned. The modern corporation thus takes itself very seriously indeed and is quite uninhibited about placing restrictions on adult lifestyles which, if the state attempted them, would be denounced as a serious infringement of individual liberties.

Finally, an eighth feature – again a fairly recent innovation – of the modern corporation is its increasingly self-conscious commitment to a kind of internal egalitarianism (this probably originated in Japan). Thus all members of staff have to wear ID cards, even easily identifiable bosses and they frequent the same canteens. They are on first-name terms – managers and workers alike; they refer to each other as colleagues rather than bosses or subordinates; and – perhaps the most recent innovation of all – they increasingly share 'open plan' offices. It is remarkable how often companies resort to crude social engineering, even though they would secure best results by leaving people to their foibles provided they deliver the goods.

THE TOTALITARIAN temptation to make people conform to a model is as much a capitalist corporate vice as a communist one. The laudable aim of the open-plan office was probably to make everyone feel more equal, and allow a freer exchange of opinions and information across the table, when in fact it just made them feel more uncomfortable and inhibited. This commitment to equality is, of course, entirely bogus, and is occurring at a time of unprecedented inequality over the thing that matters most to employees – pay. Everyone in a company knows who the boss is, and the fact that he is paid vastly more than themselves, and that they have to watch what they say in his presence. But equality is the trendy corporate thing to do, or, in office-speak, the name of the game.

As with Weber's laws of bureaucracy, so the eight new features of the modern corporation have one striking thing in common: they were also features of the now nearly defunct bureaucratic communist state, as described earlier in this book. Thus: recent communist decision-making was usually collective, not dictatorial; within communist hierarchies, careers were made and broken by internal disputes over arcane points of theory that usually bore no relation to the outside world. Communist promotion was based on hierarchy and the protégé system; loyalty and secrecy were virtues second to none in communist systems. The cult of anonymity was imperative except for those at the very top; perks and status were central to the communist system of internal reward and communist systems could be very priggish – while ruthless towards their enemies. Finally, of course, communism paid immense lip-service to a phoney cult of equality.

There is a ninth and fundamental similarity between the modern corporation and the now moribund communist system: empire-building and turf wars. Just as at the top of the communist hierarchy there was vigorous competition between the major components of the system – the party; the bureaucracy; the army; the security forces – so at the top of major private corporations there is fierce infighting between its key bureaucracies, usually its industrial, marketing, personnel, finance and legal departments.

Broadly speaking, the age of the industrial manager, running his company to produce what the market wants, is over. Personnel was never traditionally strong, and is weaker now that the union challenge has diminished. The marketing side has had its moment of glory, as this was briefly seen as the key to whether a product sold or not; but all too often marketing was treated as a little flamboyant by stodgy corporate bureaucrats. The finance department is now extremely powerful, both because of the current obsession with free-market economics and because it wields the axe in a recession.

The Japanese have convincingly shown that huge finance departments are not only an expensive luxury in themselves, usually outweighing any savings they make, but a major hindrance to corporate growth – not a view shared by the West. Finally, legal departments are now beginning to boom, as so much of corporate affairs is determined by the legal minutiae of takeover battles.

Within these bureaucratic wars, only the industrial managers and marketing men (plus sales, always on the lowest corporate rung) can be said to be primarily concerned with what ought to be the main purpose of a company – to produce competitive goods that people want to buy in the marketplace. The rest are parasites. As with the much bigger communist bureaucracies, the day of the local cadres who actually represented the wishes of the people has long been eclipsed. The modern corporate boss is as divorced from the men who pay his huge salary – the customers – as any communist boss from his cadres.

THREE HUGE QUESTIONS remain: in spite of all the similarities, why is the modern corporate bureaucracy a much more competitive animal than its communist counterpart ever was? Unlike the latter, why does the corporation appear to be thriving? And, given the similarities, is there a real danger that capitalist corporations may go the way of their communist rivals?

The capitalist corporation is undoubtedly more efficient, seriously flawed in some respects perhaps, but its state counterpart was more so. There are three key differences between capitalist and communist bureaucratic corporations that explain this: the former has ultimately to balance its books; the actual job of its employees is to expand business; and, the existence of competition, while far from pure, does condition the corporate environment.

As already observed, there are qualifications to all three. The bigger a corporation, the easier it is for a department to expand for essentially empire-building motives which have nothing to do with producing and selling goods on the market. Thus, many managers spend the bulk of their time in bureaucratic infighting rather than expanding the business; and competition can be severely restricted or even crushed altogether by size. But if a major capitalist corporation did all of these things – and some have – all of the time, it would eventually be in trouble.

Even such giants as IBM and Coca-Cola have had to cut back as their markets slowed; even these two have had consistently to find ways of expanding their sales, and to become more competitive, after years of dominating their respective markets. The major corporations are ultimately responsible to the markets in the way that the major communist bureaucracies were never responsible to the people – although many short-sighted managers have failed to see this.

The mistake is often made of comparing an idealized small or medium-sized private sector firm with a bloated communist or state sector enterprise. There are four quite distinct types of enterprise, two in the private sector, two in the public sector: the small and medium-sized enterprise struggling in a competitive market; the giant private corporation; the giant state enterprise; and the state-run public service. The 'pure' ideal of private enterprise is represented only by the first.

Michael Heseltine, a successful entrepreneur-owner himself, as well as Britain's President of the Board of Trade, captures the early days of his own small, but now substantial, enterprise:

> There is nothing quite like starting your own business: the sense of independence, exhilaration and confidence that prompts you to the first steps, and the loneliness with which you return again and again to the bank manager. He knows what you are going to say. He has heard it all before. You do your best with arguments that have been rehearsed by others a dozen times that day and often rejected. He makes a judgement about you. Sometimes you are lucky.

Friday is crisis day, when the wages must be paid. The other six days are devoted to selling the product and collecting the cash. The entrepreneur lives on his wits, his nerves and ultimately his determination to see it through. It matters as few experiences can ever matter. There are many ways up but only one way down.

The rules are elementary. The bills can either be paid, or not. The creditors can either be kept at bay, or not. The product either works, or it does not. The scale of the thing seems huge because the stakes and the price of failure are very high.

It is not surprising that attitudes forged in such a climate engender self-reliance and a certain intolerance of advice. You come to believe that if you can survive in this jungle, you must have a destiny. Success creates intolerance of the slower-moving, orderly minds of bureaucrats or of anyone who lives in the non-wealth-creating parts of the economy. You pay the taxes; they spend them. You take the risks; they make it harder for you.

I remain deeply committed to the virtues of a private enterprise system. I have competed in the business world and I know the disciplines it imposes. There is no substitute. Nothing drives an organization to greater efficiency than fear of a lost order. The market-place sorts out men from boys and entrenches power in the hands of the consumer, to whom the producer becomes servant. You work for your crust, or there is no crust.

The giant corporation, which dominates the economic scene, has the three competitive features already described, although it is lacking the immediate pressure of the marketplace. If a giant corporation does make a mistake, then starts to lose money, it will generally, after a long time-lag, be restructured in the interests of making more money, with the emphasis on lower costs, greater efficiency and higher sales.

A classic example was Britain's *Daily Telegraph*, its largest up-market newspaper. As market leader of the 'quality' newspapers, with a circulation of well over one million, it was astonishing that, by the mid-1980s, it was not highly profitable. It suffered from three problems: a huge printing bill, derived from the restrictive practices of the printing unions; excess costs from a staff that had grown too large; and massive financing costs on an overambitious, but imaginative, decision to invest in a new printing plant.

Those factors brought it to a low point of vulnerability and financial weakness; the proprietor, Lord Hartwell, was forced to seek funds from an outside investor, Hollinger's Conrad Black, a Canadian. Black made firm the option to put up more money, and secure a controlling stake, unless there was an immediate improvement in the *Telegraph*'s fortunes – a situation which failed to materialize. He took it over, slashed costs, and soon reaped the substantial benefits of a new printing plant, coupled with the end of restrictive practices among printers, following their defeat at Wapping.

This was an example of the 'bottom line' function of the market. When even a large company is about to run out of money, the axemen, the industrial consultants and the outside investors move in. In other respects it showed the deficiencies of the market, too: that matters should have been allowed to get so bad; and that, had the *Telegraph*'s credit been a little more positive at the crucial moment, the take-over would have been avoided. The newspaper's debt was largely the product of a far-sighted, if too ambitious, investment project that paid off in the end. Western banks, however, are rarely far-sighted. Certainly the reduction in staff costs helped return the newspaper to solvency, although it may have contributed to a lower quality product in some respects. (Overseas staff were reduced and the *Telegraph*'s offices were moved to the East End from central London, diminishing its contact with the main stories; both these moves proved of dubious benefit to the newspaper.)

Did the product improve, or sell more? It continued slowly to lose circulation and, while toying with a slightly different format, retained many of the same readers as before. Yet within the *Telegraph*, as within any large bureaucracy over time, there were undoubtedly savings to be made: the tendency in times of plenty is to take on more staff than you need, and in times of recession to shed staff. The great capitalist enterprise has this degree of accountability to market conditions at least.

THE SECOND WAY in which the capitalist bureaucracy is different from the communist bureaucracy is in company policy. In good times, a capitalist company is interested only partially in its main purpose of selling goods in the marketplace; the rest of the time it is more concerned with internal squabbles and personalities; the same is true of the communist system's basic commitment to equality and the betterment of peoples' lives. However, when the system is in difficulty, the original goals are the objectives by which performance is measured. The capitalist goal is a highly productive one; the communist goal is unattainable and actually anti-productive.

The corporate bureaucrats, like communist bureaucrats, are more concerned about their own position in the pecking order and their status when things are going well. When things are going badly, their job is to produce and sell, while the job of a communist bureaucracy is much harder to define. The lower echelons in a capitalist corporation will be motivated to produce and sell. The lower echelons in a communist bureaucracy will be motivated to work harder, through coercion, for the 'general good'. It is hardly surprising that the cruder, more basic, more human capitalist motive – self-betterment – wins over the vaguer, more coercive, more unpopular communist one. Carrots always were more effective than sticks (something some managers have not understood). There is thus a significant difference between the systems.

But it does not detract from the fact that the actual structure of the organization is not very different. Nor, in practice, was communism really based on selflessness. The system had long been forced to introduce exactly the same enticements as exist in any capitalist corporation for its executives, the main reason for climbing up the communist ladder being pay, perks, special shops, housing and privileges.

The third and key difference between the bureaucracies is the competitive environment. Where only one contractor – a government one – can bid for a contract supplied by the government, there really is very little reason for him to get his act together. He can settle into a cosy relationship with his client, in which one will accept a shoddy service and the other will provide it. In addition, in such a situation, the company providing the service has not the slightest reason to improve its performance or find other clients; it cannot. Once the job has been done, the employee goes home.

Private industry is, or should be, constantly engaged in the search for new clients. In the private sector, even the giant corporation is run to some extent by the need to find competitive suppliers and to compete for tenders – except in the not infrequent cases where it is in a monopoly, cartel or dominant position. Michael Heseltine's discussion of an early example of privatization is worth quoting at length:

> My eyes were opened by the burden on the defence budget of the two Royal Dockyards at Devonport and Rosyth, where there were clearly severe management problems . . . The urgent need was for effective, accountable management and we decided the best way to achieve it quickly was to keep the land and assets in public ownership, and invite tenders for commercial management . . .
>
> Enthusiasm, I know, can sound like doctrinal obsession, so let me restate what I regard as overwhelming reasons why many organizations should be moved from the public to the private sector.
>
> The first is that, in the public sector, there are few of the commercial challenges and comparisons which show whether the cost of a service, which may be only a routine activity such as building or consultancy, is properly competitive with what the private sector can offer. You cannot know that the price is not right unless there is competition and an arm's-length relationship between customer and supplier. This the Government cannot have with its own limb, the PSA; nor until now could the Royal Navy with the Royal Dockyards, or the Army with Royal Ordnance. The clearest example of the

weakness is again in the Dockyards. There was no budget of cost, only a record of what had been spent. Indeed, an awkward hurdle in the way of bringing in commercial management was the cost of introducing accounting systems.

These were essential to enable proper comparison with the private yards, or pre-contract estimating, to be undertaken.

The second point is that, within such organizations as the PSA and the dockyards, there are skills which are directed solely to the limited objective of serving the Government's purpose, in these cases maintaining either warships or estates and offices. The scale of the job is defined within the limits of one programme and one purse. There is none of that thrusting for wider opportunities which is the natural activity and essential strength of the commercial world . . .

For a measure of the inefficiency that has characterized at least this area of public sector activity, there is no need to look further than the figures for absenteeism. On average each employee in the dockyards was taking four and a half weeks' paid, unauthorized absence a year. That reflects upon the management. The cost of the extra overhead falls on the taxpayer. The attitude to work which absenteeism on this scale reveals and engenders dramatically affects the quality of service that the Royal Navy can expect. It must also have set a style and approach which percolated into the wider local economy.

Private sector stimulus would long since have cured this. After the initial trauma of achieving acceptable levels of efficiency the private sector will seek to expand its business because that is its nature. The nature of the unregenerate public sector business is not to exert itself or change but to remain as it is, inefficient, inert and unenterprising. That is a burden on local society and the national economy which we can no longer tolerate.

Even the biggest bureaucratic corporation, while prone to many of the same tendencies, is unlikely to find itself in quite such a passive position as a state one (although this has been true, in particular, of the giant American defence contractors). There is a great convergence between the capitalist and communist systems, but the differences should not be minimized.

The final category of organization is the public sector institution. This does not pretend to make money, to balance the books. It does not exist for that purpose. It includes the welfare services, defence, the police and other necessary public services. The difficulty with this category is to find any proper system of accountability: profit cannot be the measure, but this type of spending can be highly inefficient unless properly accounted for and audited – even if the purpose is entirely worthwhile. It is mistaken to apply purely private sector disciplines to the necessary parts of the public sector, much of which is overstretched in its provision of key services. In Britain imaginative steps have, however, been taken towards the creation of an 'internal market' in the health service.

THUS THE TWO bureaucracies – excluding the 'pure' private sector, competitive small and medium-sized enterprises; and the 'pure' public sector, providing real public services – remain fairly similar in structure, but with some differences. There is a considerable convergence of the two systems. Are the giant bureaucratic corporations of the West as much under threat as were the giant Communist corporations of the East?

The answer, when taken together with the globalization of capitalism, is yes. Domestically, the giant corporations are getting dangerously remote from their own natural constituencies: the customers; the workers; the shareholders. Internationally, they often behave more like colonial freebooters than the respectable guests of their host countries. On the world financial markets, there is a kind of all-powerful tide crashing about, destroying domestic national economic policies for no apparent reason. This tide is governed largely by speculative movements and guesses, not economic logic. In banking and finance, this has long been the case. This has always been the case in such areas as commodity broking and international trade. Coupled with the breakdown of the Cold War bipolar structure, the threat is of a global Hobbesian 'state of nature', a free-for-all in which the strong are dominant but not all-powerful – global anarchy in place of the tidy, if occasionally frustratingly, ordered postwar world.

What in practice does this mean? What could the increasing escape of the great capitalist corporations from political control and the growing impotence of national governments – even as they become more democratically representative – result in? What are the consequences of America's withdrawal from the world, and Europe's failure to fill that gap, for the emergence of more assertive backward nations and for the spread of nationalism, the rogue state, terrorism, nuclear proliferation, and drugs, to name but the major challenges?

It is worth examining a doomsday scenario, because catastrophe is not just possible but probable unless these problems are identified and acted upon. It is time to outline the worst possible case.

PART FOUR

Restoring Order

CHAPTER ONE

THE GLOBAL STATE OF NATURE

WHAT COULD GO seriously wrong in the new world panorama? The globalization of capitalism is inherently dangerous. To recap on each of the areas in which this is occurring: There is the impact of currency flows, overriding all but the strongest economies. If this persists, the impotence of the governments of major industrial countries, as well as Third World ones, to pursue their own economic policies, will become apparent. A widespread disillusion with the democratic process would not be far behind. Democratically elected governments would, quite simply, be seen to be unable to deliver. They would have to qualify their election pledges with the proviso 'assuming international circumstances permit'.

This is a new state of affairs. Up to now, overseas economic problems have had major repercussions; and of course the Depression in the 1930s ricocheted across the world. But over the past forty years the world economy has been more or less stable, mistakes were usually home-grown, and spendthrift governments were to blame for such things as devaluation and inflation. Today this has been transformed: governments can be more or less silly, but the whim of the international financial markets determines the success or failure of national economic policies.

Conservative governments in Britain, Italy, Sweden and France, a liberal one in Ireland, and a Socialist one in Spain were successively picked off in an almost unprecedented volley of crises in 1992–3; it strains credulity to believe that they were all mismanaged and deserved their fate. Perhaps they all had bad governments and mistaken policies – although these varied enormously. But a far more convincing explanation is that governments were not really in charge: they had been buffeted by forces over which they have no control. John Major, Carlo

Ciampi, Carl Bildt, Eduard Balladur, Albert Reynolds and Felipe Gonzalez were not wild or incompetent: it is just that they were not in charge. This knowledge is liable to discredit leadership in long-established democracies, and all the more so in countries with new democratic traditions. Small wonder that a survey conducted by the European Commission in 1993 found that a record 55 per cent of voters were dissatisfied with the way their country's democracy works.

What are the dangers in practice? Diminishing electoral turnout, decreasing participation in elections, a rise in support for extremist parties, a resort to political violence, direct action or to utopian solutions are a few of the obvious ones. In Germany and Italy these things are already happening. In Britain, France and Spain they are beginning to. Even in America, the Ross Perot phenomenon can be partly ascribed to the seeming impotence of government in the face of larger forces.

In the great number of countries that are recent converts to democracy, its fragility is apparent. In much of newly democratic Latin America, Eastern Europe and Asia, it will take only a few years' awareness of the politicians' inability to dominate events for authoritarians to reassert themselves. There is no reason, given the sheer size of arbitrary international flows, to suppose the new democracies will last long. The prospect is of a reversion, for a time at least, to simple-minded regimes.

In the West, the democratic tradition is now so deeply ingrained that this is unlikely. But lesser consequences could flow: in particular the growth of an underclass within America, and to a lesser extent in Britain and Germany, would pose a major challenge to the social order. The danger this poses is of a sharp increase in crime, particularly in the inner cities, the growth of effective no-go areas, and occasional social and political explosions. In the United States, the Los Angeles riots could multiply; in Britain, summers of hatred could be repeated.

Let us turn to the next example of capitalist globalization: the debt crisis. Here, a decade of crisis and falling living standards has yet to produce a major political explosion, which is remarkable. Part of the explanation is the traditional passivity of ordinary people in Latin America and Africa; it is an attitude born of centuries of poverty and repression. But there is also a time-lag involved. People do not take up arms immediately; they hope things will change for the best. The debt crisis, although apparently concluded to the satisfaction of the bankers, continues remorselessly to grind down the living standards of a large part of the underdeveloped world.

Maybe there is no limit to the extent to which people will suffer in silence, especially in Africa: hunger induces passivity. However, with the coming of more representative regimes and democracies, ordinary people began to have more hope that their leaders would indeed represent their interests. It is only when it becomes apparent that their politicians have little real power that the possibility of social explosion exists. If this occurs, the armies waiting in the wings are likely to move out of their barracks. This time, however, military intervention would be different: in Latin America and Africa military intervention has traditionally been seen as the response of the Establishment to the failings of democratic populists. If it happens now, after years of moderate democracy, it will be seen as virtual proof that democracy does not work in such societies: armies in Latin America and Africa could be very long in taking their leave.

The third move towards the globalization of capitalism is in the spread of the multinationals. As observed, the difficulties associated with this have been less than devastating so far, falling far short of the prediction of the doomsayers in the 1960s. But this state of affairs may not continue. In America, Britain, large parts of Europe and much of Asia, evidence of resentment towards the multinationals is beginning to mount. The problem already provokes interest in newspapers and among political parties in these countries. There is an element of hypocrisy present, in that most of the critics welcome the jobs and prosperity the multinationals bring, while objecting to their statelessness and the local power they wield. The multinationals could become a major target of local anger once again, if economies continue to worsen, even though this would itself help to accelerate the deterioration.

The final major area in which capitalism is becoming globalized is trade. The eruption of trade wars between the three major economic blocs, already under way, has huge political consequences. If increased trade continues to benefit Asia, particularly Japan, at the expense of America and Europe, protectionism seems inevitable, helping to push the world towards economic stagnation, huge job losses, and an effective tax on consumers and efficiency everywhere. The danger of America, Europe and Japan fighting a major trade war against each other is likelier than ever, one in which both America and Japan, incidentally, have an interest in frustrating European integration.

Thus the globalization of capitalism carries with it the seeds of worldwide political instability: if such instability occurs, the tendency in much of Latin America, such parts of Africa as are democratic, and in Asian countries like South Korea and Thailand, will be to revert to military rule. Elsewhere, there might be a temporary hardening of authoritarian regimes, from Middle Eastern monarchs to Chinese colonial masters in Tibet to Confucianists in Japan.

The huge advances of the 1980s would be reversed, as societies discovered that there were few material benefits in their being democratic because whatever government they voted for was forced to do much the same by international economic circumstances. In places like China and Brazil outright popular anger and demonstrations against the multinationals could not be ruled out.

If such a reaction breaks out against the globalization of capitalism, there is every prospect of popular outbursts in the United States and Europe against Asian commerce and investment penetration, leading to trade wars, retaliation and tit-for-tat protectionism to appease the electorate. The dangers of a major contraction in world trade need no underlining. Again, the possibilities of a popular reaction towards overseas investment penetration are considerable.

THE DANGERS OF global anarchy are just as serious, if not more so, in the security field. The first part of this book showed how, as the disciplines of the Cold War have faded, nationalism and lesser conflicts are now bubbling to the surface. With astonishing short-sightedness, the first reaction of Western governments (except France) to the diminution in tension in central Europe has been to throw away the armour that made it possible and slash military spending, none more so than in the United States, which has already withdrawn fully two-thirds of its forces from Europe, and shows a disturbing obsession with the Pacific region.

President Clinton declared in November that there was no region in the world more important to the United States than Asia: 'The time has come for Americans to join with Japan and others in the region to create a new Pacific Community.' Warren Christopher, the Secretary of State, declared bluntly that 'Western Europe is no longer the dominant area of the world.' Washington, he said, had decided to shed its 'Eurocentric attitude'. Yet Western Europe still accounts for 60 per cent of overseas profits of American firms, half their overseas investments and 65 per cent of all foreign investment in America. In Britain, the white paper, *Options for Change*, resulted in substantial defence cuts, some reversed.

In practice, while the enormous conventional forces drawn up in Central Europe were a deterrent but never likely to be used, force is likely to be much more necessary today to intervene in regional conflicts. Western security policy is a shambles: a kind of halfway house where NATO is still drawn up against an apparently non-existent enemy, but without the mandate to intervene where it should – in regional conflicts. No mission is prescribed for NATO beyond the old adage that an attack upon one is an attack upon all. It is an alliance bereft of purpose and meaning. No one is more responsible for this inertia than NATO's military establishments, particularly America's, which display an obsession with not taking casualties amounting to a phobia. General Colin Powell, the former American chief of staff, is the personification of this. Yet military bureaucrats should consider that, while every consideration must be made for protecting the lives of the men under them, there can be little justification for maintaining large armed forces, and the NATO structure itself, unless the threat of their deployment, which implies a willingness to accept casualties, is a real one. Most Western armies are volunteer, and most soldiers accept the risk as part of the job. A war machine that can never be used is much worse than no war machine at all, because it is hugely expensive to maintain.

It should be the most urgent task of post-Cold War security to decide what the NATO forces in Europe are for; otherwise they will slowly dribble away, leaving nothing but a series of competing national defence policies that at best would be ineffectual, and at worst in rivalry with each other. The end of the Cold War removes the really compelling sense of national danger and urgency that has kept the United States fully committed to Europe. If American forces there are run down any further, it is hard to see the United States returning to a continent where it was always historically difficult for administrations to commit their forces, and which many Americans now consider is less important than the Pacific theatre.

The crisis over Bosnia underlines the problems. For the United States, Bosnia is a minor civil war in Europe, and therefore ultimately Europe's responsibility. However, decades of dependence upon an American-led NATO has created a European inability to act separately in the military sphere. Thus, when America took no action, Western Europe was paralysed, lapsing into bitter squabbling about the desirability of action, followed by a manifest lack of co-ordination over what should be done.

Yet it was not to be expected that the Europeans would be able to agree on a common policy in a matter of months, after decades of being warned that any such development would result in an American withdrawal from Europe. American partnership in, and leadership of, a common Western system of collective security remain essential. Leadership does not mean passing the buck as soon as a challenge arises. It was particularly mistaken for America's Secretary of State first to announce America's intention of taking action on Bosnia, then to fly to Europe only to be dissuaded from doing so. Western European countries will not initiate major collective security action because they are too accustomed to the role of follower.

If America wants a global system of collective security to work, then it must take prime responsibility. Of course, if the Americans are indeed withdrawing into a period of isolationism – and the signals given out by the Clinton presidency are mixed – Europe must try and assemble its own defence structure through the European Union or the Western European Union. Differences of national interest and of perception make it unlikely that this will be effective for a long time to come. But there may be no alternative.

Far better, though, for the United States to go on accepting the reality understood since Franklin Roosevelt – that in an increasingly smaller and interdependent world a continental global superpower has huge responsibilities. America cannot retreat from a world in which security is globalized: if it does, the challenge will be much worse when it has to re-enter. America's challenge is to provide leadership once again, and to give NATO the purpose it now lacks.

One of America's top military thinkers, the director of national security studies at the Hudson Institute, General William Odom, in his remarkably candid book on American military policy after the Cold War, *America's Military Revolution* (American University Press, Washington DC, 1993), gives a sober but telling warning:

> United States defense policy and military forces are in the midst of the greatest transition since the decade following World War II. Will the chaotic and wasteful pattern of imprudent reductions that had to be reversed for the Korean War and the defence of Europe be repeated? Disturbing similarities mark the beginning of the current transition. The Persian Gulf War caught US ground forces in the reduction process, although not as far along as they were at the outbreak of the Korean War. In the period immediately after the Gulf War, the defence budget process appeared to be driven more by domestic politics than by strategic purpose.

Odom argues that America has three choices in the post-Cold War period: Pax Americana – a continuing high-profile role as the world's policeman; 'America First' – a reversion to isolationism; and a policy of 'economy of force and comparative advantage' – intervening where it is most necessary and where America has a comparative advantage, preferably in concert with its allies.

To Odom, Pax Americana seems impossible because of its high cost and lack of public support. He favours the third, more limited option, but warns sombrely that it is by no means impossible that America will opt for isolationism.

> The 'America First' option, a retreat to a new isolationism, is conceivable. It may prove unavoidable, especially if the domestic economy remains stagnant or declines for several years. However, many factors work against this choice. Some of America's foreign commitments and entanglements are not easy to break. Some of them have strong domestic constituencies. Others enjoy a cultural and sentimental basis. Finally, isolationism likely would have a negative impact on the US economy because it could easily prompt protectionist trade policies.
>
> Nonetheless, one should not take excessive comfort in these factors. They could be too late in their impact to wake up the public to their reality. And they could fail to find sufficiently compelling spokesmen in the debates over our foreign policy.

Worryingly, the traditional isolationist right is far from alone in its view:

> The political left in America has had its version of global disengagement proponents. Paul Kennedy's judgement that the United States is in danger of the kind of imperial 'overstretch' that brought down previous great powers found considerable resonance among liberals. Samuel Huntington sees relatively little danger from those who say America is in decline because, as he puts it, they wake us up in time to fix the problems that might bring that decline. More dangerous, in his view, are those who take too much comfort in victory in

the Cold War. They create a sense that the game is over, we won, and we can go home and celebrate.

Unfortunately, there is a real possibility that a *de facto* alliance between these two wings of the political spectrum could cause the United States to opt for isolation, the second of the three strategic choices. The domestic economy, if it continues to worsen, will give the isolationist sentiments of both the left and the right enormous appeal among voters.

THERE IS NOTHING academic or remote about the new isolationism: it was outlined chillingly by American columnist William Pfaff in June 1993:

> Today there is no physical threat to the security of the United States. Such threat as exists is to the country's economic well-being and comes from allies, Japan and Western Europe.
>
> There is no great idealistic motivation today for international involvement. American feelings are rightly but ephemerally engaged by human suffering in Somalia, Ethiopia or Bosnia, but these are affairs whose causes are indigenous and seemingly beyond the ability of others to much influence. There certainly is no great crusading answer to African misery and anarchy or to Balkan hatreds.
>
> The Clinton administration maintains and manages the international obligations already in place, with a bias toward their reduction. Budget and risk-assessment both dictate the run-down of overseas bases and foreign commitments. The administration offers an increased emphasis on human rights and environmental issues as its contribution to foreign policy, but this usually yields when it meets practical obstacles, as in Mr Clinton's decision not to withdraw most-favored-nation trade status from China because of its rights abuses.

Unease was not stilled in May 1993, when a senior Clinton administration official, off the record, asserted that 'it is necessary to make the point that our economic interests are paramount' over America's traditional foreign policy interests. With limited resources, America must 'define the extent of its commitment and make a commitment commensurate with those realities. This may on occasion fall short of what some Americans and others would hope for.' The same official asked candidly if 'people are dying [in Bosnia] because the United States could do more if it wanted to? Yes.' But the stark truth, in his view, was that, 'We don't have the leverage, we don't have the influence, the inclination to use military force' in dealing with 'middleweight powers' after the end of the Cold War.

These remarks were quickly disavowed by the State Department and the White House, but they clearly reflected a strong current of feeling there; this view shows an alarming reversion to the belief that intervention abroad is a luxury. In practice, every previous attempt by the United States to withdraw from the world has been rudely awakened: the longer-term costs to the United States have always been greater than American deterrence in advance.

THERE CAN BE few more poignant signs of how the strategic map of Europe has changed than the decision at NATO Headquarters Allied Forces Central Europe, in Brunssum, Holland, to drop the term 'Edge of the Battlefield' to describe the boundary between East and West Germany where eight NATO divisions were long drawn up to face an attack that, over four decades, never came. With the unification of East and West Germany, those forces were left facing a virtually non-existent army of around 150,000 men, now reduced to just 50,000 and merged, without trace of its former self, into the West German armed forces.

'This process is from west to east', one of Germany's most senior generals told me brutally, as he described how retraining, re-equipment and re-education were annihilating the East German army's separate, goose-stepping identity. Prussia has been conquered by Schleswig-Holstein, Bremen, Hessen and

Bayern, and Bismarck must be turning in his grave. The Russian forces in East Germany became isolated garrisons, protected from the ire of ordinary East Germans and gradually thinned down until their evacuation. Under the terms of reunification, NATO forces as such cannot be stationed in the old East Germany (although the German forces there are to all intents and purposes be a NATO appendage). So whither those huge armies along the Rhine, all dressed up with no one to fight?

The activity at NATO headquarters these days has, in fact, been frantic, as the Alliance seeks to establish a role for itself. The Alliance's planners are refreshingly realistic. It is accepted that the threat from Russia in the new Europe is 'very remote indeed' and that the prospect of a surprise attack by Russian forces along the central front, after the conventional arms treaty signed in Paris on November 1990, is non-existent. The treaty, made possible by the Russians' astonishing decision to drop its remaining condition that limits be imposed on the number of sea-based aircraft, pushed much of the Russian armour necessary for an attack in central Europe beyond the Urals; any build-up on the central front will violate the treaty and be instantly visible.

Should the Russians ever reassemble their forces, they would suffer from the disadvantage of having lost their buffer zone in Eastern Europe; Czechoslovakia has redeployed its forces from the NATO front to face a possible threat in the east. NATO has succeeded in imposing a limit of a third of any country's forces allowed on foreign soil within Europe. The only country affected is Russia, and the implications are staggering. From a superiority of Warsaw Pact conventional forces of around two-to-one in 1989, the Russians, bereft of allies, have accepted a ceiling of some seven armies between the Urals and their western borders, compared with combined Western and East European forces of some fourteen armies.

The strategic equation in central Europe has, in effect, been stood on its head. Indeed, with the Czechs, Slovaks, Poles and Hungarians seeking membership of NATO – which is being refused for fear of unnerving the Russians – the only possibility of conflict seems to arise through a Russian reinvasion of one of its former satellites; that, too, is remote. The shadow of conventional war has been lifted from Europe.

A nuclear deterrent is being retained by NATO for two good reasons. First, the Russians are keeping a major, if reduced, stockpile of long-range missiles, as well as short-range missiles. Second, while the Alliance has scrapped its short-range nuclear artillery and not modernized its land-based missiles, it retains airborne weapons to provide the cover to reassure the Americans that their forces would never be left unprotected in Europe.

Now that the walls of Jericho have come tumbling down, it was only a matter of time before Western public opinion demanded not just a 'peace dividend', but the virtual dissolution of the Alliance (the Warsaw Pact being dead already). Fortunately, NATO planners have risen to this challenge and are arguing persuasively that, while NATO must be drastically restructured, it would be dangerous to do away with the Alliance entirely. NATO knows, in effect, that it is fighting for its life; its arguments are by no means purely special pleading.

Why NATO? One answer is that while the Russian threat has diminished radically, it has not disappeared. It will remain a formidable nuclear power and the most effective conventional power on the Euro-Asian continent. Until democracy and stability are guaranteed there, the West will be unwise to drop its guard altogether.

NATO also discerned a new role for itself during the Gulf crisis as an ideal co-ordinator and staging post for the rapid projection of forces to world trouble spots, in particular the Middle East and the possible flashpoints between the newly assertive nationalities of Eastern Europe. Troops and equipment were removed from the central front for deployment in the Gulf; crises such as that in Yugoslavia today or, potentially, between Hungary and Romania, beckon. The experience of forty years of co-ordination will be invaluable in forging such an interventionist force. It will not necessarily go under the banner of NATO, which might be viewed with hostility in the Third World.

NATO also has two major political roles to play: it remains

the only forum that directly engages America in Western Europe and inhibits a retreat across the Atlantic which, in almost any scenario, could be dangerous; and its continued existence is crucial to preventing what senior generals discreetly call the 'renationalization' of national armed forces – in particular Germany's, with all the dangers that it implies.

The outline of a new NATO begins to emerge from the rubble of half a century of confrontation in central Europe. The redundant armies on the central front are being slimmed down almost beyond recognition: current thinking envisages a reduction of the eight front-line divisions to just two 'guard' divisions, backed up by highly mobile, much smaller brigade-sized 'reaction' units, probably stationed outside Germany altogether, amounting to a further two divisions, with one heavy mechanized division behind that. Flexibility and mobility will be the key features of the new NATO units, for use in emergencies or further afield. The slimmed-down forces will be integrated between NATO countries, both to save money and to make their continued presence in Germany more acceptable. The thinking is that the Germans will be much less likely to invite NATO forces to leave their territory altogether – public hostility is already growing sharply to low-flying and pollution – if German forces are blended into the Alliance, both inside and outside their country.

The French upset NATO planners by precipitately announcing their intention to withdraw from Germany in 1990; longstanding attempts exist to integrate France into NATO under the umbrella of the Western European Union. Many Europeans – including Jacques Delors, the President of the European Commission – have advocated setting up an embryo European defence organization; yet even if this gets off the ground, it will be a long time replacing NATO. Alliance planners have been equally slow to respond to Soviet overtures for military cooperation with NATO – although liaison with the Soviet armed forces is growing.

The alternative to the radical overhaul now being considered may be no less than the neutralization of Germany and its 370,000-strong armed forces, followed, probably, by the withdrawal of American troops from Europe. This would be a recipe for renewed instability. The very vigour with which NATO is responding to the need for complete overhaul suggests that the Atlantic Alliance is indeed worth preserving in a slimmed down form to meet the challenges that are rearing their heads around the globe.

TWO KEY QUESTIONS remain. What is the actual mission of NATO; and how should its interventions be legitimized? Up to now, the rule of thumb for American-led force projection around the globe has come to be dominated by what might be labelled the 'Vietnam syndrome'. Prior to the Vietnam war, the United States intervened massively when it saw fit. After the Vietnam débâcle, there was a dangerous period of virtual American inaction, followed by a series of interventions carefully crafted to meet three criteria: they should be in America's direct national interest; they should command popular and international support; and any action should be capable of success with as few American casualties as possible. Of the three, the last is overwhelmingly the most important, and is desperately dangerous once aggressors have understood its implications.

The seven main American interventions since Vietnam have been Lebanon, Grenada, Libya, Panama, the Gulf, Somalia and Haiti. Lebanon was, admittedly, a snakepit and President Reagan withdrew as soon as he sensibly could. It is hard to see how intervention could have worked there, or what it was designed to achieve: there were too many warring factions, none of them in the right, and the American force was too small. Grenada was successful because of the overwhelming deployment of forces, although the Americans made a number of serious military mistakes. Swatting the Libyan gadfly was immensely popular in America, and as no ground troops were involved, fully met the third requirement. In Panama overwhelming force was used – it was the biggest commitment of American military might since Vietnam – to crack a very small but hard nut, General Manuel Noriega and his cronies in the National Guard. American casualties were minimal.

In the Gulf War a truly massive aerial bombardment softened up the enemy to the point where resistance was likely to be small when American ground forces attacked: it was a uniquely tilted battlefield, involving a vulnerable enemy with obsolete weaponry, exposed as sitting ducks in the desert. Somalia passed the test of being an intervention supported by public and international opinion because of the pressing humanitarian need to relieve the famine there, but was clearly not essential to American interests. When the UN forces there were increasingly drawn into a complex factional shooting war, it was announced that American forces would soon be withdrawn. In Haiti, a ragtag militia of local thugs was finally intimidated by overwhelming American military might into surrender – hardly a great achievement for American arms.

In Bosnia, the surface perception was that none of the three tests were met: it was not a vital national interest for America in the way that Gulf oil was; there was no serious pressure to act from public opinion – although almost certainly this would have rallied round, in view of the suffering there, if a lead had been taken; and it was believed that the casualties would be unacceptably high without much prospect of withdrawal or a clearly definable objective, although a strong case can be made the other way.

However, the key point was that by signalling to the Serbs that aggression would go unpunished, and then indeed doing nothing beyond assembling files for unrealizable war crime tribunals, aggression was at every stage encouraged. The clear message sent out to would-be aggressors during the Gulf War – invade somebody else's territory and a coalition of far more powerful outside forces will retaliate – had been muddied by Bosnia. The temptation to invade your neighbour's patch was far more powerful in the post-Cold War period because the superpowers in the past kept a restraining hand on their client states, fearing that local conflict could spark superpower confrontation. Now nobody seemed to care – or at least that was the message from Bosnia: go in and beat up your neighbour if he is weaker.

What clearly follows is that America's careful handpicking

of suitable cases for intervention in the post-Vietnam era is out of date in the post-Cold War age. It must be revised, or wars will start breaking out all over the place. New rules must be put in place; the next section will outline those rules. If the present situation continues – a timorous, divided America; a quarrelsome, emaciated NATO, without any clear sense of what it is supposed to do; and a green light to the Milosevic's of this world – there will be a rash of local conflicts, some more serious than others. To reiterate: if NATO does nothing, it should pack up its bags.

It is possible to envisage endemic nationalist strife in the southern Soviet Union, where some thirty separate ethnic conflicts are already under way; possible ethnic and territorial disputes in Eastern Europe; tribal and separatist fighting in much of Africa; and continuing wars for the spoils of oil in the Middle East, as the Arab–Israeli dispute dies down. In a world without proper policing – neither American nor Russian – war could become widespread and endemic.

A FURTHER, more hypothetical problem needs to be addressed. Can the West really be confident in its assumption that there are no more areas of potential strife between the major powers with the collapse of the Soviet Union? No, and as long as there is any possibility of such conflict we must be ready for it, or the military challenge of such an adversary would come as an overwhelming shock to global security.

The United States, Britain, France and most of Europe's middle-aged military powers can be safely classified as 'defensive' – that is, are unlikely to attack another country unless they are themselves attacked. They are also committed to democracy, which acts as a major reassurance against militaristic behaviour; by and large electorates are much more concerned with the quality of public sector services and the reduction of taxes than engaging in military adventures.

A slight question mark must hang over Italy, Spain, Portugal, Greece and Turkey. Italy, after a long period of unprecedented postwar political stability under the dominant

Christian Democratic party, is now undergoing a massive upheaval, a 'peaceful revolution', in which the tumbrils that are carrying away an entire political generation are the anti-corruption probes currently under way by the judiciary. Four parties have benefited from this: in the north, Silvio Berlusconi's new right-wing grouping, Forza Italia; and the populist, secessionist 'Northern League'; as well as the ex-Communist party, the Left Democrats; and in the south, the neo-Fascist Italian Social Movement.

While the campaign against corruption is admirable, its consequences may be less so. Italy's foreign policy might be unpredictable under these new nationalist parties. It is hard to see Italy ever re-embarking upon a campaign of colonialism abroad, as under Mussolini – today's global environment would not permit this. While Italy's political traditions are thankfully at variance with the kind of bloodletting now racking Yugoslavia, the dangers of secessionist strife and a more nationalist foreign policy are not entirely absent.

Spain and Portugal are converts to democracy of less than two decades' standing, and still have armies with old traditions of intervention in politics. Even so, both countries were ruled by nationalist dictatorships for most of this century, which did not engage in any offensive military adventure, and the threat from this quarter is negligible. Greece and Turkey remain at each other's throats on a variety of issues, and conflict between the two cannot be ruled out. However, the problem and its possible fallout are largely regional in scale.

In Europe, the danger of large-scale war really concerns three powers: Germany, the Ukraine and Russia. Germany today is one of the pillars of the Western alliance: it is firmly anchored in both NATO and the European Union. Its commitment to democracy over the past forty-five years has been second to none: it has built up a stable and prosperous middle-class society dominated by two moderate parties of centre right and centre left. If the Social Democrats were to return to power, possibly in alliance with the Greens, Germany's commitment to NATO might be called into question; but this seems unlikely, and the Social Democrats anyway have a tradition of moving to the centre when in government. Any suggestion that it could re-emerge as a predatory nationalist power seems far-fetched.

Yet the issue needs to be addressed, if only because Germany's own leaders devote so much time to it. With the removal of the Soviet threat, the external reason for Germany's commitment to NATO has been removed. In addition, public opinion in Germany is far from certain of the benefits conferred by the European Union. Opinion polls show majorities objecting to any strengthening of the Union, with large numbers of voters wondering why Germany continues to be a member at all.

The reasoning appears to be that Germany is much the strongest country in Europe, and so even better placed to get its way outside the union than in. Allied to this is a hankering after the country's traditional interest in countries to the east, which is toned down at the moment by community membership: Germany, in this argument, would have a freer hand to play in the development of Eastern Europe's primitive economies if not bound by European rules. These views have little resonance inside the opposition Social Democratic Party, and are held only by a minority within the ruling Christian Democrats.

The Chancellor, Helmut Kohl, nevertheless had to underline in November 1993 that European fears of a resurgent Germany were 'a reality, whether we like it or not. We can only dismantle them step by step, and we can only do so under the firm roof of Europe'. Europe, he affirmed 'is our destiny'. He was responding to what Gunter Verheugen, the Social Democratic Party whip, argued was 'an anti-European mood in Germany which is very easy to exploit'.

The threat of the far-right Republican Party winning a fifth of the vote in Bavaria prompted the leader of the Christian Social Union there, Kohl's powerful coalition ally, Edmund Stoiber, Bavaria's Prime Minister, to argue that the government showed 'unrealistic dreaming' about European integration. 'We are no longer striving for a European federal state. I want a simple confederation. That means the nation states maintain their dominant role at least as far as internal matters are concerned'. The old need for Germans to 'seek a new identity' as Europeans in the immediate post-war period 'when it was often felt to be a burden to be German' was 'past'.

Kohl reminded Stoiber pointedly that a third of Germany's GDP came from exports, three-quarters of which were bought by Germany's EU partners. According to Kohl there is no alternative to European unity. 'In the long term I am firmly convinced that this is also a question of war and peace. It's a great mistake if people think that the horrific pictures from the former Yugoslavia are limited to that area of Europe, or that racism, nationalism, chauvinism and xenophobia in other parts of Europe and in Germany have been banished once and for all.' Kohl argued that it was necessary to complete the political underpinning of European unity 'if the evil spirits of the past' were to be kept under control in Germany. The Chancellor's warning could hardly have been stronger, more apocalyptic, or more pointedly directed primarily at his fellow countrymen. A prominent German NATO general admitted privately that Germany's membership of the European Community and NATO were essential to resisting any return to 'nationalist temptations. The right is still very much alive in Germany.'

Some of the anti-Europeans in the United States have been unconsciously stoking up this new German nationalism: there is a view among some planners in Washington that the bilateral American–German relationship is much more important than America's relationship with other European countries, or with the union itself, particularly because this serves to obstruct European integration. While pro-Western and pro-European forces are firmly in the saddle in Germany at the moment, the prospect of an isolationist, disengaged America, an introspective, curmudgeonly Britain minding its own business and picking holes in community policy, a European Union drifting apart, and an increasingly nationalist Germany pursuing its own policies is not entirely remote – and chillingly reminiscent of the climate in the 1930s.

While any real friction between France and Germany, or between the latter and its eastern neighbours, remains highly improbable, the fluidity of the situation in central Europe remains worrying. Germany may be tempted to make Eastern European countries its economic and political satellites, which would alarm Russia. German economic penetration of the Ukraine would be particularly disturbing.

The Ukraine itself is a loose cannon: although potentially rich, it has undergone few of the structural reforms embarked on by Eastern Europe and Russia, and is languishing economically. Its fear of Russia and its quarrels over control of the Black Sea Fleet and nuclear weapons could push it into the German orbit. Russia itself, which proved unable to intervene in Eastern Europe in the late 1980s, seems extremely unlikely to be able to do so with diminished forces for the foreseeable future, much less pose a threat to Western Europe.

But Russia's frictions with the Ukraine could conceivably lead to conflict one day: in the event of a more nationalist leadership taking charge, or the armed forces exercising a greater role and pushing Mr Yeltsin in a more nationalist direction, even war with the Ukraine could not be ruled out (although the latter is in no state to fight it), as could an attempt at reintegration with Russia. The eastern part of Ukraine, heavily populated by Russians, may attempt to secede. Conceivably, this could lead to tension with a more nationalist Germany. For the latter the priority must be a good working relationship with the Russians to obviate any fears that its economic expansion eastward is directed against them, or could become a nationalist threat.

The challenge of Germany's relations with East and West is huge in the long-term, and the maturity of the countries involved suggests that the whole issue can be resolved peacefully: but Western defence planners cannot rule out the possibility of tension along Germany's Eastern borders of a much more complex kind than those of the Cold War, fuelled primarily by nationalism. In view of the size of the powers involved and the fact that nationalism, not ideology, is involved, the West would have to be circumspect about involvement. The best way to prevent any such friction arising is to seek to anchor Germany all the more firmly in the democratic, co-operative counsels of the European Union and of NATO. The French, the Italians and moderate Germans recognize this.

THE OTHER AREA of potential conflict between major powers is East Asia, where as many as four significant military powers will be jostling each other in the new millennium: Japan, China, Russia and Korea, the latter possibly reunited. For several reasons the area is likely to become highly unstable geopolitically in the near future. The end of the Cold War has unfrozen co-operation between them against a common enemy, and has led to domestic calls in the United States to reduce its military presence in the Far East.

While Russia has made no reductions in its Far Eastern forces and has rescinded its doctrine of no first use of nuclear weapons, a gesture presumably aimed at China (and, possibly, Iran), the other three have been engaged in a major build-up of their armed forces, as have others in the region.

In April 1993, Indonesia bought a third of the former East German navy. Malaysia has acquired a large number of Russian fighter aircraft. China has increased its defence spending by half in just two years, and in 1993 raised spending by some 15 per cent. Singapore's arms spending rose by 23 per cent in 1991. Japan has continued to increase its defence spending steadily.

Taiwan, Thailand and South Korea have all boosted defence spending by more than 10 per cent. Taiwan recently bought 150 F-16s, has been shopping for around seventy-five French fighters, and has been buying submarines, anti-submarine helicopters and surface ships. There appears to be something suspiciously like an arms race going on between China, Taiwan and Japan – with Russia taking care not to reduce its military presence in East Asia.

There exists no security pact between these countries, or even any effective forum for economic co-operation. All are traditional enemies (this century, remarkably, each has fought each of the others at least once) and some have long-standing territorial disputes with one another; China with Russia, Russia with Japan.

Their recent surges in economic development have not been accompanied by a growth in political maturity; only South Korea has a tentative form of democracy, while Japan and Russia may be getting there. The spectacle of ambitious, newly rich, quite large military powers in furious competition against one another and busily expanding their armed forces is disturbing.

It is possible to see a configuration of conflict between any of them: China and Japan are increasingly interdependent economically, but have a long tradition of suspicion and rivalry. In an astonishingly frank recent attack, one of Japan's top defence experts, Professor Nishihara, accused China of seeking to become a 'hegemonic power trying to establish a militarily dominant position in Asia'. Korea and Japan, while close today, could become major economic rivals, and if Korea moved into China's orbit, Japanese passions would be inflamed. Russia's relations with Japan remain cold because of the Kurile islands dispute, and in spite of a recent reconciliation between Russia and China, the two are intensely wary of one another.

Again, the size of the parties involved would make outside intervention in any conflict between them difficult; but such are the economic interests in East Asia, particularly America's, that the United States would have difficulty staying out. The priority must be prevention: the establishment of a framework of security and economic co-operation for the region that permits the peaceful resolution of disputes. The United States is understandably reluctant to get involved in any deterrent security guarantees that commits it to sending in forces to police disputes; yet for nearly half a century, America's commitment to South Korea and Japan amounted to precisely that. Because such a commitment existed, war was avoided for a long time.

As IF THIS were not bad enough, there are three other major new security problems: nuclear proliferation; terrorism; and narcotics. All are global and directly threaten the interests of America and Europe. On nuclear proliferation, the spectacle is of a small boy, the International Atomic Energy Agency, trying to keep his finger in the hole of a very big dyke. The nuclear club, initially limited to the United States, the Soviet Union, Britain, France and China, now has at least four comparatively recent members – India, Israel, South Africa (which however now claims to have scrapped its formerly secret nuclear programme) and the Ukraine (which is probably handing back its nuclear arsenal to Russia).

In addition, at least two major countries would be capable of assembling a formidable nuclear armoury in a comparatively short space of time: Japan and Germany lack nuclear weapons because of political inhibitions, not because of any shortage of materials or technology. Pakistan may already have a nuclear capability, while Argentina and Brazil could acquire one at short notice, although they may not wish to do so. A host of unsuitable countries are seeking to acquire the bomb and these include Libya, Algeria, Iraq, Iran and North Korea. For any of these five to acquire nuclear weapons would be extremely serious.

But there exists no formal sanction to prevent them getting the bomb. Most countries have signed the Nuclear Non-Proliferation Treaty. But there is nothing to stop them abrogating it, as North Korea nearly did in 1993. The controls on the export of nuclear technology and materials have always been extraordinarily hard to enforce, in spite of valiant efforts by the IAEA, and are likely to become more so, with material and know-how being exported from a Russia which no longer needs them. The only real checks on the spread of nuclear weapons are the inhibitions of the countries concerned and the threat of unspecified sanctions by the West.

The one effective sanction for a country like Iraq or North Korea is the threat of the use of force. The Israeli raid on Iraq's Osirak reactor, and the American strike at its Gulf War nuclear facilities, performed this function; and the Americans threatened North Korea with force. There seems a perfectly good case for spelling out the consequences of the acquisition of nuclear weapons by certain states: people like Muammar Qaddafi,

Saddam Hussein, the Kims of North Korea or Iran's mullahs simply cannot be permitted by the responsible international community to possess the bomb. Nor can any country likely to fall into extremist hands – which makes one deeply uneasy about Pakistani or Algerian possession of the bomb.

Yet as the Third World grows more technologically advanced, the pressure to acquire nuclear weapons will intensify. This conjures up a world in which the United States has increasingly to contemplate pre-emptive strikes, and of course would be unable to act in the case of allies such as Pakistan. This is deeply unsatisfactory: to deal with what is likely to be a steadily more widespread problem, the United States requires a clear policy of stated deterrence against the acquisition of nuclear weapons, backed up by its allies and the rest of the international community.

This is complicated by a visceral Third World response: the complaint that only developed countries are permitted to retain nuclear weapons. This should be ignored: an international understanding on the subject is far preferable to a series of American strikes against countries about to acquire the bomb. One of the main goals of American diplomacy today must be to give the Non-Proliferation Treaty deterrent teeth, lessening the need for conflict and misunderstanding in the future. There should be no tacit deterrent: most countries would support the Americans on this matter. The threat of local nuclear war between, say, India and Pakistan, or attempts to intimidate the Gulf by a nuclear-armed Iraq or Iran hardly bear thinking about.

Thus a long-term strategy is required. Star Wars technology might give those who operate it the capacity to destroy nuclear missiles around the globe before they arrive. The United States will remain in charge of this, co-operating as much as possible with other military powers – as is now the case with Russia. The purpose of the technology should be superpower co-operation, not competition, aimed at deterring and enforcing the use of nuclear weaponry around the world.

Without such co-operation the possibilities are truly horrendous: this is one decision the world community cannot afford to funk. A second point follows, however. The possible proliferation of such weapons requires that the superpowers should not divest themselves of their own nuclear weaponry. For responsible nations to be defenceless while irresponsible ones acquire them would be an invitation to disaster. However, as Paul Nitze has argued, 'smart' conventional weapons will be all that are required to cope with nuclear threats from second-rank powers.

As far as possible, international organizations and other countries should be consulted before the use of Star Wars or action against the spread of nuclear weapons. The United States will not renounce its authority to use them when necessary without consultation, as every minute may be precious in a crisis and deterrence depends on effectiveness. But in setting out the occasions for their deployment, in explaining when they might be used, the widest possible international consensus should be gathered. The Soviet involvement in Star Wars is a first example; Japan, in particular, should be brought into this.

THE SECOND SUBSIDIARY global challenge is terrorism. This seems to occur in cycles, with moments when it seems on the retreat and others when it suddenly resurges. It is clear that it is not going to go away. If the Palestinian threat decreases in the wake of the Israeli–Palestinian settlement (although it might actually recur if Islamic militants opposed to the settlement take on the Palestinians), there are always new conflicts, such as the rape of Bosnia or the Kurdish people, not to mention the horrors in the south of the former Soviet Union, all of which adds fuel to the fire of terrorism and motivates extremists.

Terrorism has been fought with an efficiency that seemed barely possible two decades ago: the occasional outrage has to be set against the fact that, for example, several million flights take off and land safely every year. But there cannot ever be any reason to relax vigilance or fail to improve anti-terrorist techniques. One of the greatest strides forward in fighting terrorism has been the end of Soviet and Eastern bloc sponsorship or passive support of extremist groups, which helps to explain the decline of recent terrorist activity. If indeed the mainstream

Palestinian organizations can rein in their extremists, that will also be a great advance. Western countries should take care to identify potential terrorist trouble spots before they emerge. Both Bosnia and Tibet, with entirely justifiable causes, could nurture extremist movements one day.

THE THIRD, LESSER, challenge to the international order is narcotics. The international drugs trade is huge, and comes from two main sources: the Golden Triangle through from China, North Thailand and Burma, the origin of most of the world's heroin; and the cocaine trade – and to a lesser extent the traffic in marijuana – originating principally in Colombia, Bolivia and Peru.

The heroin route runs overland, across India, Pakistan and Afghanistan, and up through Iran, Kurdistan, Turkey and Bulgaria to its main distribution points in Italy and Sicily. The cocaine trade up to now has mostly travelled up to the United States through Mexico and the Caribbean. But as the crack-down by the United States against the trade has intensified, cocaine is increasingly transported to Spain and Portugal for the European markets.

The United Nations is the obvious organization to co-ordinate the campaign against the international drugs trade; but because of its scale the problem is now one of international security. The invasion of Panama was primarily directed at the drugs trade; in Peru and Colombia, American anti-narcotics advisers are highly visible. There can be little doubt that China colludes in the huge harvest of poppies in its southern region. There can be no doubt, either, that the problem has to be tackled at both ends – production and consumption.

The argument over drugs has often threatened to degenerate into a North–South one, as grower countries argue that they have no need to cut back on valuable sources of earnings for their farmers just because Americans and Europeans have acquired the narcotics habit, and have deemed drugs illegal. Certainly the United States will have more clout in controlling drugs at source if it provides help for narcotics growers to diversify into legitimate crops, and if it shows a greater disposition to tackle the problem in the United States.

Of course there are other major global challenges: overpopulation, migration, environmental problems, and the arms trade to name but four, which are best tackled through international co-operation as well as domestic programmes. But those identified here – the global security problem, nuclear proliferation, terrorism and narcotics – are the four horsemen of the modern apocalypse, the ones that require urgent world action. Taken together with the globalization of capitalism, which risks causing international recession and economic anarchy unless controlled, they constitute a huge agenda for the beginning of the third millennium.

CHAPTER TWO

BACK TO DETERRENCE

IT IS TEMPTING to believe that there are imaginative, original solutions to these awesome problems. In fact, the answers are straightforward. However, the process of acquiring the political will to implement them is much more difficult.

On terrorism and narcotics there is already a system of international co-operation which has often scored major successes, but which needs to be deepened and given greater resources. On nuclear proliferation, the rudiments of a system of control are already in place but a more explicit statement is needed on the consequences of the spread of such weapons to deter those that might be tempted to acquire them. The potential acquisition of nuclear weapons by a country outside the terms of the Non-Proliferation Treaty needs to be treated as a violation of the international order which would be on a par with an act of aggression.

On the issue of global security, in a world bereft of the disciplines of the Cold War, the position is a mess but there are three elements which would help to reorder it. The United States and its NATO colleagues have to spell out a new doctrine of when intervention is justified in a regional conflict. It is essential that a structure of deterrence across potential conflict epicentres be set up to make clear to potential aggressors before, rather than after, the consequences of their actions; this should be accompanied by an effective system of international arbitration, for which the UN might be suited. Finally, the mechanisms of deterrence need to be put in place, and must command the widest international support possible, without in any way paralysing the intervention process itself, which must be rapid, effective and preferably American-led.

The first element can be dealt with quickly. The United States remains overwhelmingly the most effective military power in the West and has no challenger for the job. The *ad hoc* interventions already practised by the Americans in alliance, for example, with Britain and France, have been entirely dominated by the former. No American ally can have anything but a marginal role to play in advising the United States when to intervene, because they bear the overwhelming brunt of the costs and the numbers.

However, consultation should be made as effective as possible. The Americans have, frankly, got their own way all too often. But a world without a policeman at all would be awful to contemplate. Equally, the United States has every right to expect its allies to contribute, if, because of the constitutional restraints in Germany and Japan, not in men, then in money. For intervention to succeed, leadership from the United States is necessary for the foreseeable future.

Nor, in spite of domestic rhetoric, can the United States afford to abdicate from the world, in view of the costs to itself and the world disorder which would follow. America initially attempted to shut itself off from global conflicts in 1914 and 1939 before being sucked in. It cannot afford to do so even briefly now, or it would have failed to learn anything from the past. The machinery for intervention remains: that of American consultation with its allies through NATO followed by an *ad hoc* alliance of those prepared to take part, without any need for the full alliance to concur, or any provision for veto or majority support. Military intervention cannot be decided by democratic vote in a large and cumbersome alliance. All for one and one for all was an appropriate doctrine when a Soviet threat endangered all of Western Europe. It is not appropriate for regional intervention where some countries may have major interests at stake and others none at all. Nevertheless, NATO, with its colossal experience of deterrence, remains much the best framework for intervention.

The second element, regional deterrence, is the most important of all: since 1948, much of the world has operated under a system of deterrence, which has served to keep international disputes in order. This system has now disappeared. Most areas of the world were governed by fear of superpower confrontation, or the withholding of client status. This no longer applies – hence the emergence of medieval nationalist and ethnic rivalries. It is clear, on humanitarian grounds alone, that this will have to be regulated by a structure of deterrence across most of the world's trouble spots.

This seems hard, in some respects: the West, and the Americans in particular, can hardly afford to be involved in dozens of conflicts across the globe of no direct national interest to them. But in another respect it is easier: these conflicts are never likely to be on the global scale that deterrence in Europe required: most are tiresome, difficult and murderous little local confrontations. But the purpose of the deterrent structure is to prevent them breaking out at all – and here NATO has shown the way. If possible local antagonists are impressed, well before the conflict, with the knowledge that aggression will immediately invite massive retaliation from outside, such conflicts are less likely to occur.

In most of the major American postwar interventions, misleading signals were sent as to whether action would be taken – and the consequence was a much bigger intervention than would probably have been necessary at the outset. This applied to Korea, Vietnam and the Gulf. If, however, defensive alliances were already in place, then the consequences of aggression would be apparent to potential perpetrators.

So, for example, if a formal defensive structure existed throughout the Gulf which guaranteed the territorial integrity of all the states in the area, with an intense probability of Western intervention if this were violated, there would be much less likelihood of matters reaching this threshold. This would need to be buttressed by a proper arbitration mechanism, for which the United Nations, with its interminably legalistic approach, would seem perfectly adapted.

In the event of a dispute over oil, for example, a state could go to the UN and seek binding arbitration. In the event that this failed, and one country invaded another, the international community – America and its allies – would be obliged to intervene massively against the aggressor. But it is important that the UN, while performing a mediating role, should not have the sole power to authorize such intervention. This should be left to the military powers themselves, or the threat of intervention would not be credible. Further, in view of the undoubted limits on the projection of American military force, such deterrent alliances should be constructed on a regional basis.

It is possible to envisage a full security alliance of deterrent guarantees, based on the threat of Western intervention, in such key areas as the Gulf – in particular Saudi Arabia; in the Far East, again guaranteeing the territorial integrity of each nation there, which would be largely policed by the Americans, with minor European and Anzac involvement. The old Soviet Empire would remain the sphere of influence of the Russians, necessarily so, but the West should seek to impose diplomatic restraints on future Chechnyas. So too Africa and Western Europe, with former European countries primarily responsible for their own former colonial territories, but with limited American and Soviet support. Finally, the UN should be empowered to recruit a volunteer short-stay intervention force from its members, to police humanitarian crises in which there are virtually no national interests involved. These would be low-level militarily and authorised by the Security Council: Rwanda springs immediately to mind.

Indignant criticism will no doubt bubble up at this juncture: such interventions would be impossible, because of the difficulty of identifying aggressor and victim, because of the impossibility of fighting several wars at once, because of the problems in securing domestic support for faraway wars, and so on. In addition, the real problem is that both America and Russia – never mind Europe – cannot see why they should get involved in other people's conflicts where their national interests are not directly at stake: with such guarantees of security, they risk being sucked into wars.

Yet this is defeatist thinking, and there is no other way in the long run. For nearly half a century the world was committed to mutual nuclear annihilation – something far worse than intervention in regional wars – and as a result no conflict occurred. There may have been an element of bluff in this: would a serious crisis or invasion of Western Europe really have triggered an overwhelming nuclear response by the United States? Neither side dared take the risk, so it did not happen. Similarly some rogue state in the Third World might test the threat of massive Western intervention – but most would not take the risk.

If a deterrent structure is in place around the world, the chances of conflict are far reduced, even if occasionally the 'police force' will have to be called out. A Saddam or a Milosevic is likely to think twice before attacking if he fears massive retaliation: in both cases, before launching wars of aggression, not only was no deterrent structure in place, every indication was given that there would be no retaliation at all.

Regional deterrence and intervention may be a much easier task than global deterrence during the Cold War. General Odom argues that the nature of American force projection will be changed radically as a result of developments in technology, in many ways making intervention overseas easier than in the past. Aircraft have intercontinental ranges, ballistic missiles can strike against distant powers, satellite and other means of surveillance allow American forces to 'spot' targets thousands of miles away. America can now contemplate long-distance war. The distant tactical operation centres, which managed war close to the actual site of conflict, can now operate on minute-by-minute directions from the National Military Control Center at the Pentagon and the White House.

Naval warfare is changing radically: instead of the need to maintain a huge, expensive and vulnerable surface fleet, missiles can target enemy ships and submarines from land. Similarly, the old idea of a separate air force, charged with strategic bombing, may be obsolete. The impact of such bombing was always open to question. The Gulf War showed that co-ordination between ground forces and air attack was now necessary to the extent that the old distinction between the services – with its interminable arguments and costly duplication of resources – may now be actually harmful.

In fact the effectiveness of the massive aerial softening-up

Cumulative Destruction of Equipment in the Gulf War

	Tanks		APCs		Artillery	
Original	**4,550**		**2,880**		**3,257**	
22 Jan	14		0		77	
27 Jan	65		50		281	
1 Feb	476		243		356	
6 Feb	728		552		535	
11 Feb	862		692		771	
16 Feb	1,439		879		1,271	
21 Feb	1,563		887		1,428	
23 Feb	1,688		929		1,452	
24 Feb	1,772		948		1,474	
25 Feb	1,865	(41%)	992	(34%)	1,462	(45%)
26 Feb	2,040	(45%)	1,009	(35%)	1,505	(46%)
27 Feb	3,708	(81%)	1,856	(47%)	2,140	(66%)
1 Mar	3,847	(85%)	1,450	(50%)	2,917	(90%)

Source: US Department of Defense APC = Armored Personnel Carrier

bombardment of Iraqi forces, before the ground attack was launched, is open to question. The accompanying chart shows that the great majority of military equipment was destroyed during the ground offensive, not during the aerial bombardment.

Another lesson of the Gulf War is that the only country capable of large-scale military intervention around the globe is America, because of its clear lead in the unromantic field of logistics and force lift. Odom argues:

> At present, no country other than the United States has the means to provide adequate logistics for a major campaign far beyond its borders. This fact puts serious limits on where all armies except those of the United States and its allies can fight in the world. The logistics challenge lies not only in a state's capacity to provide supplies at great distances. It also includes capacity to produce certain kinds of weapons and equipment, to afford to stock them in adequate numbers, and

> to expand production of at least some of them, all in a fairly short time. Complexities in the production of new weapons raise serious questions about the adequacy of traditional approaches to surging production during a crisis or war. The World War II pattern has lost much of its validity for present industrial and technological realities.
>
> The experience of the Gulf War revealed that the United States' military had not prepared adequately for strategic lift to provide the necessary projection and supply of its forces. Iraq fortunately allowed the United States the time necessary to overcome its shortfall in strategic lift. The imperative conclusion is that strategic lift and logistics are fundamental elements of modern military power. They distinguish minor from major powers, and major powers can be reduced to minor status in some conflicts if they do not plan for sufficient strategic transports and stocks of matériel.

Odom argues that despite this America still has a long way to go in developing both air and sea lift capabilities. Another problem is that modern 'smart weapons' cannot be rolled off civilian production lines, hastily converted to military use, in the event of general mobilization. Unless huge stocks of these sophisticated weapons are built up, a sustained war would quickly see the use of smart weapons tapering off into simpler, mass-produced, more old-fashioned weaponry. America's technological edge might thus fade in the event of a long war: Odom believes that quality of weaponry is much more important than quantity – where in some areas it lagged behind the Soviet Union during the Cold War.

The requirements of modern weaponry also make the United States dependent on some foreign sources of technology, unless it pursues hugely costly policies of making itself self-sufficient in technology. The three countries essential to America's modern arms technology are Japan, Germany and Korea. The United States thus will need access to at least one of these three in wartime. In the highly improbable event of hostilities between America and Japan (which could blockade Korea), the United States would have to be careful to have the Germans on its side. In the event of hostilities with Germany, America needs good relations with Japan.

In addition, Odom argues, America's space capabilities make its participation in any major allied military engagement absolutely essential.

> Space-based systems played a greater role in the Gulf War than is generally appreciated. Both communications and intelligence means in space were critical determinants of the campaign. The global positioning system for ground navigation in the desert also depended on space components. The military uses of space in this regard promise to become more important. Although most of these capabilities were developed to deal with a NATO–Warsaw Pact conflict, they have proven very adaptable to small wars in the Third World. They give the United States and its allies advantages that are easy to underestimate.
>
> Some of the new technologies, particularly for intelligence and space, cannot be fully exploited unilaterally by the United States. Co-operation with allies, especially in providing ground stations, adds to their capacity. During the Cold War, some of these capabilities became a kind of 'public good' within US alliances. For the United States to enjoy them, they had to be shared with other states. This is likely to remain true in some respects for the indefinite future. It is not an exaggeration to say that modern technologies for warfare require coalitions of states for their most effective use. The implications of this are important, particularly for some second-level powers. Within coalitions including the United States, such powers enjoy much more military potential than would be possible outside such coalitions. Any plans for an independent European military coalition inevitably will mean a decline in the military potential NATO has given Western European states. A European coalition would lack the space capabilities, the *en-route* basing for force projection to distant regions, and other features. These technical realities are often ignored in policy debates about alternative military alliances in the post-Cold War era.

On the nuclear front, the collapse of the Soviet Union creates the possibility of virtually eliminating nuclear weapons carried by bombers, which are much easier to defend against than are those carried on ballistic missiles. The latter should be based in mobile launchers, not silos, and, together with submarine-based missiles, would provide an adequate defence against a shrunken Russia or any other conceivable nuclear power. With Star Wars technology still in a much earlier state of development than generally realized, it is necessary to retain an adequate defensive structure against ballistic missiles.

Odom assesses America's military needs at about twelve divisions, one corps being required for Europe (down from two), while Korean forces should be maintained at present levels, as much to retain America's key presence in Asia as to deter North Korea. The army should also have a corps of three divisions that could be deployed anywhere in the world within thirty days. The necessary airlift and sealift must be provided for.

Odom eloquently argues why it would be counterproductive for America to shed its global responsibilities:

> First, the US domestic economy, not just the defence industries, is interdependent with the economies of Europe and Japan. Although this has long been conventional wisdom, the implications are seldom fully explored. Those economies would not have prospered as they have if the United States had not provided a security structure that permitted old adversaries to co-operate economically.
>
> Second, the world is in the midst of a revolution in military affairs driven by new technologies. Although military coalitions have been imperative for Western security for a long time, this military technology revolution makes them all the more so, both for operational reasons and for defense industrial reasons . . .
>
> Beyond the bounds of NATO and the US alliances with Japan and South Korea, the trend is toward more conflicts, more small wars, and less international order. The end of the Cold War has facilitated and perhaps accelerated that trend.

Although many of these conflicts may not directly affect US security interests, some already have.

These . . . realities mark a major break in the international system, revealing forces that are likely to hurt US interests, both domestic and foreign, unless they can be contained, arrested, or eliminated. They show why American foreign and domestic policies are interrelated in ways that disallow trade-offs between them. The choice to give domestic policies all the priority while relegating foreign and military policies to relative neglect simply does not exist. Unless the international challenge of the post-Cold War period is successfully met – creating a climate in which the industrial democracies can continue to enjoy economic growth – there will be far fewer resources available to deal with domestic problems. It has become fashionable to assert that America must be strong at home before it can be strong abroad. The United States cannot be strong at home, however, unless it is strong abroad . . .

Diplomacy alone will not suffice. It must be backed with adequate military power.

. . . Introducing such new thinking into the American defense debate will not be easy and may prove impossible. If it does, America is in for a decade of declining economic performance, increasing political and economic competition among nation states, and perhaps not major wars among the industrial democracies, but certainly wars on their peripheries that provoke the democracies to quarrel over what to do and thereby prevent them from doing anything. The trend has already been made apparent in Europe by the war in what was Yugoslavia. Given the sluggish nature of all Western economies, the weakening of NATO coincident with the dimming prospects of European political and military integration, and the large reductions already in progress in US military capabilities, one can argue that the United States may have already missed the opportunity to create a new world order. Perhaps America has won the Cold War only to lose the peace.

> In my own judgment, the United States has not yet lost the peace, but time is running out. Americans must get on with the debate because there will not be as much time now as there was after World War II to reverse the tendency to retreat to isolation in North America. Nor does the United States have the relative economic advantages enjoyed at that time. The United States today, nonetheless, has more resources to engage in international leadership than most public discussion suggests.

Odom's warning could hardly be more sombre. His analysis points to a world in which America must remain engaged, and in which its allies militarily cannot do without it; and in which rapid, short-lived intervention in regional conflicts becomes increasingly possible.

America's new medium-term military strategy, announced in September 1993, envisages keeping 100,000 troops in Europe and 98,000 in South Korea. The navy will continue to have a global role in the Pacific, the Mediterranean and off South-West Asia, but, sensibly, fewer aircraft carriers will be used. America's submarine force will be reduced from eighty-one to around fifty. The army will move in brigade rather than divisional strength, with more pre-positioning of equipment abroad and at sea. The American navy and air force will develop together a new generation of attack jets with four-fifths identical parts and weaponry.

Neither the United States, nor Russia, nor Western Europe can afford to let the present vacuum of responsibility after the collapse of the Cold War structures continue: a world of regional wars that could even involve nuclear confrontation between other countries is otherwise in prospect, which would permit none of the big three the luxury of isolation. Security pacts, a mechanism of arbitration supervised by the UN, with the prospect of overwhelming deterrent force projection by the major powers, each taking prime responsibility for its own area of the world, are the long-term keys. This is authorizing the developed world to intervene to prevent carnage in the developing world; otherwise the developed world will be shirking its responsibilities – and in an increasingly shrunken world, it can only get away with that for a short time. This is not the new colonialism; it is the new responsibility.

THE STRANDS OF a post-Cold War security structure can now be brought together. If anyone a decade ago had suggested that America would be entering a new period of domestic self-obsession, non-intervention abroad and isolationism, that Western Europe would watch idly as a war of aggression and 'ethnic cleansing' took place on its borders, that massive reductions in European armaments would be under way while NATO would be struggling to find a role, he would have been thought a pacifist crank by most defence experts.

Yet all of these are happening now, made acceptable by the reduction in the Russian threat, even as other military challenges loom on the horizon. These threats are not confined to the multiplicity of newly rich, politically backward societies increasingly throwing their weight about in the Third World. Any survey of global security has to consider the possibility that in a new age of nationalism, Japan, whose outlook and institutions were little changed by the Second World War, could one day pass over from being a Western ally to a security threat, and that Germany, now suppressing a wave of street-level nationalism but increasingly assertive in its unified state and impatient of European co-operation, could similarly one day pose a security challenge.

The Soviet threat seems much diminished and history suggests that even a return to the *ancien régime* would result in a primarily defensive posture, owing to economic weakness: if the Soviet Union was unable to hold on to Eastern Europe in 1989, it seems unlikely to be able successfully to reinvade it in the future. It would only be tempted to try by the emergence of a German challenge in Eastern Europe; much likelier is conflict between the new and down-at-heel nationalist state of the Ukraine and Russia, which would be dangerous but not uncontrollable.

Global security is moving into dangerously uncharted new waters. How can it be steered? A new global security structure must be based on the following premises:

THE UNITED STATES should remain a major interventionist superpower and the leader of the Western alliance. Only America has the global force projection to assume this leadership role. Economic rivalry between the three major blocs should not obscure the need for Europe and Japan to accept America's military leadership. Neither Europe nor Japan can enforce global security without America. Nor can America do without allies or, in an increasingly interdependent world, retreat into global isolation.

NATO PROVIDES a well-tried organizational framework for co-operation between the Western allies which also anchors America to the European continent. It must act as the foundation of a new European security structure. NATO also serves the immensely important function of keeping Germany's armed forces in full alliance with its Western partners. The British-led Rapid Reaction Force is precisely the kind of development that NATO needs. The integrated Franco-German-Belgian Eurocorps, while a welcome development, also helping to dilute any reversion to German militarism, cannot be a substitute for NATO as a whole for many years to come, if ever. But for NATO to deserve to survive at all, in the face of public scepticism, it must be ready to intervene militarily where necessary. Otherwise its soldiers may as well be sent packing, and thereby save taxpayers a lot of money.

The Eurocorps, founded in November 1993, is based in Strasbourg, a city which has changed hands four times in 125 years. The Eurocorps has around 600 men, due to increase to 45,000 or so by October 1995, containing a mixed Franco-German brigade, plus separate tank divisions for each country, and a mechanized infantry division from Belgium. The Spaniards, who are observers, are expected to join soon. In addition to the Eurocorps, southern European countries have been staging joint military operations, and Britain and Holland are forming an amphibious force. Helmut Willmann, the Eurocorps's first commander, says it is intended to become the military arm of the European Union; but, he says, it is available for NATO and UN operations as well. Britain may eventually co-operate with this, and its growing détente with its natural ally in Europe, France, is to be welcomed.

Britain is down to a single corps with only one armoured division in place on the Rhine; the RAF seems likely to remove its group headquarters from Germany, and may pull out altogether. Klaus Kinkel, the German foreign minister, believes that the North Atlantic Co-operation Council embracing both NATO and the Warsaw Pact, should take on an operational role for joint manoeuvres and deployments in crisis regions. He is surely right.

The Western European Union cannot provide a substitute for an American-led NATO. It would be transparently absurd to set up a full WEU command alongside the NATO one – for the WEU has no overall commander, command, control or communications facilities, formal headquarters, intelligence, surveillance, sea or air transport, logistics or infrastructure; to set one up would be ruinously costly, as well as duplicating existing arrangements. Instead, NATO's American supreme commander, SACEUR, should have a European general on his staff as deputy commander in charge of WEU forces, with a separate planning staff located at NATO headquarters in Brussels, which could take over the NATO levers in the event that a wholly European operation was decided upon without American participation. This is as far as the European pillar should be taken at this stage: units from the new Eurocorps and the British-Dutch amphibious force would be made available to the WEU when necessary, as well as British and NATO forces stationed in Germany.

The WEU's most significant role is in drawing the French back into NATO military structures while preserving the fiction that they are not placing men under American leadership of the alliance. According to a senior French officer, 'We are ready to participate provided we are not put in front of ready-made decisions from our American friends.' France, he said, had shed all its 'taboos' over NATO. 'Nothing serious can be done on the ground in Europe without the participation of French forces,' he added grandiosely. France has raised its military spending to 3.6 per cent of GDP in 1993–4, uniquely among NATO countries, under its dynamic young defence minister, François Leotard.

It is deeply undesirable that the three competing economic blocs – Europe, America and Japan – should become military rivals as well. Far better for NATO integration to cut across economic rivalries, and for NATO to be able to enlist assistance from allies around the globe, such as Russia and Japan.

NATO's FIRST PURPOSE must be defined as the continuing defence of Western Europe in the (highly improbable) event of attack from Russia and in the (marginally less improbable) event of conflict between one of its members and another (for example, Greece and Turkey, Germany and one of its neighbours).

NATO's NEW MISSION needs to be spelt out as providing for the enforcement of deterrence: in practice, some degree of apportionment of global tasks is necessary. The United States alone should be responsible for the enforcement of security in its own hemisphere, America and European NATO for Eastern Europe and the Middle East; European NATO and America for North Africa; the United States and Europe for sub-Saharan Africa; the United States, Japan and ASEAN for East and South-East Asia; Russia for the former southern republics of the Soviet Union; the United States, Europe and Russia jointly for South-West Asia and the Indian subcontinent.

A SERIES OF DETERRENT security alliances based on non-aggression and the resolution of disputes by peaceful arbitration needs to be set up, covering each of the following areas: Central Europe; the Balkans; the Gulf, North Africa; India–Pakistan; and East Asia.

MILITARY INTERVENTIONS, while making use of the full NATO infrastructure if necessary, can be decided upon by the United States and one or more of its senior NATO partners. The decision-making process should be flexible, rapid, and compact; the full concurrence of the alliance should not be necessary and no country except the United States or the three European members of NATO – Britain, France and Germany, acting together – should have a veto on such action. European NATO countries should have the power to act in crises where the Americans prefer to stay out.

WHILE THE WIDEST possible support should be canvassed for any military intervention, the UN should possess no power of veto, nor be placed in operational charge of any such action. The UN role should be limited purely to peacekeeping operations particularly in areas of no strategic significance involving low-intensity operations (like Rwanda) and its new role as arbiters in international disputes, with no major enforcement role: it is entirely the wrong organization for the job. Obviously, the views of UN members and the judgment of UN arbiters about the rights and wrongs of a particular dispute would be taken into account by the enforcing nations, which would most often, however, act against the party that resorted to force to settle such a dispute, regardless of the arguments themselves.

NATO NEEDS TO BE reformed so as to provide three levels of security co-operation and authority in enforcing the new security system: at the centre, the United States would provide leadership – which must be in the interests of global security, not the narrow interpretation of American national interests; the second circle should consist of America and its traditional NATO partners. In the third, wider organization needs to be created, based on the Conference on Security and Cooperation in Europe and the rather fuzzy Partnership for Peace, perhaps termed the Northern Alliance and consisting of the existing members of

NATO; Eastern European countries which wish to join, including the Ukraine and the Baltic States; the Soviet Union; and Japan.

The current argument about whether NATO should be extended eastward would be resolved by the creation of a wider, looser framework which, embracing the old NATO as well as Eastern Europe and Russia, could not be seen as directed against Russia. Clearly, Russia would have to provide guarantees of non-intervention against other member states to belong – although, for reasons already stated, a Russian reinvasion of Eastern Europe seems neither probable nor practicable except in the unlikely event of a threat from Germany (a dispute with the Ukraine would be another matter). It is far preferable to retain Russian goodwill by including it in a wider alliance, defusing tensions with its neighbours and giving the armed forces a new, constructive role.

NATO's CONVENTIONAL global deterrent needs to be underwritten by a nuclear umbrella capable of deterring and, if need be, preferably using conventional missiles, striking at Third World countries that might use nuclear weapons in any conflict. Such a system could ultimately be space-based.

ONCE THE DETERRENT structure is in place, while NATO intervention would be highly probable in any given conflict, it would not be automatic: any such intervention would have to take account of the degree of provocation of the attacking party, local circumstances, the extent to which the enforcing countries were tied down elsewhere, the scale of the operation and so on. For deterrence to be credible, intervention must usually take place; but the final decision would be left to the United States and its *ad hoc* group of allies.

These principles are the backbone of a new global security system that is desperately required to prevent a slide towards a series of dangerous regional conflicts in the Third World which would inevitably in the long run suck in the major industrial powers. It would be tragic if the opportunity offered by the new military co-operation between previously competing superpowers were followed by a new age of nationalism and an abdication of responsibility, resulting in global chaos and conflict.

Now that the Russians are no longer against us – and the best way to ensure things stay that way is to give their armed forces a new and constructive role – and now that conflicts are likely to be on a much smaller scale, although more numerous, it ought to be easier, rather than harder, to police global security. The Western alliance is groping its way blindly forward in the unfamiliar landscape of the post-Cold War world; it will find the path more easily if it takes off the blinkers of the attitudes of the past four decades, and does not rear up in horror every time a nationalist mouse runs under its feet.

Even the Clinton administration shows signs of being shamed into a more active foreign policy, while part of the Republican Party, to its credit, is urging one, rather than reverting to its traditionally isolationist, pro-business attitudes. Yet what if Odom's worst scenario proves correct and America is indeed entering a period of historical self-absorption and isolationism? Then Britain, France and Germany, Europe's big three, will have no alternative but to reach out to their great cultural and geographical neighbour, now-democratic Russia, and beyond it, Japan, for a new alliance of the older world powers in friendly competition with the United States.

The interests of all five, in a world where none harbours territorial claims on the other (except for the minor Russian–Japanese dispute over the Kuriles) are closer than many think, and could be closer than any of these countries has with a United States hell-bent on business expansion at the expense of its global responsibilities. It would not be in America's interests, economic or otherwise, for Western Europe to look East rather than West for its allies. This alone should ensure that America's period of post-Cold War self-indulgence comes to an end and that it reaches out again to Europe and the world.

CHAPTER THREE

POLICING THE JUNGLE

THE GLOBALIZATION of capitalism presents greater challenges still. There are two entirely separate approaches to the problem. The first is supra-national regulation; the second, the recognition of internal responsibility by the major corporations.

The first is the easier to tackle. The entire history of the development of capitalism has been characterized by the gradual evolution of state intervention to obviate its excesses: anti-trust regulations in the United States, social legislation in Britain and so on. The business enterprise is both necessary and crude: necessary because without it the organization does not exist for the creation of wealth and jobs, crude because the main objective of its owners and management is to maximize profits, and they have no obligations beyond that.

Society has to impose its own obligations through regulation – obliging capitalists not to destroy their local environment through pollution, to house workers in decent conditions, not to employ children and so on – without destroying the dynamics of capitalist wealth-creation. The global firm has to a large degree escaped national constraints – not in these fields (although major Western firms are much less scrupulous about observing them abroad than at home), but in the way it moves investment about arbitrarily, devastates economies with profligate lending, clobbers them with unfair trading practices, permits globalized industry to be dominated by a few huge firms and, in the field of currency trading, allows speculation that knocks national economies off course, for no better reason than the herd instinct of the market. All these phenomena require new means of control; otherwise the law of the jungle is back, at a time when most countries have become more democratic, because most economic decisions have been taken out of governments' hands.

The key is a decisive strengthening of international regulatory organs. The shape of this is obvious. The world is increasingly dividing into three giant trading and economic blocs – the Americas, Europe and its dependencies, and Japan and Asia. Only these giant clusters are going to be capable of controlling international flows. Indeed, co-operation among the three may be necessary to harness the really powerful forces – for example, currency movement or multinational investment. It is not impossible to see even Japan allying itself with the other two blocs if the major economic forces cannot be overcome by them acting alone. Of course, the embryo of such co-operation already exists in a host of international forums, such as the G7, the UN, the IMF, GATT, the World Bank, the OECD and so on.

But, as with the UN in the security field, there is little real commitment to such multilateral institutions. The only real hope lies in deals between the three main economic groupings – the three world superstates. It is already evident that these exist: the American superstate, NAFTA, joins 250 million Americans with 87 Mexicans and 25 million Canadians. America provides some 85 per cent of NAFTA's GDP, Canada 10 per cent and Mexico 5 per cent, yielding a combined total of $7 trillion a year. The European superstate of some 350 million people, produces a combined GDP of more than $6 trillion a year. The Japanese superstate, with its three-quarters share of the output of East Asia, has a population of 120 million and an output of $3.5 trillion.

Some people argue that if China, Hong Kong, Taiwan and Singapore are taken together in a 'greater China' bloc, their exports are equal to those of Japan and could exceed them early in the millennium on the current 7 per cent average growth rate over the past thirty years. The Chinese could outstrip the GDP of either Germany or Japan. However, only Hong Kong is scheduled to join mainland China in 1997; the others seem likely to retain their independence. China's underlying weakness is exposed by the fact that its per capita GDP is still about a fifth of America's and a sixth of Japan's. It is true that 50 million Chinese who live overseas have a huge share of the regional Asian economy: 80 per cent of foreign investment in China comes from Taiwan, Hong Kong and Singapore. Companies owned by overseas Chinese account for around 70 per cent of the private sector in Singapore, Malaysia, Thailand, Indonesia and the Philippines. But Japanese dominance is currently undisputed.

LET US RETURN to each example of the globalization of capitalism in turn. In terms of currency trading, major reserve currencies are obviously far more powerful than smaller ones. A speculative flow can overwhelm a currency as large as the French franc. It can even slightly lower the value of the dollar or the yen, although almost invariably changes in these can be ascribed either to deliberate policy by their central monetary authorities, or to entirely understandable phenomena, such as the American twin deficits, or the Japanese trade surplus. In other words, the major currencies are affected by rational movements of money markets, rather than the capricious speculation that knocks about the smaller currencies. A unified Euro-currency would enjoy the same privileged position (to some extent the mark already does).

The failure of national governments to control speculative currency flows would not apply to the dollar, yen and Euro-currency. The three main currencies could float freely against each other or, more likely, as is already beginning to happen, be managed so that a massive Japanese trade surplus is compensated for by a rise in the value of the yen, as negotiated between the monetary authorities. Currency rates are too unpredictable and fickle to be permitted total freedom: where sudden movements can destroy the export strategy of a perfectly competitive economy, some stability must be introduced.

The world's economy should be managed and monitored as intensively as a national economy: already the embryo of global economic management exists within the G7 group of major industrial nations. A G3 group – America, Europe and Japan – could work much more effectively to iron out destructive currency fluctuations, shortages of global demand, economic overheating and the dangers of protectionism. Recently the world has been experiencing a surplus of liquidity and a shortage of demand – on a smaller scale, the classic ingredients of recession that helped to cause the depression in the 1930s. This is because of a curious combination of orthodox economics that were fashionable in the 1980s, the implosion of demand in the non-Asian Third World that followed the debt crisis, the deflationary impact of Japan's trade surplus which is sucking demand out of the system, and the recessionary impact of high European interest rates needed to pay for German unification.

It may prove impossible to get Japan to alter course significantly through reflation, although Keynesian tinkering has been tried there in the wake of the bursting of the 'bubble economy'. But in the future it should be possible, for example, for the Americans and Europeans to agree on a concerted increase in demand by both economic blocs. If the Japanese won't play ball and increase their own straitjacketed domestic demand, both Western blocs could indulge in a joint devaluation against the yen that would prevent Japan reaping the export benefits of greater demand in their economies. To some extent this is already happening. This is the kind of global economic management that becomes possible in a world of three superstates, replacing the current free-for-all on the foreign exchange markets. G3 would be much more effective than G7.

The arguments for and against a single European currency are well rehearsed: it will come as no surprise to the reader that the author of this study favours a single currency as the best means to protect individual nation states against speculative currency flows – and also to end the massive interference with free trade of fluctuating national currencies. One condition must apply to the creation of such a currency: an effective regional and industrial policy that ensures there are no massive transfers of wealth to the centre – a tendency in any superstate.

Currently, without agreement on a single currency, the

European Union has the worst of all worlds. A single currency is in the making already: the German mark is becoming Europe's reserve currency while the rest bob about half-drowning in its wake; and there is no effective industrial and regional policy to compensate for the growing centralization of capital flows around Germany.

A greater role for the state in Europe requires government structures with much more satisfactory accountability than is provided by the present unelected Commission. The structures of this can be argued about, but their outline is clear: an elected executive, chosen either by the European Parliament or directly by the people; a more powerful parliament containing a senate elected by national parliaments; and a European central bank whose governors would be chosen by the nation states, but which would be accountable to parliament.

It is a matter of semantics whether to label this federalism or not. Ironically in the United States and Germany, federalism was a term implying the decentralization of authority to the constituent states, as opposed to a more centralized confederal state like Canada. In America, that most varied and parochial of societies, there is much grumbling about Washington and the federal government, but few people really consider it a remote and bullying central authority. In American elections there is greater participation in local and governorship races, as well as congressional battles, than in presidential elections. This is entirely healthy: people are concerned about the running of their state more than the remoter political battle in Washington. The same would undoubtedly be true of a European state.

In Iowa and Alabama there is no sense of resentment about dealing in dollars printed in Washington. The reverse is true: people know they are dealing in a strong, hard currency. The same would apply to a common European currency. Countries could even retain their national names for it – pounds, marks, francs and so on – provided one unit is worth exactly the same as another and could circulate freely across Europe.

In Asia we are already seeing the evolution of a 'yen zone', willy-nilly. As Japan becomes the dominant economic partner in the region, responsible for some 70 per cent of its GDP, and regional trade is increasingly carried out with Japan rather than the United States, the advantages of having local currencies pegged to the dollar are diminishing.

The great advantage in the past was that the exporting countries of East Asia ensured that their products never became uncompetitive in America as their currencies descended with the dollar, while, as the yen rose, they became more competitive in Japan. But as the volume of their trade with Japan increases, so does the disadvantage of being paid in appreciating yen, rather than depreciating dollars, and people are choosing to hold yen to facilitate transactions. The Japanese government, previously opposed to the concept of a yen zone, is now sympathetic.

The problem of creating one is, however, more complex than with Europe. Many fear that Japan's domination of the regional economy – much greater than Germany's in Europe – would create a one-sided arrangement between Japan and little local satellites. Now with the growth of China's economy and the possibility of Korean union, there will be at least two other major economies in the region, with Taiwan and Singapore some way behind. The relationship may become slightly more equal, which makes for an easier one.

APEC, the Asia–Pacific Economic Community, which first met in Seattle in November 1993, has much more modest goals than the European Union: its own internal report circulated in advance of the summit argued that:

> The creation of APEC in 1989 represented a critical first step in the process of filling an inter-governmental institutional vacuum. The time has now come to use the organization much more extensively to promote the economic interests of its members. It could thereby promote their security and political interests as well. APEC should adopt a bold new vision for the future of the Asia–Pacific. This would provide a clear – and even dramatic – substantive mandate for the institution.
>
> The proposed Asia–Pacific Economic Community would not seek to replicate the evolution of the European Com-

munity. We see neither a need nor a practical possibility of creating a single internal market. We do not envisage a common currency or a common foreign policy. We do not even advocate a customs union.

Nonetheless, few Europeans – and even fewer observers elsewhere – believed in the 1950s that Europe could overcome its vast cultural differences and tragic history to unite economically. Today we take Europe's common market as an established part of the landscape. It is quite feasible, if difficult and ambitious, for the Asia–Pacific Community to achieve the more modest course we propose in the decades ahead.

The issue of the links between the super-currencies and the countries on their periphery is also crucial. There could be nothing more dangerous globally than if the three superstates become exclusionist, leaving the developing world to the predatory forces of currency speculation which they have escaped. Any global co-operation between the three economic superpowers must provide for the possibility of third countries attaching themselves to the arrangement, and thus enjoying currency stability. This would be crucial to the establishment of a yen zone; the United States has been enlightened in bringing Mexico into NAFTA. A European currency should offer linkage agreements with Eastern European currencies currently outside the community and with Third World countries traditionally associated with Europe.

One key aspect is that the superstates must always be ready to bring in outside countries as they become economically mature enough to benefit from membership: in the long term, the European superstate could reach out to embrace Turkey, much of Eastern Europe and even, possibly, the Ukraine and Russia. The American superstate could reach down into Latin America; and the Japanese one could extend to Indonesia and much of South-East Asia. Meanwhile, currency association agreements would bring much stability to those on the periphery.

Sub-Saharan Africa deserves special mention. Africa must be taken in paternalist partnership by Europe. With the end of colonialism, and the passing of proxy wars like that in Angola between the superpowers, it has become the world's neglected, stagnant backwater, sinking – in spite of some commendable local efforts at reform – even deeper into poverty, malnutrition and strife for control of scarce resources. As commodity prices bump along the bottom and the debt burden mounts, large parts of Africa are, quite literally, returning to their pre-colonial past.

The average African today eats a tenth less than he did twenty years ago, according to the UN Food and Agriculture Organization. While African populations have risen by around 3 per cent a year since 1970, annual production of staple cereals has grown by less than 2 per cent annually. The amount of cultivated land per person has fallen by half over the past two decades. Some 34 million Africans in fifteen Sub-Saharan countries suffer from what the FAO genteelly calls 'exceptional food emergencies' – virtual starvation. The average Ethiopian eats 1,500 calories a day in food – 300 calories below FAO's minimum recommended intake.

Life expectancy in the two most recent African flashpoints – Rwanda and Somalia – is forty-six years. Four-fifths of Rwanda's population live in absolute poverty, as does three-fifths of Somalia's. The average Somali attends just three months of school, while the average Rwandan spends fourteen months there. Rwanda's average population growth is 3.3 per cent a year, or 8.5 children per woman, in the country which already has the highest population density in Africa. Food production in both countries has plummeted by a fifth in the past decade.

That grim prophet of capitalism, Malthus, has found his laboratory at last in Africa, where genocide could be classed as at least restoring the food–population balance. In nearby Zaire, law and order has deteriorated to the point where the country is effectively under the control of marauding armed bands of soldiers. The celebrated Kenyan author, Ali Mazrui, has even advocated 'a once unthinkable solution: recolonization . . . Even the degree of dependent modernization achieved under colonial rule is being reversed,' he points out. 'External recolonization under the banner of humanitarianism is entirely conceivable.'

Few would go so far. One self-interested incentive for

Africa's northern neighbour, Europe, to help develop the continent is to create more developed populations capable of consuming Western products. Another is precautionary – to help stem the increasing flow of migrants from the continent. But it is also humanely incumbent upon prosperous Europe to assist towards developing a huge continent whose living standards seem to be slipping back to those of the nineteenth century. It was never likely that countries abandoned in a rush by the colonial powers, endowed with only a handful of university graduates, would modernize themselves by their own efforts. It would be a tragic historical irony if continuing neglect causes Africa to look back to the age of colonialism and superpower competition across their territories as a golden age.

THE INCREASINGLY tempestuous world economy would be radically changed by the establishment of the three main currency blocs (it is already three-quarters there) and a global pact between them to manage their currencies responsibly. The present picture of huge funds sloshing their way about the world leaving devastation in their wake would be transformed. If all three were prepared to agree annual exchange rate targets, based on rational criteria, such as trade flows, interest rates and so on, and were prepared to support each other with the massive reserve funds at their disposal, there would be relative currency stability; the size of the available intervention funds would reduce the margins for speculation considerably. In itself this would greatly facilitate international trade; currency instability has been one of the single biggest obstacles to the expansion of world trade in the post-Bretton Woods period. There would be an end to destructive currency tidal waves.

In addition, the herd, and irrational instincts of the market, would be replaced by more measured economic planning. Of course the market would still have a role: where exchange rate targets were out of line – as, given the fallibility of all human institutions they sometimes would be – the market would probably anticipate the necessary corrections. Given the size of the currencies concerned, financial flows would have a relatively small impact, helping to prompt a more realistic readjustment. The wild fluctuations against smaller currencies would be things of the past: size confers stability.

The state of nature would have been brought under control: the biggest beasts in the jungle would have imposed a measure of order in which they no longer grappled fiercely with each other while the interests of the weak went unprotected. The best guarantee of order throughout human history has come when the biggest accepted responsibility for enforcing it. Co-operation between the three biggest animals in the jungle is indeed the only realistic way of bringing order to it. To rely on a toothless United Nations to do the job is pure moonshine, although there is a significant role for financial institutions like the development banks and the IMF.

THE SECOND ITEM on the global economic agenda is world finance. International bank lending seems to be recovering slowly from the debt holocaust. With the drying up of financial flows to the Third World, banks suddenly realized that there was such a thing as sovereign risk and stampeded just as stupidly in the opposite direction, refusing to lend money because of the possibility of default, thus creating a financial drought for perfectly good Third World projects. The banks found themselves stranded as huge, inflationary money pumps looking for places to put money.

After the debt crisis, the same team brought the junk bond and secondary banking crisis in America, the splurge of the 'bubble economy' in Japan, the massive inflation of property values, creating an artificial boom which like all others ended in collapse, in Britain, and now, just possibly, another South Sea Bubble in overheating China. The flow of international bank lending globally, as of 'hot money' in bond and equity markets, is largely unregulated, and inherently both inflationary and deflationary – inflationary when it pours into a particular country or region, deflationary when it seeks to recover its loans.

The solution is to find ways of ensuring that bank lending is channelled to investment or productive purposes – which requires much greater supervision; if the banks are incapable of this, the regulators must step in.

In Latin America, for example, the World Bank and Inter-American Development banks, for all their deficiencies, are ideally placed to pass judgement on whether a particular project loan is likely to be well spent or not. The collapse of the Bank of Credit and Commerce International has exposed the scandalous inadequacy of international banking regulation in the global marketplace. Here the problem is to marry banking with fundamentally creditworthy projects in the credit-starved Third World, as well as containing the excesses of banking deregulation and the oversupply of credit in the developed countries.

The first problem is relatively easy to solve, in four practical stages. There needs to be a global resolution of the debt problem, so that commercial banks understand that they can resume lending for viable projects without the risk of these loans being swept away in a national default. This is already being part-achieved through selling Third World debt at a discount, debt-equity swaps, the writing off of debt and so on, mechanisms for which the international banking community has congratulated itself for its ingenuity. Yet because these are so grudging and partial, huge debt burdens remain, which helps to deter productive lending for fear of a repeat of the crises of the 1980s.

Another step forward would be international guarantees of lending for the right kind of projects, permitting banks to take minor risks. This requires proper inspection and regulation of those projects; as already suggested, the development banks are in a good position to provide this. Again, this is already to some extent happening because in practice commercial banks are unwilling to extend new loans except for projects which have the World Bank or IDB seal of approval; other possible supervisors are Eximbank in the United States or Britain's Export Credit Guarantee Department. After the fiasco last time, when lending was left to international banks literally chasing each other to lend money to Third World crooks, some degree of supervision is right and necessary: the 'market' proved to be a disaster.

This calls for an improved and overhauled World Bank, Inter-American Development Bank, Asian Development Bank and European Bank for Reconstruction and Development. The World Bank has in practice amassed a mass of expertise in the Third World but suffers from bureaucracy, political appointments and over-dominance by the United States, as does the IDB. The EBRD has got off to an appalling start and, in view of America's domination of the World Bank, needs to be developed to channel funds not just to Eastern Europe – its initial mission – but to the developing world.

One of the biggest global problems is reconciling the surplus of international capital with its productive use. Marx defined colonialism as a product of the search by surplus international capital for a home in the developing world. The contrary is true today: finance-starved Third World countries desperately need such money. The problem is that when the banks fight shy of such countries and channel funds into the industrial nations, they risk merely adding to inflationary pressures unless they are careful in their choice of project: the junk bond boom and the property boom were examples of that.

In fact far more non-inflationary wealth can be created in less developed countries, with their frontier opportunities, than through the expansion of credit in already prosperous countries. In the developing world this can be done through inspected, authorized lending under the eye of responsible banking institutions with experience in the field acting as catalysts for large flows of commercial bank lending. The wasteful spectacle of funds looking for a home, chasing crooks in the Third World, or in real estate or predatory take-overs could gradually be brought to an end. In its place, capital surpluses could be recycled into commercially viable Third World projects (the developed world needs schemes for recycling capital to its underdeveloped regions; but that is another subject). This would be non-inflationary, and unlikely to result in the depressing cycle of boom followed by bust.

The need for a proper strategy of bank lending in the Third World is an urgent one. At the moment the panacea for most of its ills is acquisition and investment by the multinationals or by 'hot money' in pursuit of equity and bonds.

Of course, this proposal for resumed commercial bank lending guided by, and underwritten by, the major development banks, is far from foolproof: they are far from perfect institutions. But can it be doubted that their supervision would be considerably more sensible than the profligate and naïve lending of the commercial banks during the debt crisis?

Whether the International Monetary Fund has a role in all this remains an interesting question. After the mess, those who mopped up certainly performed a useful role in restoring some confidence. But its tough, unimaginative, and often inappropriate addiction to narrow financial targets for Third World countries has possibly done more harm than good. It should revert to its proper role, not as a kind of totem pole around which the developing countries have to dance, but as an official receiver when things go disastrously wrong. The rule of thumb should be that if one country goes bankrupt while the rest remain solvent, that country is at fault. When a large number of countries go bankrupt, the international financial system is at fault and narrow-minded IMF prescriptions are inappropriate. After the debt crisis, much of the 'hot money' flowing to the Third World took the form of bonds and equity, which are just as liable to sudden panics, as in the Mexican crisis of January 1995. Then, nearly $50 billion had to be stumped up at speed by the official international financial community; the IMF might have a role in raising such money itself from the commercial market, as such cases are likely to be increasingly frequent given the size of international flows.

THE THIRD MAIN field for regulation of the global jungle lies in the activities of the multinationals. This can best be attained through co-operation between the three superstates, which have the size and market access to overawe even the largest global companies. In addition, as we shall see in the next chapter, the problem of company size and power can be addressed through making large corporations more responsible to their shareholders, customers and employees.

THE FOURTH AREA for regulation of the global jungle, the global state of nature, is trade flows, and they need not detain us long. The establishment of a tripod of superstates would do much to remove the most damaging aspects of these. If Japan could be brought on a voluntary basis into agreement with America and Europe on the amount of trade that should pass between the three, the biggest problem would have been resolved.

If not, concerted pressure by America and Europe – Japan's biggest markets – should make the country see reason; at present it plays one off against the other, and the Americans, always trying to steal a march on Europe, lend themselves to this. The Japanese trade surplus is a huge global problem, acting as a severe restraint on the world economy and is not, as the Japanese contend, entirely a product of their super-efficiency. If this sounds like trade management, so be it, provided it is aimed at removing obstacles to free trade and is not used against weaker trading nations.

The goal must be to dismantle tariffs between the developed and developing world. But where tariffs exist between the big three, a certain toughness is required to force one or another down. In the global jungle, the big three should seek to resolve their differences amicably, or all the animals will suffer: growling will sometimes be necessary, but the big three should be as kind as possible to the weaker animals, which are no threat to them.

A serious danger of this arrangement is that the three economic superpowers might appear to be dictating terms to the rest of the world, arousing anti-colonialist resentment. The extent to which the triumvirate shows itself aware of the danger, and of the importance to be derived from rekindling growth in the Third World, will determine its success.

*

THE BIGGEST PROBLEM is, however, the extent to which the global superstate itself could become too remote and detached from the ordinary person. If the nation state has been transcended by the forces of international capitalism, the global superstate needed to control the latter seems almost as remote. Communities of hundreds of millions of people are not likely to be in close touch with their grass roots: the collapse of the Soviet Union seems an awful warning of the remoteness of a major superstate from its people – as Britain's Mrs Thatcher, among others, has often pointed out.

Yet the argument is mistaken: there is certainly a danger of a non-democratic superstate – like the Soviet Union – moving too far from its people. The European Union is a largely non-democratic institution, and so there is also a danger of this in Europe. The answer is not to do away with superstates – which are essential – but to make them democratic. The United States – with some reservations – has shown how extraordinarily successful a superstate can be at retaining its roots, its contact with ordinary people, and avoiding a backlash of the kind which destroyed the Soviet empire.

Several aspects of the American system prevent it from being remote from the ordinary person, and permit a nation of 250 million people, covering an immense geographical area, from not appearing as a distant bureaucratic entity which ordinary people cannot relate to. In spite of the grumbles about Washington, most Americans are intensely patriotic and supportive of their president and proud of their system and way of life. America has many lessons to offer other would-be superstates like Europe and Japan.

The federal system, in particular, gives a remarkable degree of power to the state and local governments. Moreover, America's written constitution and supreme court enshrine a mass of liberties and rights that no one – least of all government – can tamper with. In addition, Congress, in its battles with the Executive, encapsulates a division of powers which gives the ordinary voter a feeling that he really matters, and that he is being represented. The administration is constantly being scrutinized and checked. In particular, with the whole of the House of Representatives and a third of the Senate being re-elected every two years, Congressmen could hardly spend more time nursing their districts. With every state sending two members to the Senate, no part of the country, however underpopulated and remote from the centre, feels left out.

The presidency itself, with its sometimes ludicrous over-personalization, with its travelling circus at election times, and with the genuine partisan battles between Republicans and Democrats, serves to defuse suspicion of the central bureaucracy. There has been nothing remote about men like small-town Harry Truman, amiable, shrewd Dwight Eisenhower, glamorous John Kennedy, lived-in Lyndon Johnson, clever, devious Richard Nixon, ordinary Gerald Ford, bumbling Jimmy Carter, smooth-communicator Ronald Reagan, preppie George Bush and stumbling Bill Clinton. All supremely professional politicians – as they need to be to survive the gruelling year-long American election – their obvious human failings under the spotlight make them appear close to ordinary people, and far from remote.

Finally, the power of the media, and in particular television, helps to knit America together as one nation. America shows that it is possible for a superstate to be in touch with its people – and both Europe and Japan have a lot to learn from this: Jacques Delors would not win an election in the United States. George Bush was as near to being a bureaucratic politician as any modern president – and he was not that near and did not survive that long.

In case this seems too adulatory, there are some serious defects in American democracy. Institutional paralysis is produced by the interminable battle between President and Congress, which over some issues – in particular foreign policy and the budget deficit – threatens to freeze the system into inaction. The huge range of issues in which co-operation is achieved between executive and legislature dwarfs this; and in foreign affairs presidents have often got away with acting now, explaining later. But over the deficit, Congress reinforces any president's propensity to spend and blocks any attempt by the treasury to save.

In many cases this is not objectionable: deficit financing is preferable to underspending, lack of demand and recession. But when deficit financing occurs through inflation, or through arbitrary or high interest rates, thereby hurting other economies, and becomes institutionalized, there are serious dangers and presidents and congressional leaders have to address them. Others who might imitate the American way should consider whether the balance between executive and legislature is right, or whether the latter, on this key issue, is too powerful.

Another major defect of the American system is more dangerous: while the ordinary American does not feel remote from central government, there is a perilous remoteness between civil society and a large, although in the minority, underclass: previously mostly consisting of blacks from the inner cities and the south, this now includes a large number of first-generation Mexican immigrants, poor southern whites and new European immigrants.

Galbraith, among others, has argued that all that keeps these people from revolting against the system is that they consider themselves better off than their forefathers, but that this will not apply to their children. Because the overwhelming majority of Americans are contented, the needs of the underclass are neglected; they are not a revolutionary class, in a historical sense, because they are a minority. However, the potential for mass discontent among the second generation, trapped in a cycle of poverty, should not be underestimated.

Whether Galbraith is right or not depends on whether American society provides its traditional safety valve of offering opportunities for these people to escape their predicament: the record among inner-city blacks is not encouraging. If he is right, a second Kennedy-style era of emancipation may be necessary to prevent American cities degenerating into riot zones and armed camps, where haves protect themselves from have-nots.

THE FAILINGS OF America should not blind Europe and Japan to the lesson that the superstate can be made to work, if it incorporates some essential features. Neither does, at the moment. The European superstate, because of the reluctance of the nation-states to share power with the centre, has a nominated executive, the Commission, which is no more democratic in composition than the leadership of the former Soviet Union. The executive is supposedly checked by a largely impotent parliament for which ordinary voters – unsurprisingly, in view of its lack of authority – show little enthusiasm, and by a fairly threadbare system of personal rights and legal guarantees. The relationship between ordinary people and senior government officials, because of their non-election, is almost non-existent.

Jacques Delors made a fine demon for the British tabloid press as the apparently colourless bureaucratic empire-builder he appeared to be; Sir Leon Brittan served the same role for the French press. As neither had been elected to their jobs, whatever their abilities, they made convenient Aunt Sallys. Until Europe has an elected executive, its authority will be small – as Mr Gorbachev discovered in the Soviet Union. Without major and massive institutional reform, the European Union does risk suffering the Soviet fate – becoming a superstate without popular consent.

This is not because it is a superstate or too large: it is because Europe is not democratic. It is perfectly adequate in one respect – the relationship between the nations and the centre; if anything the nations have permitted too much authority to flow to the bureaucracy, while obstructing its democratic development to ensure their own dominance. No serious person can possibly believe Europe will ever override or crush the sovereignty of the nation states, any more than the American federal government does of the states. In a democratic state, this is impossible – it could happen only in an undemocratic set-up like the Soviet Union. The European superstate should acquire control over areas where common action needs to be taken, in order to regain power over the outside forces that have diminished national sovereignty – through, for example, the globalization of the world economy. The nation state should retain sovereignty over the rest.

In Japan, a political vacuum exists because of the country's essentially authoritarian tradition of government behind a democratic façade. This may be changing; but until it does, massive tensions will continue, and the sense of alienation of ordinary people from their government is palpable.

The state of nature, the global jungle, thus needs to be brought under control by the three biggest animals acting under democratic rules, as responsible as possible to their own people because their very size runs the risk of alienating them: the United States has shown it can be done, and so it should by both Europe and Japan – or they run the risk of going the Soviet way.

CHAPTER FOUR

REFORM FROM WITHIN

But there is a second way of imposing order on the state of nature: and that is for the middle-sized powers within it, the major corporations, to become responsible to their own constituencies. This needs immediately to be qualified: one is not proposing any real change in the structure of what might be called the dynamic private enterprise, the small or medium-sized company competing furiously in the market. For these, the issue is whether they can survive; they are already intensely accountable to the market. To compete they may need the inspired, striving leadership of a dictatorial individual. It is the already established bureaucracies in the giant corporations, barely accountable to the market, that need to be made more responsible, or they risk arousing the same kind of hostile reaction that led to the collapse of communism. At present they are controlled by only one of their three constituencies, and are distantly accountable to another.

Self-appointed corporate management runs the show, subject to its demonstrable failures in the marketplace – but, as suggested, this is much less likely for a giant company than anyone else. Most managers are obviously motivated by the desire for self-enrichment and status, but it is also true that many have the corporation's interest at heart (although this is not true of today's predators). Most managements cannot be described as ill-motivated, because very often this is not the case, although there are plenty of people about whose purposes are simply to maximize their earnings irrespective of the corporate good.

But, equally, the management clique is responsible to no one. As in a communist bureaucracy, it chooses its own successors, it makes the decisions, it rewards those who respect the system and it punishes those who dissent. In terms of financial size, it may be the equivalent of a small country and, in terms of numbers, of an army. It is unashamedly authoritarian and believes that its efficiency derives from this fact. It has very little contact with the free market: its size enables it to manipulate the market and its bureaucratic structure, where possible, stifles individual initiative.

How then to make it responsible, and to whom? All three constituencies need to be brought into play. The time has long since come for those who provide capital to be given a louder voice. A shareholder today has only two rights: depending on the type of shareholding, the right to a say in the choice of directors; and the right to sell his shares if dissatisfied with the performance of the company. In fact the right of participation in the choice of directors is barely exercised at all by most shareholders. It is difficult for them to attend company annual general meetings, difficult for them to vet the often over-simplified accounts they are presented with, and even more difficult to understand who is responsible for what decision, in the light of the almost total secrecy that generally swathes corporate affairs.

Only very occasionally, when companies have very high profile management or very visible failings, are shareholders motivated to exercise their rights – Britain's Lonrho being one example, Ratner's another (although both were simultaneously victims of boardroom coups). Directors are usually selected by the management, with the shareholders' formal consent – and a docile lot most of them are. They are, however, wholly incapable of ruling the corporate roost and are selected for their importance – or self-importance – and passivity, not for their ability to represent the shareholders vigorously.

So shareholder power, if it exists at all, consists of voting with their feet, abandoning companies in visible trouble, which is why shareholders so often get stung. As already noted, a company's financial results are not necessarily the best guide to its good management and profitability – under-investment or the sale of assets, detrimental to the company in the long run, may be used to puff up a company's annual results. Often the accounts are the last thing to show the company's weaknesses. Perhaps the most classic rip-off by the professional managers of the men who put up the money and then sat back, expecting to reap large profits, has been the experience of many syndicates in Lloyd's of London; devious professionals can sting absentee investors.

That said, there are two things happening in Britain to the stock market which both tend towards greater accountability. The first is the growing power of the institutional shareholder – the pension fund, the unit trust, the building society and so on; the second is the dispersal, through privatization, of millions of shares among ordinary people. The institutional shareholder is no less a corporate bureaucrat than the company he invests in. But he knows what he is looking for, and is unlikely to invest in a company which he views as unsatisfactorily managed.

The small shareholder has very little say at present, and the very atomization of shareholdings makes it easy for the management of the new privatized corporations to ignore him. So far most privatized companies are doing well in terms of share prices and dividends. But if these companies start doing badly, thousands of small investors will be affected, and it cannot be long before they demand an explanation: it is not easy for a bus driver or bank clerk to ring his stockbroker and sell his shares if he scents a whiff of trouble in the financial press. But he can join with his fellows to make his voice heard.

This is heartening at a time when most companies lack any form of accountability to those who put up the money for them. In Britain the Cadbury Committee, reporting in May 1992 on ways to improve company accountability, argued in favour of self-regulation, while accepting the need for legislation if this failed. The Committee recommended setting up a nomination committee for each company, dominated by the non-executive directors, with the task of coming up with the names of new directors. They also recommended that an audit committee should be set up for each company consisting of non-executive directors alone, with direct access to the company auditors, reviewing half-yearly results and looking at the internal control systems of companies before they are put to the board. Finally, a remunerations committee for each company should examine the issue of executive pay. They pronounced:

> Shareholders are entitled to a complete disclosure and explanation of directors' present and future benefits, including stock options and stock appreciation rights, and of how they have been determined.
>
> Accordingly, we recommend that in disclosing directors' total emoluments and those of the chairman and highest-paid UK director, separate figures should be given for their salary and performance-related elements and that the criterion on which performance is measured should be explained.
>
> In addition, we recommend that, in future, service contracts should not exceed three years without shareholders' approval . . . this would strengthen shareholder control over levels of compensation for loss of office.

This would safeguard against executives deciding their own pay. Auditors should be encouraged to report their suspicions of fraud to the investigatory authorities. However, the committee accepted that there was concern about the lack of a direct link between auditors and shareholders, and that the need to secure a commission from a company often overrode an auditor's perception of his duty to the stockholders.

Both institutional investors and mass investors should demand two more things: that directors be submitted to contested annual re-election by postal ballot – exactly what is now required by law of trade unions; and, a much greater access to information about the company than presently available. 'Creative accounting' can obscure the truth about all but the most ineptly managed company: the regulations requiring disclosure of company information need to be much tougher, and the company accounts much more transparent and accessible for inspection by the ordinary shareholder.

As observed, there is little demand for this when things are going well; there will be when they go badly; as in some newly privatized companies they surely will. Finally, chief executives should be appointed directly by the shareholders – not through the directors as at present, because they are effectively chosen by the executives. This will generally be a formality, but could give shareholders power in the event of a major problem.

THE SECOND MAIN 'constituency' in a company is the market. For small and medium-sized business, this works fine. Capitalism is at its most efficient, and most impressive, in the efforts of single individuals creating dynamic and thrusting companies against all the odds placed against them by the big boys, the giant bureaucratic firms: entrepreneurs like Crosby's Tim Beardson, who has set up from scratch a multimillion dollar stockbroking company in Hong Kong, or Hugh Ehrman, pioneer-king of Britain's mail order knitwear business. Even within major groups, individuals can sometimes flourish if given enough autonomy and initiative: the thriving offshoots created by men like Schroder Wagg's Andrew Williams, Rothschild's Nicholas Banzsky and Guinness's Simon Duffy spring to mind. Yet major companies can manipulate the market to a great extent, although not entirely. The market can be made more efficient, through anti-trust and anti-monopoly legislation, at a global level through action against anti-competitive practices such as predatory mergers or anti-competitive cartelism, and finally through greater consumer action and awareness.

In the United States consumer awareness has actually strengthened competition and corporate effectiveness through increased sales. There is nothing radical or anti-capitalist about insisting upon free competition rather than rigged markets; indeed, this is to return capitalism to its first principles, the ideals of Adam Smith. Modern free marketeers like Hayek appear to believe that markets are free if left to themselves; in reality, markets have to be supervised in order to preserve the freedom of the many from the predations of the monopolistic few. Consumer legislation is being increasingly recognized as not just beneficial to the consumer, but to the producer.

*

THE MODERN CORPORATION also has responsibilities to the workforce. Traditionally its attitude to management has been confrontational and, frankly, extremely crude. In response to the employers' attitude that its objective is to provide goods at the lowest possible labour cost, workers banded together to deny employers their labour and demanded better pay and conditions. They also formed the backbone of socialist political organizations devoted to their interests. The struggle was for the most part successful at the beginning of the century and in the immediate postwar period.

However, the massive expansion of the state machine, and the inflation caused by soaring labour costs, provoked a backlash that reversed the tide in the employers' favour, and caused a major erosion of trade union power. The unions are now in decline, their membership falling, reluctant to indulge in strikes in America and across Europe. This would be welcome news, but for the feeling that employers are increasingly reverting to their old high-handed attitude of hiring and firing and squeezing as much labour for as little pay as possible. Technically, innovation has made it possible to maximize productivity, increasing industrial tasks for workers on new machinery for no increase in pay.

The decline in union power has not been so dramatic that it is impossible for employers to overstep the mark. They might take a leaf out of the Japanese example. The latter have introduced new plant into Europe with no-strike agreements: in exchange they offer job security, reasonable pay and facilities to air grievances. This paternalistic approach, while in some ways unsatisfactory, is infinitely preferable to management methods, imported mainly from the United States, where labour is viewed as just one of many disposable costs of production. Labour is the key to any successful business, and the best results will be secured if workers are treated as human beings.

While the organization of any firm requires a chain of command and a clear definition of management authority, some innovations would greatly improve the climate. One is a much greater diffusion of information to the workforce. Unnecessary secrecy can only render management decisions much more difficult to apply. In addition, the presence of one or two directors directly representing the interests of the workforce (not simply able employees who have made it from shop floor to boardroom), but not endowed with any power to block board decisions, would assure the workers' interests were not misjudged or overlooked.

The Japanese practice of offering workers – and management – across-the-board pay cuts instead of compulsory redundancies, when a firm is in difficulties, would do much to secure the loyalty of a workforce for whom unemployment is a far greater evil than lower pay. This would encounter resistance from traditional unions, of course, whose primary purpose is to secure higher pay for the existing workforce, rather than to represent the interests of all workers in a country, employed and unemployed – unions themselves are a major source of unemployment – but it might be popular among the rank-and-file. These innovations would not, of course, make management responsible to, or representative of, the workforce in any way; a company has to have an authoritarian structure. But they would give the workforce some influence in decisions that directly affect it.

THESE THEN ARE the three great areas of change necessary to avoid a state of global economic anarchy early in the next millennium: the establishment of superpower policing to prevent conflicts breaking out all over the world, through an efficient system of regional alliances and deterrents, backed up by the threat of major superpower intervention; the regulation of the global economy through co-operation between the three economic superstates of the next few decades – America, Europe and Japan; and the reform from within of the capitalist corporation.

The alternative to these changes is hardly worth contemplating. It includes one or more of the following: American withdrawal from its global responsibilities; growing rivalry among the European nations; the spread of a host of ethnic and nationalist conflicts across the globe (already under way); possible confrontation and war between quite major powers –

for example, Pakistan and India, China and Japan, Russia and Japan, Iran and Iraq (again), or either with Saudi Arabia, possibly involving the use of nuclear weapons. Further, a renewed offensive by international terrorism; or the expansion of narcotics trafficking, with its huge social consequences for the developed world, to uncontrollable proportions.

On the global economic front, there is the prospect of the bitter legacy left by the debt crisis in the developing world, erupting into savage confrontation with the developed world. This would involve: the seizure of multinational assets, the collapse of major multinationals, attacks on Westerners, and the degeneration of the world economy into a trading confrontation between America, Europe and Japan, with profound recessionary consequences; the growth of widespread disillusion even among long democratic electorates; and the reversion of many new democracies to populism and authoritarianism. It might further result in explosions of crime or rioting by the underclass, reinforcing the impression that governments are simply unable to govern; the disintegration of the European Union into a free-for-all in which Germany dominates its weaker neighbours and even perhaps ends up in confrontation with its rivals, France, Britain and Russia.

Global disorder would be in prospect. Some of these things are already beginning to happen with the thawing of the Cold War's glacial grip. The concept of a 'new world order' is not just some hollow phrase employed by a now discarded American president. It is essential because the old world order – which for all the danger of nuclear confrontation saw the world through a period of relative peace and a surge in prosperity – has collapsed. Without a new world order there will be no world order.

The list of areas of global concern outlined in this book is not, of course, exhaustive: population, the environment and the global arms trade are enormously important. But these problems have been extensively discussed in the past. The challenges outlined in this book have not been much discussed and are, I believe, immediate and extremely serious.

*

DOOMSDAY – global anarchy, the state of nature, where the strong prey on the weak unchecked, where the powerful neglect their responsibilities and the world becomes a dangerous, unpredictable and inequitable place, the undoing of all the great strides towards international order that over the past forty years replaced a world riven by world war and the murderous ideological disputes of this century – is a real possibility if we do not rise to the occasion. Thirty years of world wars, economic crises and social disorder followed the collapse of the last world order in 1914. The consequences of not acting in time are terrifying.

This in turn requires political leaders and corporate bosses capable of lifting their eyes above the daily political and economic grind to sense the dangers and take evasive action. There are only a few signs that this is happening in the global jungle of international security, none at all in that of international economics.

This is the challenge for the planet as the sun sets on the old millennium and the dawn of the new beckons. Will it be the red dawn of danger, of countless conflicts and economic hardships, or the brightness of a new, gentler, more ordered age for humanity?

INDEX